AIR ACES

The Lives and Times of Twelve Canadian Fighter Pilots

DAN MCCAFFERY

James Lorimer & Company, Toronto

Photos for this book were gathered by PHOTOSEARCH.
Photos courtesy of the Department of National Defence and the National Aviation Museum.

Canadian Cataloguing in Publication Data

McCaffery, Dan

Air aces

ISBN 1-55028-322-7 (bound)   ISBN 1-55028-321-9 (pbk.)

1. Fighter pilots — Canada — Biography. 2. World War, 1914-1918 — Aerial operations. 3. Canada — History, Military — 20th century. I. Title.

UG626.M33 1990   358.4'3'0922   C90-094002-6

James Lorimer & Company, Publishers
Egerton Ryerson Memorial Building
35 Britain Street
Toronto, Ontario M5A 1R7

Printed and bound in Canada

6 5 4 3 2 1 89 90 91 92 93 94

Contents

Acknowledgements   v

Introduction   1

World War I

1.	Arthur Royal Brown	11
2.	Ray Collishaw	27
3.	Alan McLeod	49
4.	William George Barker	59
5.	Bob Leckie	79
6.	Billy Bishop	93

World War II and Korea

7.	George Beurling	117
8.	Russ Bannock	137
9.	Vernon "Woody" Woodward	151
10.	Buck McNair	165
11.	Wally McLeod	177
12.	Omer Levesque	191

Conclusion   207

Ace Lists   213

Aircraft Glossary   223

Endnotes   227

Bibliography   232

This book is dedicated to my mother, Veronica (MacDonald) McCaffery, who always told me there's no such word as "can't."

Acknowledgements

This book would not have been possible without the help of fighter pilots from both world wars and the Korean conflict who shared their experiences with me. First and foremost, my thanks go out to Russ Bannock, Canada's second highest scoring ace of World War Two, and to Omer Levesque, the nation's only ace in the Korean conflict. Those two courageous and humble old warriors reached back nearly fifty years to tell me the stories of their youth, answering every question in detail and without the slightest hesitation. Their recollection of minute details and their willingness to share inner thoughts about such touchy subjects as killing and fear, added an important dimension to the book.

Two former Spitfire pilots, Robert Hyndman and D.J. Dewan, took the time to write to me, providing valuable insights into what made Canada's highest scoring 1939-45 ace, George Beurling, tick. First World War veterans Roger Neville and George Stirrett, now both deceased, supplied me with fresh information about Billy Bishop, the top gun of the Allied forces in the 1914-18 war.

I would also like to thank Will Chabun, in Saskatchewan, the talented *Regina Leader Post* reporter who brought to my attention an important interview he conducted with former Spitfire pilot Don Walz, who flew with ace Wally McLeod.

Special thanks to Curtis Fahey, who has always had faith in my writing, and who urged me to write this book. Thanks also to Virginia Smith and Tim Dunn at James Lorimer & Company, for helping me work the bugs out of the manuscript.

The staffs at the University of Western Ontario library, the historical branch of the Department of National Defence and of the Toronto Public Library were also most helpful.

Finally, heartfelt thanks to my wife Val, and special friends Mary-Jane Egan and Dave Anderson, whose support is deeply appreciated.

Introduction

This book is about a dozen young Canadian fighter pilots who gained "ace" status in the nation's three air wars of the twentieth century.

Canadians are, the world has been told so often it now believes it, a rather boring people with a colourless past. Indeed, our own history teachers have helped foster this myth, cramming youthful minds full of tedious details about constitutional conferences, the goings-on of stuffy nineteenth-century politicians and the precise date on which John Cabot discovered Newfoundland. While American school children learn about the pioneer exploits of dashing heroes like Daniel Boone and Davy Crockett, Canadian youngsters are expected to develop a sense of national identity by reading about the Charlottetown conference of 1866. We're a conservative people who believe in peace, order and good government. Or so the story goes. But the proponents of this well-accepted theory would have a difficult time explaining why it is that staid Canada has produced, by far, more air aces per capita than any other nation on earth.

An ace is a fighter pilot who has vanquished five or more enemy aircraft in individual duels above the clouds. Although the figure seems modest enough, the fact is that only five per cent of all wartime fighter pilots ever become aces. And yet that select group of experts is responsible for destroying half of all the airplanes lost in battle! They are the absolute cream of the crop and, since air fighting began, the very best of them have always been Canadians.

That isn't just so much bombastic nationalistic rhetoric. The raw statistics speak for themselves. In the First World War, for instance, five of the British Empire's top ten fighter pilots came from the Dominion. In all, 127 Canadians became aces during that awful conflagration, accounting for a staggering 1,500 victories. In the Second World War, when victory totals generally dropped,

Canada still produced 160 aces, who racked up another 1,021 kills. In Korea, the handful of Canadian fighter pilots proved themselves virtually invincible, destroying or damaging twenty Communist MIG jets, without loss. From February, 1917, when Toronto's Eddie Grange destroyed his fifth German Albatros over northern France until March, 1951, when Montreal's Omer Levesque shot a MIG down in flames over North Korea, Canada amassed 288 aces.

The definition of a "victory" changed as battle planes became more sophisticated. In the First World War, pilots were credited with victories, or "kills," if the enemy plane they engaged was seen to crash, go down in flames, or simply fall away out of control. In the Second World War and in Korea, a victory was only awarded if the enemy was seen to crash — or if the pilot was spotted bailing out.

The top guns came from all ten provinces, from big cities, small towns and right off farms. They came from every educational and ethnic background. Some were unreasoning rebels like Billy Bishop and George Beurling, while others were cool professionals like Russ Bannock and Ray Collishaw. Some, like Wally McLeod, gloried in fighting while others, like Roy Brown, detested it. If they had anything in common it was that they were all Canadians and, collectively, they were better than the fighter pilots of the nations they flew with and against.

Some Canadian historians have tried to downplay their remarkable achievements. One of the better ones, Ronald Dodds, has even gone so far as to suggest Canada's aces were not superior. "Their record speaks for itself without attempting to endow them with mysterious abilities lacking amongst those many others who flew with and against them,"[1] he wrote in his classic book *The Brave Young Wings*.

Such modesty is typically Canadian and perhaps even admirable. Certainly it is easier to swallow than the excessive flag-waving of some other nations. Unfortunately, however, it isn't accurate. There is simply no getting around the fact that Canadian pilots were vastly more talented than those from other countries. Over the Western Front in the First World War, the top-scoring Allied ace was Ontario's Billy Bishop, with an astounding seventy-five kills. On the Italian Front, the top gun of both sides was Manitoba's William Barker, with fifty-three victories. The leading two-seater ace of the war was Andy McKeever of Ontario, and the most dangerous naval airman of either side was British Columbia's Ray Collishaw. The leading zeppelin killer was Bob Leckie of Toronto. In fact, Canadians shot down six of the twelve dirigibles lost by the Germans during the whole war. When the enemy replaced zeppelins with the fabled Gotha bomber, everyone thought the new ships were invincible until Prince Edward Island's Wendell Rogers sent the first one down in a ball of fire.

By the war's end, Canada, with a population of only eight million people, had produced four super aces with fifty or more kills each. Germany, by contrast, had three and France and England just two each. The United States had none at all, and the leading American flyer, the much-celebrated Captain Eddie Rickenbacker, wouldn't even have made the top ten on the Canadian ace list.

In the Second World War, Quebec's George Beurling was the most spectacular Allied ace of them all, once destroying twenty-eight opponents in only fourteen flying days. Along with Canadians Wally McLeod, Buck McNair, Johnny Williams and Moose Fumerton, he broke the back of the Axis air armada hurled against the tiny island of Malta. Indeed, those five Canadians destroyed more than seventy German and Italian planes over the besieged rock in the middle of the Mediterranean Sea. Even in the Pacific, where few Canadian airmen saw action, British Columbia pilot Robert Gray managed to win a Victoria Cross and become the only Allied serviceman of the war to have a statue erected in his honour by the Japanese! In individual dogfights against the leading enemy aces, Canadians came out on top, time and again. Roy Brown probably killed the German ace of aces, Manfred von Richthofen. Barker shot down the second-highest scoring Austro-Hungarian pilot; Collishaw slew a thirty-victory German ace and Bishop vanquished two leading enemy pilots. Beurling killed the most famous Italian ace flying in the Malta campaign. The noted British historian, Denis Winter, faced the issue of Canadian superiority head-on, declaring that 1914-18 airmen from Canada were "more talented" than those from the rest of the Empire. "By the end of the war Canadian pilots had the lion's share of killings: Bishop 72, Collishaw 60, Barker 59, McLaren 54, McElroy 46, Claxton 39, McCall 37, Quigley 34, Carter 31, McKeever 30 — without such scores the R.A.F. list would have been thin gruel."

Why has such a peace-loving nation done so well in the grisly blood sport of aerial dogfighting? Even today, it's difficult to say for certain. C.G. Grey, editor of the authoritative British magazine *Aeroplane,* speculated in 1917 that Canadians had "inherited the spirit of self-reliance and the love of adventure — two qualities which go far to make up the composition of the ideal aviator." Perhaps just as critical, he continued, they had better "hands and eyes. It is important to note that Canada has not really a large town-bred population, and even those who have been more or less bred in towns have not been brought up in the murk and gloom of British manufacturing cities. The clean air, the clean winters and brilliant summers of Canada have produced a healthier race with better eyes than our own town-bred people."[2]

Grey went on to suggest that Canadian sports such as skating, tobogganing and sailing helped develop better co-ordination. Many find these theories questionable, but in their own time they may have been convincing.

Reasons for Success

The main reason for the success of the Canadian fighter pilots can be found elsewhere. While many European air forces discriminated against men from the so-called "lower classes," Canadian flyers faced no such social preconceptions. The British, Germans and French believed in the officer class and they drew most of their pilots from it. Also, they promoted and publicized the people with the "right" accents. Therefore, a man with a "proper" Nottingham upbringing, like Albert Ball, was lionized in the British press for shooting down forty-four German aircraft, while Edward Mannock, a working-class individual of Irish-Catholic descent, was able to score seventy-three times and never get mentioned in the newspapers of the United Kingdom. That he was the top-scoring British ace wasn't even generally known until several years after the war.

The Germans did much the same. They gave the most ink, the promotions, the decorations and the best airplanes, to Prussian pilots. Their highest gallantry award — the Ordre Pour le Merit — was only available to officers. Men from Bavarian squadrons were treated to haughty contempt by Prussian aristocrats. The Austro-Hungarians were the same, refusing to make high-scoring ace Josef Kiss an officer because, in civilian life, he had been from the working class. The leading Belgian ace was a count and the top-scoring German a baron. That was all well and good for the propaganda mill, but it stifled many brilliant pilots.

Canada's flamboyant young pilots were not held back by such foolishness. They were, for the most part, more vigorous and daring than the pampered aristocrats found in many other air forces. Canadians even outperformed American pilots in the First World War, because they were better-trained and had been in the war longer — the United States didn't get into the fighting until 1918. In the Second World War, although Canada produced more aces per capita than the Americans, the disparity was much less noticeable.

By the Second World War, the European air forces themselves were characterized by less discrimination, but Canadians still did better than those from other countries because, in the 1920s and '30s, no profession was more prestigious than that of pilot. No schoolboy could grow up without reading or hearing about Canada's legendary First World War aces, or its equally heroic 1920s bush pilots. When war came in 1939, young men swamped RCAF recruiting stations. While the army and navy occasionally had trouble finding enough men to fill the ranks, the air force had to turn them away in droves. That, in turn, meant it could take its pick of some of Canada's most talented young men.

The aces became famous in the First World War, after the opposing armies bogged down in a bloody stalemate. Trench warfare caused the mass slaughter of literally millions of men by poison gas, artillery fire and machine guns. It was dirty and de-humanizing, and it produced very little opportunity for individual heroism. The newspapers of the world, in a desperate search for individual champions, turned to the sky. Flying was still new in 1914, and most people thought, quite correctly, that you had to be something of an adventurer just to take one of the flimsy crates of that era off the ground. The planes were made of wood and canvas, and were held together by piano wires. One bullet through the gas tank would send them down like a torch, and the pilots had no parachutes. People were fascinated by stories of individual duels above the clouds, much as we would be today to read of astronauts fighting in outer space. Before long, the leading aces became household names, provided that they had the proper public image. In every country, the best-known war hero was a fighter pilot, and not a general, soldier or sailor.

By World War Two, this hero worship had diminished somewhat. In many ways, this was because people realized flying had been more pioneering, more adventurous and more dangerous in the earlier conflict. The 1939-45 aviators flew in closed cockpits, protected by armoured plating and parachutes. Also, the average person could no longer imagine himself in the role of fighter pilot. The little open-cockpit biplanes of the First World War had only seven instruments in their cockpits, and anyone could learn how to fly them in just a few weeks: they weren't much more complex than today's ultra-light hobby planes. The Second World War machines, on the other hand, were far more sophisticated. In fact, there were thirty-five instruments in the cockpit of a Spitfire. Besides that, society as a whole was more mature and better-educated. The propaganda of earlier times didn't go down as well. People accepted that the war was necessary to stop the Nazis, but they no longer relished stories about efficient killers. Therefore, the aces, while still well-known, were no longer lionized. By 1950, when the Korean War came along, aces hardly received any publicity at all. As a result, a First World War hero like Billy Bishop is better known in Canada today than George Beurling. And Omer Levesque, the Korean War ace, is completely unknown.

My interest in Canada's fighter pilots began at an early age. My dad had been a Second World War air gunner and, as a boy, I developed a fascination with air combat. That interest was rekindled as an adult when I set out to write a biography of Billy Bishop. The book took eight years to complete, and, when I was finished, it was clear to me that Bishop was by no means the only great Canadian ace. It was very obvious that men from the Dominion had been the best Allied pilots in both world wars and in Korea.

I tried to determine what it was that made them so special. To do that, I decided to investigate the backgrounds of twelve of the best of them. I wanted to find out not only what they had done, but what was it about them that made them so strong, energetic and brave. As well, I was curious about what it was that made it possible for them to kill fellow-humans with such apparent casualness. I wanted to know what distinguished them from bullfighters, boxers and others who win fame through the use of brute force. And finally, I was determined to find out if they were really heroes at all, or merely bloodthirsty killers.

Now that Canada's wars have been won and fighter pilots are no longer needed, it has become fashionable to degrade them. The National Film Board even went so far as to produce a documentary suggesting Bishop was a fraud. When my book, *Billy Bishop: Canadian Hero* was published in 1988, presenting fresh evidence confirming his exploits, I was attacked by some critics as a hero-worshipper. They didn't question my findings, but suggested that Bishop was no longer a hero because, as one of them put it, "the values under which he lived and fought are no longer living." It seems to me unfair to question someone's heroism because the war they fought in appears now to have been unnecessary.

I am convinced that this heroism still has important meanings for us today. We can all learn and take heart from the courage of Canada's aces.

I have interviewed surviving aces from all three wars, read their combat reports, letters and diaries, and examined newspaper and magazine reports from an earlier era. The finished book will, I believe, give Canadians a better understanding of the men who wrote such a unique chapter of the nation's history.

Dan McCaffery
Sarnia, Ontario
March 1990

World War I

ONE

Arthur Royal Brown

Arthur Royal Brown was the last man on earth you'd expect to be a successful fighter pilot. For one thing, he was a pacifist at heart — appalled at the thought of killing other human beings. For another, he was physically weak. As a boy, he avoided contact sports like the plague. While his schoolmates played football, hockey and lacrosse, young Roy contented himself with sailing and footraces. When he became an airman, he was constantly bothered by a nervous stomach and a nagging ulcer. Always frail, he was a sensitive, shy man given to intellectual pursuits. If Roy Brown were in the Canadian air force today, he would likely be dismissed by his peers as "a wimp." Yet this unassuming fellow was credited with shooting down Baron Manfred von Richthofen, the greatest German fighter pilot of the First World War.

Brown was born in 1893 in the village of Carleton Place, thirty miles west of Ottawa. Flying was in its infancy, and Roy quickly became fascinated with newspaper accounts of the new airplane. As soon as he was old enough, he left home and headed to Dayton, Ohio, telling friends he was "off to see the Wright brothers." Orville and Wilbur Wright had invented the first motor-driven, heavier-than-air machine in late December, 1903, when Roy was just nine years old. Flying was a dangerous game in those days. The planes used four-cylinder engines capable of only twelve horsepower. But they didn't need tremendous capacity because the planes weighed less than 800 pounds. Young Roy had to sign papers absolving the Wright Flying School of any blame should anything happen to him. He also had to pay for his lessons, which were expensive, and that meant doing menial labour around Dayton. He loved flying and spent every spare moment in the air. When he couldn't afford a lesson, he hung around the hangars, studying aircraft engines and badgering the Wrights for information about the planes. Eventually, he got his pilot's licence and headed home — one of the few Canadians who had ever flown a plane.

When war broke out, in 1914, Brown was determined to fight it in the sky. He joined England's Royal Naval Air Service and sailed for Europe. But disaster awaited him in the United Kingdom. Despite his experience, it was decided he wouldn't go on active duty until he'd spent some time at the big aerial dogfight school at Chingford. There, flying the old Avro 504, he had his first crash. It was almost his last. In a scene right out of the movies, he was hauled unconscious from the wreckage by ground personnel just seconds before his biplane exploded in flames. Brown's back was broken and he spent several painful months in a hospital bed. When he was released, he walked for a time with a cane, and then with a cumbersome back brace. Nevertheless, he was able to wangle his way into an active squadron and, in February, 1917, began to fly patrols over the coast of Belgium, where he engaged in fruitless searches for the evasive German torpedo seaplanes, or conducted boring escorts of lumbering Allied bombers.

But when he did get his chance, Roy Brown made the best of it. Flying the outdated Sopwith Pup on July 17 near Dunkirk, he spotted a lone German Albatros D-3 scooting gingerly along, a few thousand feet below him. The "Pup" had only one gun, compared to the Albatros's two, but the Canadian didn't hesitate for a moment. He dove down on the unsuspecting German and triggered his Vickers from fifty yards. The enemy pilot crumpled in his chair and the D-3 fell away, completely out of control.

Brown didn't show the exuberance that rookies usually demonstrated after their first kill. There would be no grandstanding for him. Indeed, he had little use for the show-off antics of pilots who looped over the airfield or fired off signal flares before landing if they had registered a victory. To him, the grisly business was not a sport. "I love flying, not killing,"[1] he told a friend. Indeed, those who knew him best said he could never have accomplished much as an infantryman, because he would have had to see the men he killed, close up. As a pilot, he could concentrate on downing a machine, and that's exactly what he did.

Whether he enjoyed it or not, Brown's easy first victory may have given him the impression that aerial combat was a lark. He found out soon enough that such was not the case. The Royal Flying Corps was taking a terrible drubbing on the Western Front and, that fall, Brown's naval squadron was rushed to the main theatre of war to help stem the tide. After months of mostly non-eventful patrolling over peaceful waters, the air service pilots were being thrown into a savage death-struggle, in which each of them would be expected to engage in three or four dogfights a day. The life expectancy of newcomers was just eleven days. Casualties quickly mounted, and morale plummeted. But Brown, of all people, did very well. He may not have been much of a fighter but he was an above-average pilot. In battle, German pilots found they couldn't keep him in their sights for more than a split second. He'd been flying for years and he whipped his little Pup around with ease, quickly darting out of harm's way and gaining the upper hand on less-experienced flyers.

On September 11, he demonstrated his skill to the whole squadron, smartly outmanoeuvring an Aviatik two-seater before sending it down in flames for his second confirmed victory. Before the month was out, three more opponents fell before his gun, making him an ace.

More impressive still, Brown won the Distinguished Service Order, the British Empire's second-highest award for gallantry in the face of the enemy. He won the coveted decoration for an extraordinary act of courage. In the midst of a fierce battle, his gun jammed and Roy dove for his own lines. Looking back over his shoulders to see if any adversaries were tailing him, he caught sight of a lone British pilot trying to fend off four determined Albatroses. Brown wheeled around and came charging back into the fray like some berserk pit bull. He came within two feet of ramming one of the startled Germans and all four of them scattered. In the resulting confusion, both he and the Englishman made good their escape.

By late November, having survived several more close calls, he was granted leave and sent home to Canada. But just after Christmas, he was back on a ship, headed for England. The boat had hardly docked when he received orders immediately transferring him to the front. He arrived at a time of grave crisis: the German high command, in a desperate gamble, had launched a massive offensive all along the front. They knew they had to score a knockout punch before American troops, who were just beginning to flood into Europe, could swing the tide of war in favour of the Allies. Their attack drove the British and French armies back forty miles in just a few days. This was shocking: in four years of fighting, the lines had hardly moved at all, and generals considered an advance of a few dozen yards to be a great victory. The bombastic English commander, Douglas Haig, issued orders decreeing that every man should fight to the death.

Brown very quickly found himself in the thick of the fight. Posted to 209 Squadron, Royal Air Force (the air service and the Royal Flying Corps had been amalgamated to form the RAF), he flew as many as four missions per day. This meant taking part in nerve-wracking ground-strafing attacks, designed to beat back the waves of German infantry: a pilot couldn't be given a more thankless assignment. To be effective at all, he had to dive within a few feet of the ground, where he was an easy target for anti-aircraft gunners. And any enemy planes that came on the scene would have the all-important advantage of height. Moreover, there was little glory in the work. The Sopwith Camel pilots plunged into long columns of advancing grey-clad soldiers, cutting them down with ruthless bursts of fire. Brown openly admitted that he was sickened by the work; nevertheless, he did it well. He had long been one of the best pilots on the Western Front and he was becoming a crack shot. No one knows how many ground troops he killed during this period, but it is known that he shot down seven more German planes.

The men who flew with Brown liked him enormously. He had a self-deprecating sense of humour and was genuinely humble about his achievements. Indeed, he had the reputation of submitting victory claims only if he was certain the enemy plane had been destroyed. In fact, on at least two occasions, he received credit for victories only because fellow-pilots had witnessed his kills and filled out reports.

The squadron commander, C.H. Butler, realized he had a mature, responsible individual on his hands, and named Brown a flight commander. But the twelve-kill ace didn't welcome the promotion. He was finding the strain of daily combat difficult to cope with, and the responsibilities of command weighed further on him. Indeed, Brown was on the verge of cracking up. He had several close calls, including a half-dozen unsettling encounters with a green Fokker triplane. Brown was flying a Camel with a cherry nose and, whenever the pilot of the green Fokker spotted him, he made straight for the Canadian. On two occasions the sharpshooting German had riddled Brown's Camel with bullets, shaking him up so badly that he had to be helped from his seat after landing.

Brown found a new problem on his hands when he returned from a patrol in mid-April. An old school buddy, Wilfred "Wop" May, had joined the squadron, and Roy feared for the rookie's life. May had gone to college with Brown and the two had been fast friends. May was an extrovert who loved a party. In fact, he was two days late reporting to the squadron because he had become involved in a wild drinking binge on his way to the unit's base at Bertangles. Major Butler was so furious that he ordered May back to England, dismissing him as a "bloody fool." As the crestfallen Albertan stepped out of Butler's office, he walked right into Roy Brown. He tearfully explained his predicament and asked Brown to go to bat for him. Roy did so at once, literally begging Butler to let May stay. He didn't want to see his friend killed in action but, in those days, such a fate was considered preferable to being sent home in disgrace. Butler reluctantly agreed, only because he held Brown in high esteem. But he insisted that May must fly as a member of Brown's "A" flight.

On April 20, Brown led May and the rest of the flight on two offensive patrols. The first one was uneventful but, during the second, they ran headlong into a Fokker triplane. Brown drove it off after a short skirmish but, when they got back to the airfield, he looked exhausted. One of the men who saw him that day was ace Ray Collishaw. Collishaw belonged to a neighbouring squadron and had come over for a visit with Brown, who was an old friend. He remembered a handsome, black-haired, square-jawed pilot full of joy for flying. The man he found that afternoon was utterly different. There were grey hairs in his head, he had lost twenty-five pounds and his once-sparkling eyes were now bloodshot and sunken in his face. Brown admitted he'd been living for more than a month on a diet of milk and brandy. He said he had already had a nervous breakdown and that he was suffering from a severe ulcer.

Collishaw was shocked and begged his friend not to fly any further missions. But both men knew that was impossible. The war was out of control. Enemy troops were threatening Paris, and no one could get out of combat with anything less than a battle wound. Combat fatigue was simply not understood in those days.

Still, as far as Collishaw was concerned Brown was incapable of further fighting at the time. He recalled, decades later, that "Brown was definitely in a bad way, both mentally and physically, and he was both nervous and had lost his nerve."[2]

Oliver LeBoutillier, an American who flew in Brown's squadron, had a similar impression. He said the Canadian was "fast developing a full-blown ulcer."[3] Brown's "reserves had been drained" by the strain of daily combat, he added. But he "never complained, he simply carried on and kept his troubles much to himself." LeBoutillier said the whole squadron was in a bad way. It wasn't uncommon for a flight of pilots to collectively down a bottle of Scotch on the tarmac just prior to dawn patrol. And there was no diversion after battle was over. Bertangles, in the words of one pilot who was there, was "a dirty forsaken hole." There was no hot water, meaning that pilots had to travel to Amiens just to get a bath. Many went for days at a time without bathing. They were forced to sleep in tents because there were no permanent buildings, and the airfield was usually shrouded in a thick fog each morning. It was a dreary spring with plenty of cold air, rain and mud to add to the bleak surroundings.

A Similar Ordeal

Forty-five miles away, at Cappy Aerodrome, the pilots of Jagdstffell 11 were suffering through a similar ordeal. Their quarters were little better than those at Bertangles and, like the Allied flyers, the men of Baron Manfred von Richthofen's Flying Circus were completely exhausted. They only kept going because their leader, the fabled Red Baron, wouldn't let them quit.

Richthofen, a stocky, handsome young man with blond hair and an easy smile, had earned his nickname by fighting in a blood-red Fokker. Like Roy Brown, he was just twenty-five. And like the Canadian, he was tired. Richtofen had been at war since August, 1914, when he first crossed into Russian territory on the back of a cavalry horse. Later, on the Western Front, he had that horse shot out from under him by a Frenchman: the episode convinced him that there was no future in the cavalry, and he applied for a job in the Imperial Air Service. He got one — in the back seat of a bomber on the Russian Front. Richthofen was a good shot and, although he was merely a gunner, he quickly showed his stuff, shooting down an enemy plane. He applied for pilot's training and was accepted. But after winning his wings, he was sent to a two-seater squadron and ordered to carry out mundane reconnaissance duties. Still, he managed to shoot down a fast French fighter plane and that convinced authorities to post him to a single-seater outfit.

Transferred to Jasta Two, (a Jasta was a German fighter squadron) under the leadership of the legendary Oswald Boelcke, he quickly blossomed into a top-notch fighter. Richthofen downed an English two-seater on his first mission and, after that, Allied planes began falling like raindrops before his guns. He closed out 1916 with sixteen victories to his credit, and among his victims was Major Lanone Hawker, a Victoria Cross winner and the leading British ace. Given command of his own Jasta in 1917, the Red Baron went on the rampage. He killed English ace A.W. Pearson, a Military Cross winner, on March 9, and then, in an almost unbelievable display, shot down twenty-one Allied planes during the month of April. Despite suffering a rather serious head wound on July 6, he was back in action later that summer, adding more victims to his score. By year's end, Richthofen was the world's leading ace, with sixty-three kills to his name. He had a reputation as a pilot who would close in point-blank to obtain a victory.

When the Germans launched their big attack in the spring of 1918, the Richthofen Circus was at the forefront once again. The Red Baron mowed down another seventeen planes, adding Major Raymond-Barker, yet another English ace, to his total on April 20. As he went to sleep that night, he had eighty confirmed conquests to his credit. But Richthofen wasn't very excited about his achievement. His old head wound still bothered him and he was depressed over the loss of so many friends. He could list the names of dozens of flying mates who had been killed in action. Once a rather swaggering, arrogant fellow who openly boasted of his victories, he now wrote: "I no longer possess an insolent spirit. It is not because I am afraid, though one day death may be hard on my heels; no, it is not for that reason, although I think enough about it. I am in wretched spirits after every battle. When I set foot on the ground I go to my quarters and do not want to see anyone or hear anything. I think of this war as it really is, not as the people at home imagine, with a Hurrah! and a roar. It is very serious, very grim."[4]

April 21 dawned cold, foggy and damp. Both Richthofen and Brown saw the thick fog and went back to sleep. Each hoped that it would last all day, giving them a merciful rest.[5] But by 9:00 a.m. the skies had cleared, and they were forced out of bed. Brown awoke after only five hours of restless sleep. He was suffering from a severe stomach pain and a badly inflamed colon. Later, he admitted it was all he could do to sit up in his bunk. The Red Baron, never an early riser, wasn't physically ill. He always took good care of himself, never going to bed drunk or staying up too late. Nevertheless, he was mentally tired and could only continue because of his strong sense of duty to the fatherland and to his men.

On the flight line, Richthofen was annoyed to find an army band in attendance to salute his eightieth kill. Richthofen no longer took any pleasure in the slaughter, and the tribute disturbed him. Nevertheless, he was in a playful mood with his men. He kicked the leg out from under a cot set up outdoors on the flight line, dumping a sleeping pilot on his butt. When another man set the cot upright and lay down, Manfred repeated the prank. The two junior officers got their revenge by tying a huge wooden wheel chock around the tail of Richthofen's pet dog. When the hound came mournfully up to his master dragging the wheel chock, the Baron patted him lovingly on the head. At that moment, someone snapped a photo and Richthofen's sour mood reappeared. He always considered it bad luck to have his picture taken just prior to takeoff. He then looked around for his cousin, Wolfram. The younger Richthofen was going on his first sortie, and Manfred warned him to avoid combat if at all possible. He was to turn for home if Allied planes were spotted.

At almost the same moment, Brown was giving similar instructions to May. At 9:15 a.m. fifteen Sopwith Camels roared down the runway at Bertangles and headed east. A few minutes later, two flights of Fokker triplanes left the ground at Cappy and flew west. In a bizarre twist of fate, both formations ran into enemy two-seaters shortly after takeoff. Brown and his men piled into a pair of Albatros two-seaters. The Canadian ace fired a few bursts but his bullets failed to find their mark. However, one of his men, Merrill Taylor, shot one of the enemy down in flames. The second

German dove into a cloud and fled. Richthofen, meanwhile, led his men into an attack on two Australian R.E.8 two-seaters. The Red Baron's marksmanship was no better than Brown's. The Australians, however, shot down one of the triplanes and then escaped. The Red Baron, fuming over the loss of a man, and the getaway of the R.E.8s, regrouped his pilots and continued the patrol. Roy Brown, displeased with his own shooting, signalled his flyers to get back in formation and made a course for German territory. The two formations were on a collision course.

Brown spotted the Germans first. He immediately signalled May to leave the area and then led 209 Squadron to the attack. Richthofen saw them coming and the two groups came together with guns blazing. Planes twisted and turned in close quarters, firing in short bursts before veering off in desperate bids to avoid crashes in midair. The fight was so wild, LeBoutillier said later, it was "like trying to catch lightning in a bottle!" Brown got cracks at two triplanes but failed to down either one. The little Fokkers, with their three wings, could turn more tightly than the Sopwiths, and Brown soon found both of his adversaries on his tail. Bullets whizzed past his right ear. Brown slowed his Camel down almost to stalling speed, and the two enemy planes roared right by him.

May, meanwhile, looked on from several thousand feet above the dogfight, itching to get into the thick of it. A German passed directly under his wings, but he ignored the temptation and obeyed orders. But when a second Fokker glided by, it was more than the headstrong young Edmontonian could stand. He peeled over on his side and came tearing down on top of the unsuspecting triplane. It was Wolfram von Richthofen. But, in his eagerness, May sent a burst wide of the mark and then thundered right past the German. By the time he pulled out of his dive he found himself smack in the middle of the battle. May held his guns wide open, spraying bullets all over the sky without hitting a thing, and, as a result, both of his Vickers soon jammed. He wisely dropped out of the struggle and headed for Bertangles.

The Red Baron, who was keeping an eye out for Wolfram, had seen May's Camel dive on his cousin. When May continued on into the dogfight, Richthofen's eyes followed him down. And when the rookie banked over hard and headed for home, the Red Baron was still eyeing him. Almost unnoticed, the red Fokker slipped out of the pack of whirling fighters and went after the retreating Sopwith. The Red Baron was being extraordinarily careless for a skilled veteran. It was an unwritten rule of aerial combat not to chase an opponent low to the ground behind enemy lines; Richthofen himself constantly warned his pilots against it.

By this time, May was feeling rather pleased with himself. He had fired his first shots in anger and had driven off a German plane. What's more, he had gotten away scot-free! Or so he thought. Machine-gun bullets suddenly slashed into his plane, sending up a shower of wood splinters and sounding like a whiplash as they ripped through the canvas. Glancing hurriedly over his shoulder, May caught a glimpse of a scarlet Fokker perched right on his tail. He could see the twin Spandau machine guns flashing. And just behind the guns he could make out the goggled face of the pilot.

May should have died right then and there, but the tired Baron failed to kill him with that first burst, just as he had missed the R.E.8 a few minutes earlier. May didn't wait around to see if the German ace would improve his shooting. He dove steeply away, zigzagging as he went. Richthofen stuck with him, matching each move and firing incessantly. Several more slugs smashed into the Sopwith.

Dodging and Spinning

"I kept on dodging and spinning, I imagine from about 12,000 feet until I ran out of sky and had to hedgehop over the ground" May wrote later. "Richthofen was firing at me continually. The only thing that saved me was my poor flying. I didn't know what I was doing myself and I do not suppose that Richthofen could figure out what I was going to do. We came over the German lines, troops firing at us as we went over. This was also the case coming over the British lines."[6]

Brown, in the meantime, saw May's predicament and came hurtling down to the rescue. But he was a long way from the action and May would have to survive for several more moments before his commander could save him. For his part, the rookie had all but given up. "I got on the Somme river and started up the valley at a very low altitude, Richthofen very close on my tail," May recalled. "I went around a curve in the river just near Corbie. Richthofen beat me to it and came over the hill. At that moment

I was a sitting duck. I was too low down between the banks to make a turn away from him, I felt that he had me cold, and I was in such a state of mind at this time that I had to restrain myself from pushing my stick forward into the river, as I knew that I had had it."[7]

May wasn't the only one in a state of near-panic. On the ground, people were scattering for cover as the two fighter planes came swooping down on them, their engines straining so hard that they could have popped from their mounts. Bullets from Richthofen's guns sliced into the ground, wounding two Australian soldiers. Several of the Aussies were firing back, even though they were just as apt to hit the Camel as the Fokker. Brown was now in a position to fire. He pulled out of a screaming dive barely two plane lengths away from the triplane. He couldn't possibly miss. Unleashing forty rounds, he saw the Red Baron snap bolt upright in his chair just as he roared past him.

But the Fokker remained airborne for almost another minute before crash-landing. As it came down, it was subjected to a hail of fire from below. Sgt. Alfred Franklyn was one of those blazing away and he later claimed the German crashed just after he opened up. Gunner Robert Buie made the same assertion, as did Sgt. Cedric Popkin. A rifleman who discharged a single shot also claimed the honour of downing the German ace. In any event, the Fokker did not appear to be seriously damaged and several Australian troops rushed over to it, determined to capture the pilot. When they got there, they found Manfred von Richthofen still strapped in his seat. He was stone-dead.

Word quickly spread that the dead aviator was the war's greatest ace, and souvenir hunters hacked the triplane to pieces. They carted away virtually every bit of it, taking with them evidence that might have proved conclusively whether or not the killing burst came from above or below. The best evidence, of course, was the body. But no attempt was made to open it. The doctors who examined Richthofen disagreed amongst themselves. Some insisted the fatal blow came from the sky. Others believed it must have come from the ground. But with thousands of wounded Allied soldiers to treat, there was no time to waste on an autopsy of a dead enemy. Richthofen was shipped off to Bertangles, placed in a hangar a hundred yards from Brown's hut, and prepared for burial.

When 209 Squadron landed later that morning, returning in-
dividually or in twos and threes, everyone was astonished to
discover that none of the Camels had been lost. One pilot had been
wounded in the back and most of the machines were badly shot
up. There was so much damage, in fact, that the afternoon patrol
had to be cancelled. They were all happy just to be alive.

Brown was unsteady on his feet when he climbed out of his
fighter. He filed a brief report before retiring to his quarters,
completely exhausted. It read: "Dived on large formation of 15-20
Albatros Scouts D-5s and Fokker triplanes, two of which got on
my tail and I came out. Went back again and dived on pure red
triplane which was firing on Lieut. May. I got a long burst into
him and he went down vertical and was observed to crash by
Lieut. Merrersh and Lieut. May. I fired on two more, but did not
get them."[8] It was a typical Roy Brown report — modest to a fault.
The captain made no claim to have shot the triplane down. He
said simply that he had fired on it and two other pilots had seen
it crash.

But, before the ink had dried on the document, a bitter controversy had erupted. The Australians were insisting that they had
killed the Baron. And the Royal Air Force, ever mindful of the
propaganda value of air heroes, was demanding that Brown get
the credit. In an absurd compromise, Brown was awarded a second Distinguished Service Cross while, at the same time, the
Aussies were officially congratulated in a telegram from higher
authorities.

Historians and popular writers, of course, weren't about to be
satisfied with that. "Who killed the Red Baron ?" became one of
the great unsolved mysteries of the war, spawning books, magazine articles and newspaper debates for more than seventy
years. Those who favoured the ground-gunners latched onto the
fact that Brown never actually claimed in his report that he shot
Richthofen down. He wasn't sure himself, they trumpeted. Brown,
however, was certain. A week after the historic clash, he wrote to
his father, saying "we shot down three of their triplanes.... Among
them was the Baron who I shot down on our side of the lines."[9]
Publicly, though, he refused to be drawn into the distasteful discussion. The longer it dragged on, the less he would say about it.
In later years, when asked about it, he refused any comment
whatsoever.

Brown wasn't just being modest. He realized nothing he could say would put the issue to rest. He was convinced that the more he said, the longer the controversy would rage. And rage it did. Long after the war, he was hounded by reporters. Occasionally, he received death threats from German-Americans living in Detroit. He paid no attention to them and carried on with his life, operating an airline in Ontario and Quebec. During the Second World War this relatively quiet man shocked his family and friends by running for Parliament. But, despite his fame as the man who had vanquished the Red Baron, he lost. He died of a heart attack a few years later, in 1944. He was fifty years old.

Throughout his life, Brown refused to use his main claim to fame to advance himself. As the recognized killer of Richthofen (most people in those days accepted that he was the victor) he could have gone places, had he been willing to sensationalize his exploit. But he flatly refused, going to his grave leaving many with the impression that he didn't really believe he had brought down the fabled ace.

The real reason for his reticence can be found in something Brown wrote a few years after the war. When Richthofen's body was brought into Bertangles on the night of April 21, 1918, it was laid out in a hangar. Brown was one of the Allied servicemen to pay his respects to the German that evening. When he emerged from the tent, Sgt. Lewis Gyngell recalled later, the Canadian was nauseated. What he had seen was enough to turn any man's stomach. Manfred von Richthofen, a young, handsome, courageous flyer like himself, had been transformed into a lifeless, battered corpse. His eyes were open and his top teeth were caved in by the force of the crash. There was an ugly gash on his waxen chin. Brown, staring at the body, realized that, if circumstances had been different, the two might have been friends. He wrote that: "…the sight of Richthofen as I walked closer gave me a start. He appeared so small to me, so delicate. He looked so friendly. Blond, silk-soft hair, like that of a child, fell from the broad, high forehead. His face, particularly peaceful, had an expression of gentleness and goodness, of refinement. Suddenly I felt miserable, desperately unhappy, as if I had committed an injustice. With a feeling of shame, a kind of anger against myself moved in my thoughts, that I had forced him to lay there. And in my heart I cursed the force that is devoted to death. I gnashed my teeth,

I cursed the war! If I could I would gladly have brought him back to life, but that is somewhat different than shooting a gun. I could no longer look him in the face. I went away. I did not feel like a victor. There was a lump in my throat. If he had been my dearest friend, I could not have felt greater sorrow."[10]

In the final analysis, what are we to make of Roy Brown and the Richthofen controversy? The whole truth about the dogfight may never be known, but it seems indisputable to me that the Canadian ace fired the fatal shot. Brown, to his lasting credit, would probably have preferred to have not been the one to have ended the Baron's life. The Australian claims, although made in good faith, cannot be taken seriously. Virtually every Aussie who took a pot-shot at the German claimed the honour of shooting him down. They told wildly conflicting stories, with some even insisting there were only two planes — the Baron's Fokker and May's Camel — on the scene. A few admitted Brown was there, at least for a few moments. In reality, there were no less than four Camels in the immediate vicinity and three pilots came forward with reports backing up the Canadian.

Brown's victory was not only legitimate, it was also of enormous historical importance. Most of the leading German aces who survived the 1914-18 conflict went on to become Luftwaffe generals in the Second World War. Ernst Udet and Hermann Goering are the best examples. Goering, a grossly incompetent leader, became head of the Nazi air force. Had Richthofen been alive, he would probably have been given the post. And with the highly proficient Red Baron at the helm, the Germans might well have won the crucial 1940 Battle of Britain. Had they done so, they might have been able to invade England and perhaps win the war.

On a less speculative note, Brown's kill was also important because it saved the life of "Wop" May. The rookie flyer went on to become Canada's most famous northern bush pilot of the 1920s. He won fame for supplying medicine to remote Yukon communities and for helping the Royal Canadian Mounted Police track down the legendary "Mad Trapper." May directed the search from the air, making it easier for the Mounties to nab the notorious bandit.

Brown was a gentle but principled man who got out of his sickbed to provide his men with the leadership they needed.

We should remember him most for that, and for the fact that he wasn't so much trying to kill Richthofen as attempting to save May. He hated war and killed strictly out of a sense of duty. When the fighting was over, he wanted only to get on with his life and leave the events of April 21, 1918, in the past.

TWO

Ray Collishaw

Ray Collishaw was a swashbuckling adventurer who may have shot down more planes than any other pilot in World War One. Officially, he scored sixty-eight kills but unofficially, his tally stood at eighty-one. However, what made him unique was that he transcended his limited formal education and became one of the great air-force generals of the century.

Born on November 22, 1893, in Nanaimo, British Columbia on Vancouver Island, Ray dropped out of school at age fifteen and went to sea as a cabin boy. He got his first taste of danger aboard the Canadian Fisheries Protection ship *Alcedo,* sailing into the Arctic Circle in search of a vessel from the ill-fated Stepnasson expedition that had been crushed by ice. His ship left the halibut fishing grounds, where its job was to arrest American fishermen caught in Canadian waters, and headed north to look for survivors. Sailing through the Bering Strait and into the frigid waters of the north, they found they were too late to be of any assistance. The ice had smashed the missing ship to splinters and the crew was dead. After the voyage, Collishaw applied for and received the British Polar Ribbon. Later, legend had it that he earned the decoration by sailing to the south pole with the celebrated explorer Robert Scott. The story, unfortunately, isn't true, although he did manage to get to China on one of his trips. These experiences whetted his appetite for adventure, but it was a hard life for a youngster. "You jumped to it when you were told to do something and you definitely didn't hand out any sauce to your betters or sulk about if you didn't particularly like a job that was handed you,"[1] he recalled later. Still, there was no overt bullying and the food was surprisingly good. For a lad fresh out of grade eight, it was all very exciting indeed.

When the First World War broke out, in August, 1914, Collishaw decided to join the navy. Canada's naval force was only four years old at the time, and he guessed correctly that it wouldn't be seeing much action. So he left for England, determined to sign up with the Royal Navy. In the United Kingdom, however, he saw airplanes for the first time and decided on the spot that there was more drama to be found in the sky than on the waves. But because of his loyalty to the sea, he opted to enlist in the Royal Naval Air Service rather than the land-based Royal Flying Corps. It was a decision that would cost him dearly.

In the air service young Ray quickly discovered that naval officers had little use for airplanes — or for pilots, for that matter. They were traditionalists, who believed airplanes would be of little value in warfare and, as a result, the British Columbian often found himself shovelling coal while his plane was disassembled and stored below deck. When he did get the opportunity to fly, it was on a French Caudron. It was a crude machine that was difficult to handle and he had to make several forced landings due to engine failure. If there was even a hint of bad weather, flights had to be cancelled. And like Billy Bishop, Collishaw had trouble with his landings, often levelling out ten feet above ground and then bouncing in with a resounding thump. Once, his engine cut out and he glided in for what looked like a perfect landing when — without warning — the engine roared back into life. Caught by surprise by the sudden burst of speed, the rookie pilot crashed straight into the ground. Fortunately, he was so low he walked away with only a few bruises. But despite his troubles, he was allowed to solo after only eight-and-a-half hours of air time.

But his difficulties weren't only in the air. Collishaw soon discovered that going into town for a visit could be even more dangerous than flying. German zeppelins were bombing England with virtual impunity and the populace was in an ugly mood whenever it saw an Allied airman. Several of Collishaw's friends were attacked and badly beaten by a mob when they tried to get into a Kent theatre.

Despite these trials and tribulations, he was, in some ways, more fortunate than many other rookies. He received a good deal of attention from the redoubtable John Alcock, an instructor. Alcock would later become the first pilot to fly across the Atlantic Ocean, completing the feat in an open-cockpit biplane in 1919, eight years before the famous Lindbergh flight. Alcock made Collishaw a better pilot but he couldn't stop the youthful Canadian from getting into trouble. Once, flying over the home of a comely English girl, and attempting to drop a love note, Ray's engine died. The plane crashed into a row of outhouses, covering him with human excrement and toilet paper. The young lady, needless to say, was not impressed when she got a whiff of him. "It was highly embarrassing to note the number of lavatory items which made their way back to the station with what remained of the machine," he said later.[2]

When he received his wings, he was posted to a Sopwith two-seater bomber squadron and told to prepare for long-range raids into Germany. The Allies, fed up with zeppelin attacks on London and Paris, had decided to strike back at industrial towns in the Ruhr Valley. As fate would have it, Collishaw was one of those chosen for the historic first strike on the Mauser Arms Works at Oberndorf. It was to be a major effort — by 1916 standards — with eighty planes taking part. Collishaw admitted later that he was nervous before the flight. Anyone who wasn't, he said, was a fool.

The Sopwiths were equipped with special fuel tanks that gave them an amazing endurance of seven-and-a-half hours. More than forty of them took off at dawn on October 12, accompanied by a large group of French Breguet bombers and an escort of Nieuport fighters from the famous Lafayette Escadrille. The Escadrille was a fighter squadron in the French air force made up of American volunteers. Although the United States was still neutral at this time, a handful of American adventurers were flying with the British and the French. The French government assembled all of the American pilots into one unit and named it after a hero of the American Revolution, the French general Lafayette. The Escadrille captured the imagination of the American public and reminded the U.S. that France had come to its aid in the past.

The armada of warplanes crossed the Rhine River at 10,000 feet, encountering some light anti-aircraft fire, or "Archie," as it was nicknamed by the pilots, but suffering no casualties. Then it happened. A swarm of Fokker D-3s from Germany's "Grasshopper Jasta" (so named because of the grasshopper insignia painted on the unit's planes) came diving out of the sun to intercept them. This was a crack outfit that included a young Lieutenant named Ernst Udet. Udet sent one of the French bombers down in flames that day, gaining his first victory. By the time he was finished, exactly two years later, another sixty-one Allied aircraft would fall before him.

Udet and Collishaw didn't fight each other that day, but the Canadian had his hands full with two other German aces. His adversaries included Lt. Otto Kissenberth, a nineteen-kill pilot, and Ludwig Hanstein, who would end the war with sixteen conquests. Collishaw banked to give his gunner a clear shot at one of the brown-painted ships. A short burst damaged Hanstein's Fokker and he dropped out of the fight. Collishaw, showing killer instinct in his first battle, followed him down, blasting the German with his forward gun. According to Collishaw, the enemy pilot splashed into the river below. German records say he made an emergency landing beside the waterway. In either case, he had been shot out of the sky, and the Canadian had his first victory. It was also very nearly his last, because his engine began skipping badly and he barely completed the 200-mile trip home.

Despite Collishaw's victory, the raid was not a success. Nine bombers had been lost, and very little damage was inflicted on the rifle factory. A few warehouses had been badly damaged, but the plant remained in operation. As far as Collishaw was concerned, the main benefit of the mission had been the lessons learned.

A few weeks later, he and the other pilots of Naval Three Wing put those lessons to good use, destroying three furnaces at the Hagendingen steel works. Collishaw was the last man in, dropping his bombs into a cloud of dense smoke immediately below. The strike was carried out by a much smaller force, which managed to get in and out of Germany without being detected by enemy fighters. His next raid, against the Dillingen steel works, was more hair-raising. Hit by ground fire, Collishaw glided home with a dead engine, crash-landing near Nancy in France. The plane was a write-off, but neither he nor his gunner were hurt.

Winter weather then set in, and the airmen looked forward to a rest. But Collishaw seemed to be able to find excitement and danger no matter where he was. Once, he went boar-hunting with a group of French officers and was horrified to see several Allied soldiers accidentally shot by the would-be hunters.(No boars were brought down.) Back at the base, Canadian pilots and observers took over one of the hangars and turned it into a giant hockey rink. The matches were so dirty, he recalled, that even "the most bloodthirsty" modern National Hockey League goons would have been reluctant to join in. Anyone within ten feet of the puck was considered fair game for a slash or a crunching body-check. And even more vicious were the poker games, in which several men lost every cent they had in the world. It must have been almost a relief when, in late January, 1917, skies cleared and the unit went back into action.

Collishaw's first flight was on January 23, when his Sopwith was badly mauled by a persistent and skillful Fokker pilot. None of the squadron's planes were lost in battle, but one, still carrying a bomb, crash-landed at home base. The blast severed the pilot's leg and killed three nearby mechanics.

A few days later, Collishaw himself came close to death in one of the most remarkable narrow escapes in the history of air warfare. He was ferrying a new Sopwith back to the squadron without a gunner in the back seat when he inadvertently strayed over enemy lines and was jumped by six of the fast new Albatros fighters. Collishaw didn't even know they were on his tail until reddish-brown tracer bullets began slamming into the cockpit, shattering his instrument panel. One slug actually hit his goggles, sending glass into his eyes. Partly blinded, he flew on instinct, kicking the rudder bar and twisting and turning to throw off the aim of his opponents. Barely able to see, he dove to the treetops, hoping the Germans would more cautious near the ground. One of them proved him wrong, chasing the Sopwith so recklessly that he crashed his Albatros into a tree. The other five, after seeing their comrade crash, broke off the attack rather than trying wild manoeuvres near the ground. One of them, however, carelessly strayed in front of the Sopwith, presenting even a half-blind man with an easy target. Despite the stinging pain in his watery eyes, and his blurred vision, Collishaw managed to score a direct hit, and the black-crossed machine fell minus a top wing.

The Nanaimo boy was now alone in the sky but he wasn't out of hot water yet. His vision was now almost completely gone. He couldn't even read his compass, which was directly in front of his face. Relying on the sun, he flew westward in the direction of home. After a time, still lost, he regained enough of his sight to spot large objects below. And soon after, he could barely make out an airfield just ahead of him. Letting out a huge sigh of relief, he set his wheels down and taxied up to the tarmac. As the Sopwith rolled to a stop Collishaw looked up and saw a group of men running out to greet him. That was a nice gesture, he thought, and was about to wave his thanks when he noticed they were wearing grey uniforms and brandishing rifles. Glancing over his shoulder to the flight line he saw a row of Fokkers, with their distinctive black crosses. He'd landed on a German airfield!

Wasting not a second, the panic-stricken pilot gunned his motor, whipped the plane around and roared off down the runway. Several gunshots rang out, but Collishaw managed to lift off safely. The enemy pilots scrambled into their machines, bent on catching him. Despite his head start, the Germans, in their faster single-seaters, easily caught up with him and closed in for the kill. Several bursts of fire snapped flying wires and punctured the wings of the big Sopwith, but didn't hit any of its vital parts. Somehow, Collishaw managed to evade the Fokkers in the clouds, but his eyes were now virtually closed shut and he could just make out the ground below. He flew above the trenches for several miles, not realizing that the Allied lines were only a few hundred yards away. German anti-aircraft crews blazed away at him for several minutes before he realized where he was and made a mad dash to safety.

No Permanent Damage

Eventually, he managed to land at a French airfield near Verdun. He stayed three days, having his eyes treated by a kindly old doctor who cleared the glass out by bathing them in a tea-leaf solution. Miraculously, he suffered no permanent damage.

The French government was so impressed with his escape from the clutches of enemy troops, pilots and anti-aircraft gunners that it bestowed the Croix de Geurre on him — Collishaw's first gallantry award. The British gave him a posting to a fighter squadron. It couldn't have come at a worse time. The Royal Flying Corps was being pulverized on the Western Front and several naval squadrons were rushed to the Arras sector to lend a helping hand. Collishaw arrived in February, 1917, just as action was really heating up.

Surprisingly, he wasn't welcomed with open arms by the hard-pressed RFC. Because most naval squadrons did little more than patrol the peaceful English coastline looking for zeppelins that they almost never found, RNAS pilots were held in open contempt by RFC aircrews. Canadian John Brophy wrote in his diary that the RNAS was "commonly called the Hot Air Service. And well named it is too, because they don't do a thing but spend their time in England living in palatial dwellings. They have only one station in France and do less than any RFC squadron out there. They receive Military Crosses if they fly in windy weather, and pages of hot air when they nip a Hun near Dover, who was trying to get back home. They don't even know there is a war on."[3] There was some truth to the bitter comments. Because few naval pilots had ever even seen a German plane, they were shocked to find themselves thrown into the daily grind of aerial combat. Some, perhaps understandably, reacted with cowardice. On several occasions soon after he arrived, Collishaw said later, he found himself flying alone just as a fight was about to break out. Looking around in astonishment, he would see his whole flight racing at top speed for home. When he confronted them back at base, they all claimed to have engine trouble, or to have lost sight of the enemy.

Despite the lack of support, and several unforeseen mishaps, he managed to do well. Flying a Sopwith Pup on February 15, he shot an Albatros down from seventy yards' range. The Pup had only one gun but it was extremely agile and Collishaw had little trouble getting on the German's tail. But the experience was frightening, because afterwards his engine died and he had to glide home without power. Cold weather caused him to miss several sure kills in the following few weeks. Just as he'd worked himself into position for an easy shot, the plane's gun would jam in the frigid air. It wasn't until March 4 that he registered another victory. Escorting a flight of FE2b two-seaters on a spy mission over Cambria, he attacked three Halberstadt fighters, getting on the tail of the leader before sending him spinning into the mud.

A few weeks later, on March 24, his goggles were shot from his face for the second time. To make matters worse, his gun jammed and Collishaw was forced to lean out of the cockpit, into the icy slipstream, to clear it. Without the protection of his windscreen or goggles, his features were exposed to the full blast of the prop wash and he was severely frostbitten within minutes. When he landed, his eyes were almost closed and his head had swollen to the size of a bloated watermelon. He was hospitalized in England for more than a month.

When he returned to the front in late April, Collishaw found himself posted to Naval Ten, a squadron equipped with the new Sopwith Triplane. The plane was even more handy than the Pup. Its three wings gave it an incredible rate of climb and a tight turning ability. At 100 miles per hour, it was slower than the Albatros but more than compensated with its amazing manoeuvrability. Its only real drawback was that, like the Pup, it had only one machine gun, compared to the two carried aboard every German fighter. He got his first taste of battle in the new triplane on April 28, flying three missions and scoring one kill. The Germans had never encountered triplanes before and were taken by surprise by the tight turns. Their own Fokker Triplane was still on the drawing boards and wouldn't see action for another five months. Collishaw allowed an Albatros to get on his tail before zipping around, gaining the advantage in seconds. One burst sent the enemy falling in pieces into the sea. Two days later he repeated the trick, destroying a D-3 over Cortemarcke. There was a brief lull in his scoring but on May 10, Collishaw got his first "flamer," sending another Albatros down. There was no cause for joy, however. The sight of his opponent burning alive sickened him, as he frankly admitted in his later writings. But despite the undeniable horrors of war, he had to keep fighting, and two days later he sent a German seaplane crashing into Ostend harbour, killing two young airmen.

The squadron moved to Droglandt, near the Belgian border, where it was to be thrown into the toughest fighting on the front. Directly across from them was Baron Manfred von Richthofen's dreaded Flying Circus. The Baron, who was destined to die the following April in a clash with Roy Brown, was at the top of his game, with fifty-two kills to his credit. Collishaw and his pilots would be facing the cream of the crop in the German air force. Nevertheless, the Allied flyers were in a cocky mood. Collishaw was put in charge of "B" flight, which was made up entirely of Canadians. That wasn't unusual, because thirteen of the squadron's fifteen airmen were from the Dominion. To boost morale, he ordered his men to paint their machines black. It was a direct challenge to Richthofen and his men, who were flying in bright red Albatroses. If all this seems a little ridiculous today, it should be remembered that all the pilots on both sides were little more than schoolboys. Many of them, in fact, were still teenagers.

Collishaw had four good men under his command and he knew it. Ellis Reid of Belleville, Ontario, had been a University of Toronto student when war broke out. John Sharman, of Oak Lake, Manitoba, was widely regarded as the best pilot in the service. Bill Alexander, a University of Toronto graduate, had been so anxious to get into combat that he signed up illegally, lying about his age. Gerry Nash, of Stoney Creek, Ontario, was a big, strapping farm boy with a wonderful sense of humour. The five got along famously, deciding to name their machines. Collishaw had the nickname "Black Maria" painted on the side of his ship, just below the cockpit in white letters. Reid flew "Black Roger," Sharman fought in "Black Death," Nash in "Black Sheep" and Alexander in "Black Prince." Within weeks they would be the most feared Allied flight on the Western Front.

The group went into action together for the first time on June 1, over Menin. Flying at 16,000 feet, the "All Black Flight" spotted three Albatroses droning along a few thousand feet below. Collishaw led the assault, sending one down in flames from thirty yards range. Three more Germans came to the rescue, but Reid took care of them, shooting one down and driving the other two off. Two days later, the black triplanes struck again. Flying at sunset over Lille, they pounced on a flight of Germans. Collishaw scored twice, sending one down on fire. He followed up on June 5 by flaming a two-seater. But the unit's biggest day was June 6, when Naval Ten recorded an incredible ten victories. The Black Flight did most of the damage, as ten triplanes lit into sixteen Albatroses and Halberstadts escorting a lone Aviatik two-seater. Collishaw shot down three Albatroses himself. Nash got the two-seater and an Albatros, while Reid bagged a Halberstadt. Sharman and Alexander each won a victory. Clearly, the enemy's domination of the skies during the previous spring was now history.

But the Canadians were becoming over-confident and, in battle, that can be fatal. Collishaw didn't bother to keep a close eye behind on June 9, and it nearly cost him his life. An Albatros got on his tail and destroyed his instrument panel with a burst of fire. Black Maria floated helplessly down, crashing in a heap. British Tommies who pulled the stunned Canadian from the wreckage were shocked to find him unhurt, despite the 16,000-foot plunge. Two days later, Collishaw was shot down again but his remarkable luck held. As his crippled triplane tumbled end-over-end, his

seat belt snapped and he was hurled into space without a parachute. While falling out of the cockpit he grasped frantically for
the centre-section struts, just managing to get a gloved hand on
one of them. It was a fantastic sight: the Sopwith Triplane roaring
down out of control, engine full on, while the pilot hung on with
one hand as it plunged to earth. He got so close to the ground that
he could make out individual trees, and his right arm was aching
so fiercely that he feared it would be ripped right out of its socket.
Somehow, he managed to hook a boot back into the cockpit and,
by superhuman effort, to lever himself back into his seat. Pulling
frantically on the joystick, he lifted Black Maria's nose. Too late.
The ship slammed into the ground and was destroyed. Once again,
however, Ray Collishaw walked away unhurt.

In any other air force, he would have been granted a rest. But
the RNAS didn't take shattered nerves into consideration. It sent
the Canadian right back into the fray. In a remarkable demonstration of skill, courage and resilience, he shot down two Germans
on June 14 and, before the month was over, knocked down six
more. But Naval Ten wasn't having everything its own way. On
June 26, the Black Flight ran headlong into the Richthofen Circus,
with disastrous results. Karl Allmenroeder, a close friend of the
Red Baron, shot Gerry Nash down, but fortunately the Canadian
wasn't killed. Allmenroeder, the son of a Catholic priest, had been
studying to become a doctor when the war began. Inspired by tales
of the ace Oswald Boelcke, he applied for a posting to a fighter
squadron. Before long, he was one of Richthofen's best men. In
fact, Nash was his thirtieth victim.

But, despite his victory over a member of the dreaded Black
Flight, Allmenroeder was a tired man. He'd been in combat for
months and was badly in need of a rest. He refused to take one,
however, explaining his reasons in a letter to his sister. "You beg
me urgently to take leave, but the situation at the Front is similar
to that at Arras last spring. I would find no rest with you.
Richthofen and I fly ever together, one watching the other. We
have many newcomers in the unit and I am one of the few remaining old-hands. You can imagine that he would not like me to go
and that at the moment I would not wish to go."[4] He wouldn't get
a chance to change his mind. The day after Nash was shot down
the Flying Circus and the Black Flight clashed again. And this
time the Canadians came out on top. Collishaw had made a mental

note of the fact that Nash had been shot down by a green-and-red Albatros and, when he spotted Allmenroeder, he went for him. Firing from long range, he killed the German pilot with one burst.

A Wild Melee

July came, and Collishaw continued his impressive string of victories. On July 2, he drove down an Aviatik two-seater. The enemy gunner's return fire had been accurate, and the Canadian was forced to return to base with a sputtering engine. Four days later, Collishaw and Richthofen went at it again, in one of the biggest dogfights ever seen on the Western Front. Six FE2b two-seaters from Number 20 squadron, RFC, were set upon by thirty Albatroses, including the Red Baron and seven of his men. Collishaw arrived on the scene with the Black Flight, and a wild melee developed. Two of the FE2bs were shot down, carrying four men to their deaths. But one of the FE2b gunners, Lieutenant A.E. Woodbridge, took revenge by shooting down Richthofen! One of his bullets grazed the side of the Baron's head, and he fell several thousand feet before regaining his senses and making an emergency landing in a cow pasture. Weak from loss of blood, Richthofen was rushed to hospital and was out of action for more than a month. Meanwhile, the battle continued to rage overhead. Collishaw, in a virtuoso performance, shot down six Germans. Mel Alexander got two and Reid nailed one. It was small wonder that Collishaw won the Distinguished Service Order. The official citation, in the understatement of the year, said he had displayed "conspicuous bravery and skill in leading attacks upon hostile aircraft."

One of the Black Flight members who lived to a ripe old age was Mel Alexander. He was devoted to Collishaw and, decades later, remembered him as a charismatic leader and an inspiration to others. He also painted a grim picture of aerial fighting, writing that he had "butterflies" in his stomach and was "almost panicking" on patrols. After flights, his jaws hurt from muscular tension.[5] No doubt Alexander and the rest of the Black Flight were suffering from such strain on July 12, when another full-scale brawl broke out with the German Air Force. Collishaw led the flight against three Albatroses, shooting one down. The pilot was seen to crumple in his cockpit, and the machine fell out of control.

Thirty more Albatroses flashed to the rescue and Reid, fighting like a madman, shot down two of them. Collishaw found himself single-handed against six Germans, but he somehow managed to shake them off and escape.

The flight wasn't so lucky on July 22, suffering a devastating blow. John Sharman, who by now had nine kills to his credit, was killed. In the midst of a dogfight his triplane was hit, probably in the fuel tank, and exploded in a million fragments. No trace of man or machine was ever found. Another Naval Ten pilot, from a different flight, was killed in the same combat. After this, Collishaw decided two guns were needed if the unit was to maintain its edge, and personally strapped a second Vickers onto his engine cowling. The extra weight reduced speed but he felt the added firepower more than compensated for it. And he made his point on July 27, shooting down two opponents. Reid got two more and a newcomer to the Black Flight, Nick Carter of Calgary, racked up three more. Unfortunately, the Germans were shooting back, and a British pilot named Gerry Roach, went down in flames. The fight raged for an hour — an absolute eternity in aerial combat — and when Collishaw landed he found his clothing soaking wet from perspiration.

So ended Collishaw's time with Naval Ten. After a three-month leave, he would join a new squadron. While assigned to the Black Flight, he had scored an amazing twenty-seven victories. In all, the fearsome group of six Canadian triplane pilots had shot down eighty-seven German planes while suffering only two losses themselves. It was one of the most incredible records in the history of air warfare. Still, when Collishaw arrived back in Canada, he found he was virtually unknown. Billy Bishop was on leave at the same time and he was receiving all the headlines. Collishaw rested quietly on Vancouver Island. If he was bitter about the lack of public acclaim he never let on. Nowhere in his public or private writings does he express disappointment at his lack of fame.

When he returned to Europe, in November, he was posted to St. Pol, in northern France, flying the hot new Sopwith Camel. His duties included flying cover for Royal Navy ships and escorting RNAS bombers. The Camel was notoriously difficult to fly but, once mastered, it was a dangerous opponent to face. It flew fifteen miles per hour faster than the triplane and was lightning-quick on turns to the right. Much to Collishaw's joy, it also came equipped with a pair of Vickers machine guns.

There was little action in the district, but the British Columbia ace, true to form, still managed to get into trouble. He downed an Albatros on December 19 while escorting a flight of DH4 bombers to their target. A few days later, the squadron's commander was lost, and Collishaw was appointed leader. He immediately demonstrated that high command had made the right decision when he led his squadron into an attack on the big German seaplane base at Zeebrugge. The squadron took a large formation of enemy machines by surprise, shooting down three without a loss. One of the kills was credited to Collishaw. The Canadian was then put in charge of Naval Three, which included ten Canadians among its roster of eighteen pilots. The unit was stationed at Mont St. Eloi near Arras. At first he saw little action, because he found himself swamped with paperwork but as the summer of 1918 approached he was in the air as much as possible.

Collishaw proved himself, to no one's surprise, to be a brilliant commander. He often gave credit to rookie pilots for victories that were his own. Whenever a newcomer arrived, Collishaw would take him aloft to look for enemy two-seaters. When the target was sighted, Collishaw would signal the novice to attack. Often the inexperienced fighter would spray bullets aimlessly about the sky. Collishaw would slip in unnoticed beside him and shoot down the enemy himself. Back home, the ace would slap the new man on the back and congratulate him for his "kill." The praise helped rookies blossom into competent flyers.

Despite his new responsibilities, his own string of victories kept increasing. He now favoured the head-on attack. He would charge straight at enemy fighters in a test of nerves. Whoever broke off first would expose himself to a hail of bullets. If neither gave ground, the confrontation could only end in a fatal collision. Collishaw always held his position, and invariably, the other pilot would give way. Using this tactic, he shot down two Pfalz fighters on June 11 and a pair of the new Fokker D-7s three days later. For his accomplishments, he won the Distinguished Flying Cross.

Collishaw's greatest feat came on July 22, when he and an Englishman named Leonard Rochford raided an airfield fifteen miles behind enemy lines. Each man carried four twenty-five-pound bombs under his wings and extra ammo. Rochford led the way, coming in at treetop level as he shot up the barracks, mess and hangars. When his guns were empty he dropped his bombs, setting a giant tent on fire. Collishaw, who had been providing overhead cover, swooped in next, shooting up three Albatroses parked on the tarmac. More planes were being frantically wheeled out of hangars, and a German two-seater suddenly bumbled onto the scene. The enemy pilot seemed totally unaware of what was happening, despite the fact that a hangar was on fire and two Allied fighter planes were only yards away from him. He set about landing his big machine, making a routine approach. The rear gunner was no more alert. His arms were seen to be folded and he was leaning back in his chair. Collishaw exacted the price for carelessness, shooting the enemy down in flames.

The two Camel pilots, their guns and bomb racks empty, turned for home. But Collishaw stayed on the ground only long enough to reload and refuel. He was going back to inspect the damage. As he returned to the ruined airfield, he spotted an Albatros circling overhead and shot it down. For the day's work, he was recommended for a Victoria Cross, the Empire's highest award for bravery in combat. However, when the award came through, it had been downgraded to a Distinguished Service Order. Rochford had to settle for a Distinguished Flying Cross.

Increasingly, Collishaw's fighting duties included ground-strafing, as the German army was driven out of its trenches and forced into the open while it retreated across France. Like most pilots, he hated the work, which he considered to be extremely dangerous. Not much skill was required. Even a relatively poor pilot could shoot up long columns of soldiers caught on a roadway, but a stray bullet from below could bring down a rookie or a veteran with equal ease. In one strafing attack, Collishaw saw one of his flight commanders — J.P.Hales, from Guelph, Ontario — shot down only yards in front of him. Although dogfights became less frequent, the Canadian ace kept adding to his score, shooting down four planes and a balloon during August. One victim was a DFW two-seater which he destroyed on August 9, diving below it before raking the underbelly with 150 rounds. Next day, at dusk, he saw a dozen Fokker D-7s harassing a lone Sopwith Dolphin near Bray. Ignoring the odds, he sneaked up on the Fokkers, sending one crashing into the Somme River and knocking a second down out of control. He had to withdraw, however, when his own engine was damaged by German bullets. On August 15, flying alone, he rescued a Spad pilot. Collishaw shot down one of two Fokkers attacking the Spad, whose pilot got the other.

In September, he scored five more times, beginning the month by ambushing a Fokker as it tried to sneak in behind an Allied balloon dangling above Bourlon Wood. But his most impressive fight of the month came on the twenty-sixth, when he led a low-level attack on the airfield at Lieu St. Amand. In all, thirty-six Allied planes took part, including eleven SE5s, fourteen Camels and eleven Bristol fighters. They rained ninety bombs and 8,500 bullets down on the German camp. Three hangars were set ablaze. A handful of brave Fokker pilots managed to get airborne, but most were quickly destroyed, with Collishaw getting two. One Camel was lost to ground fire, but the pilot survived. On his way home, Collishaw strafed a group of soldiers near the airfield. "All in all it was a most successful affair," he wrote.

The war was now winding down. He engaged in one more combat that month, when he attacked a balloon. Two Fokkers latched onto his tail, and it was obvious from the ease and speed with which they performed their movements that both were flown by old hands. One of the enemy shot the controls out of Collishaw's cockpit, just missing him. One of his wingmen was less fortunate and crashed.

A Tougher Time

On October 22, Collishaw was ordered to report to the Air Ministry in London and, three weeks later, the Great War came to a close. Most records give him sixty kills but don't take into account balloons, eight of which he sent down in flames. Officially, then, his score was sixty-eight. But he claimed eighty-one kills. Had he flown for the Royal Flying Corps, where confirmations were given more easily, that would have been his score. But because of the rivalry between the two air services, many of his claims were not accepted by a high command that favoured the RFC over the RNAS. RNAS pilots, in general, had a tougher time getting confirmation of their victories. They also had more difficulty winning decorations. A dozen men in the RFC, with far less impressive credentials than Collishaw, were awarded the Victoria Cross; but the British Columbian never won the coveted medal, even though he was twice nominated for it. Had he flown for the RFC, he would almost certainly have won the VC and been credited with more victories than any other pilot on either side.

Despite his shabby treatment at the hands of higher authority, Collishaw was determined to remain in the air force at the end of hostilities. Because the Royal Canadian Air Force still didn't exist, he jumped at the chance when offered a permanent commission in the Royal Air Force. Poor treatment or not, he liked the way of life. Thus, while most of the world had stopped fighting, for Collishaw, it was just beginning. Some of his most breathtaking adventures and exploits still lay ahead of him. After a lengthy leave in Canada, he was posted to southern Russia in 1919, as part of the western Allies' intervention after the revolution there. The contingent he commanded was Number 47 Squadron, RAF. Officially, all the pilots were volunteers but, in reality, no one in the outfit was given even the slightest choice. Collishaw was ordered to lead ten pilots to Nororossiiski in June, 1919. They were flying Sopwith Camels and DH9 two-seater bombers.

The main threat, at first, was from typhus. There were no medical supplies and anyone who caught the disease usually died a lingering death. Before long, people were dropping like flies. But, days after the squadron arrived, Captain J.L. McLennan of Montreal was killed by small-arms fire while attacking a balloon. Collishaw's first combat came in late August, when the Bolsheviks attempted to float troops down the River Volga in broad daylight. Attacking in his Sopwith Camel, he scored two bomb hits and sank a gunboat. He thereby became one of the few aces in history ever to sink an enemy vessel.

On the ground, the war was sickening to behold. Walking through villages that had been ransacked by Bolshevik troops, he found bodies of women, children and old men hacked to pieces and scattered about. But from the air, events looked almost beautiful. Once, he watched a spectacular cavalry charge, in which Cossacks and Muslims, with green banners flapping in the wind, thundered across the plains. From his vantage point, he said, he felt like a time-traveller witnessing a battle in the fifteenth century.

His first aerial combat came on October 9, when he shot down an Albatros D-5. The Russian pilot crashed into the Volga and disappeared from view. A few days later, he scored again, his seventieth kill. Collishaw would probably have further increased his score had he not contracted typhus aboard a train crowded with half-starved refugees. The ace became delirious and only survived because a gentle old Russian countess nursed him back to health in her cottage. He was flat on his back for several weeks before returning to action. By then, Allied troops were on the defensive, and Collishaw once again found himself heavily engaged in strafing enemy soldiers. On one sortie, four Camels caught a mass of Bolshevik cavalry on the open plains and inflicted 1,600 casualties on them. The horsemen were raked again and again by eight machine guns. With nowhere to hide, they suffered a terrible massacre, which ended only when the pilots had exhausted their ammunition.

This success — if we can apply that term to the one-sided bloodbath — was an exception. For the most part, the Allies were being kicked out of Russia with their tails between their legs. In the end, Collishaw and his men had to abandon their planes and flee aboard an old locomotive. It was a 500-mile retreat with the Bolsheviks in hot pursuit. This was the most harrowing experience of Collishaw's life. Without a plane to fight in he was out of his element. The train was loaded with diseased refugees. Dozens died and were tossed off. But the typhus continued to spread, perhaps because mothers hid dead children in their clothing rather than have them thrown from the train like sacks of garbage. To make matters worse, they were being chased by an armoured train, and rumour was that the Bolsheviks intended to castrate any pilots who fell into their hands. The evacuation was slowed down by frequent stops. Sometimes they had to repair tracks torn up by peasants sympathetic to the revolutionaries, or forage for wood to feed the engine. Women went out in blinding snowstorms, using their skirts to collect enough snow to keep them supplied with water. And more than once they were fired on by civilians as they limped through the countryside at twenty miles per hour.

Near panic broke out when the armoured train appeared behind them. A few Russian aristocrats on board the fleeing locomotive committed suicide because they feared being tortured to death. But somehow, the Allied train always managed to stay just far enough ahead of its pursuer. Once, they were almost caught. The Bolsheviks had a nine-inch cannon and they were about to fire it when a bend in the tracks saved the Allies from disaster. When they regained some distance on their pursuers, they stopped long enough to tear up the tracks behind them. That gave them some breathing room, but then, while the train refuelled at a place called Bolshoi Tomak, it was rammed from behind by a runaway locomotive sent churning down on them by the local Bolsheviks. Damage was slight, however, and they managed to make quick repairs and continue their flight. Finally, on January 4, 1920, the train limped into Crimea, ending what Collishaw termed a "nightmare journey."[6] The episode haunted him for the rest of his days; His experiences in Russia, he admitted, were far more terrifying than combat on the Western Front.

Once the airmen left the train, they were ordered to reassemble their planes and go back into action. Back in his element, Collishaw was deadly. He blew an enemy train off the tracks on February 18. A few days later, he scored bomb hits on another train, but return fire damaged his plane and he was forced to land in enemy territory. Fortunately, he came down on ice-packed snow and the ground was frozen so solid that he was able to taxi back to his own lines. By the time he left Russia, Collishaw was credited with two planes, one gunboat, two trains and a bridge. He also had three czarist medals to add to his collection of awards. That should have been enough action for any one lifetime but the ace wasn't done yet — not by a long shot.

His next postings were in the Middle East, starting in Iraq. Several Iraqi tribes were hostile to central authority at this time and rebelled against the rule of King Faisal. Because Iraq, in the words of Collishaw, was "a British mandate," the RAF was sent in to crush the rebels. Here, however, he encountered no enemy aircraft and his missions were bombing and strafing. Later, when Arab tribesmen rebelled against British rule in Mesopotamia, Collishaw was sent into combat again. The greatest danger in this campaign was engine failure behind enemy lines, a possibility that RAF pilots tried to counter by carrying notes, written in Arabic, informing captors that they could secure ransoms by releasing their prisoners unharmed.

Collishaw was disturbed to see that his men had no hesitation about bombing villages, even when women and children would be killed, but they flatly refused to drop explosives on livestock when given direct orders to do so. He considered attacks on

civilian targets to be dishonourable, much preferring to drop propaganda leaflets.

His most memorable adventure during three years of Middle
East combat occurred when he ventured into the desert to secure
water from a well. Recalling the incident in his autobiography
fifty years later, Collishaw said he descended into the cool, damp
place only to notice the walls appeared to be moving all around
him. With a sense of foreboding, he shone a yellow light on the
side of the well only to see it covered from top to bottom in hairy
scorpions. The sight made his flesh crawl but he continued to the
bottom, filled his bucket and took his leave as quickly as he could.

When World War Two began, in 1939, Collishaw was still in
the RAF, holding the rank of air commodore. Now too old for
combat, he was put in charge of air-force units in North Africa.
His main task was to neutralize the Italian Air Force, and he
wasted no time in carrying it out. The very day that Italy came
into the war, Collishaw ordered air strikes on the Italian base at
El Adem, adjacent to Tobruk. The results were devastating. Eighteen enemy planes were knocked out on the ground in just two
days. Collishaw's unit lost only three pilots. He then turned his
attention to bombing harbours, ships and concentrations of Italian
soldiers, with spectacular success. The Italian cruiser *San Giorgio*
was gutted by bombs and an enemy ammunition dump was blown
to bits.

Collishaw's fighter pilots were flying outdated Gladiator biplanes but, inspired by their leader and his advice on how to use
the sun and clouds to advantage, they shot down eight enemy
planes without a loss on August 17, 1940. Although badly outnumbered, the wily Canadian was able to turn the tide with aggressive tactics and trickery. He had only one Hurricane fighter
under his command, but he convinced the Italians that he had
many of the modern fighters by having it flown to a number of
different airfields in the desert. Italian formations kept taking
home reports of seeing a British Hurricane. He also used dummy
airplanes, built of wood and canvas, so that spy planes would see
Collishaw's bases apparently crowded with planes. And, in a
stroke of genius, he ordered single-plane raids on Italian army
units. His lone pilots caused little damage, but the Italian high
command kept receiving reports of constant air attacks and responded by spreading its own fighter forces thinly across the

battlefield. Collishaw even fitted transport planes with machine guns and bombs, and used them to attack Italian positions. Eventually, Collishaw was able to win complete air superiority in the desert. It was, in his opinion, his greatest career achievement.

After the war, he returned home and became part-owner of a mining operation in Barkerville, British Columbia. He settled nicely into retirement, saying his only regret in life was that he had taken so long to marry his wife, Neita Trapp. He had met her while on home leave in 1917 but they did not marry until mid-life because Collishaw's career kept him away from Canada for years at a time. The man who had cheated death a thousand times in five different wars died peacefully in West Vancouver in 1975, at the age of eighty-two.

Ray Collishaw's story is the most exciting of all of Canada's great aces. He was a man of incredible courage and daring who packed more adventure into one lifetime than you'd find in any three Indiana Jones movies. It is not surprising that he loved aerial combat and excelled at it. It took audacity to be a great fighter pilot and Collishaw had been daring since boyhood. What is amazing is how successful he became after the war. With only a grade eight education, he to graduated from RAF staff college and rose to the rank of air marshal. He'll be forever remembered as the brash young man who painted his plane black in an open challenge to the Germans, but he was correct in his assessment that his finest moment came when he defeated the Fascist and Nazi forces in North Africa a generation later. The term "military genius" is seldom used to describe air-force leaders. Instead, it is usually applied to generals who move vast armies in ground actions. But there can be no doubt that Collishaw was a master tactician. In the First World War, he displayed courage; in the Second World War, he demonstrated high intelligence. And in both struggles, he came through with flying colours.

THREE

Alan McLeod

The single most magnificent act of courage by a Canadian military aviator was performed by a fresh-faced schoolboy. Alan Arnett McLeod was a fifteen-year-old playing sandlot baseball in his native Stonewall, Manitoba when the Great War broke out in August, 1914. He was still a teenager when he won what many veterans consider to be the most deserved Victoria Cross ever awarded for valour in the face of the enemy.

Alan was a slight lad, unassuming and shy, but his father was a sturdy Scot who worked all his life for the Hudson Bay Company, and expected his son to take up the outdoor life. Alan enlisted in the Fort Garry Horse Regiment in the summer of 1913. He was only fourteen at the time, four years younger than legal requirement, and, with his youthful features, could have passed for a nine-year-old. But it was peacetime, and the authorities looked the other way. They let the boy groom horses, polish boots and take part in parades. It was mundane work, but he was thrilled just to be allowed to mingle with professional soldiers. "They even let me wear a uniform,"[1] he said, betraying a boyish innocence that would never leave him.

When war came, Alan naively expected to be going overseas with the Fort Garry Horse. Instead, he was told to pack his belongings and go home to his mother. The only consolation was that they let him keep a riding stick. Still, he admitted later, he choked back tears as he walked home that night. Like most everyone in Canada that summer, he saw the war as a great adventure that would soon be over. The thundering cavalry charge, with bugles blaring and sabres flashing, was the stuff of his dreams — and he was convinced he was going to miss out on the opportunity of a lifetime.

Alan was so disappointed that he decided not to take no for an answer. The boy hopped aboard a railroad boxcar and rode the twenty miles to Winnipeg, where he presented himself to the first army recruiting officer he could find, claiming he was eighteen years old. It was a comical scene. Photographs of Alan taken even four years later reveal a youth who looked like a grade nine student. The men in the line with him trying to enlist that morning were burly Mounties, rugged miners and sturdy farm boys. Many sported facial hair. The recruiter, who was middle-aged himself, took one look at Alan, threatened to spank him, and sent him home. The humiliating rebuff discouraged the boy for awhile. But, as the war dragged on and he grew a little taller, he decided to give it another try. He was still only seventeen, however, and once again he was sent back to high school.

Exactly one year later, on his eighteenth birthday, he quit school. His excited classmates and teachers threw a party for him and saw him on his way to Winnipeg. By this time, Alan's imagination had been captured by newspaper tales of aerial combat. Now, instead of the cavalry, he wanted to join the Royal Flying Corps. He still didn't look very warlike, but his birth certificate said he was old enough, so the recruiters had no choice but to accept him. He was signed up as a cadet pilot-in-training and ordered to the RFC flight school at Long Branch, near Toronto. Alan proved to be a born pilot. Like most teenagers, he had little concept of the permanency of death, and he tossed his Avro 504 training craft around the sky with reckless abandon, making a good impression on his instructors. His progress was so speedy that he soloed on June 9, 1917, with only three hours' flying time to his credit. By July 30, he had his wings and, on August 20, the new RFC lieutenant was sailing for England. He had fewer than fifty hours' flying time in his log book, including only six hours of dual instruction.

Alan had read the stories about Billy Bishop, Albert Ball and Manfred von Richthofen, and he dreamed of becoming a fighter pilot. Two of the Canadians who trained with him, Donald MacLaren of Vancouver, and Bill Claxton, of Gladstone, Manitoba, had similar dreams. MacLaren would go on to become one of the war's great aces, bringing down fifty-four enemy aircraft. Claxton wasn't far behind him, destroying nearly forty opponents. But Alan McLeod wasn't destined to share in their glory. When he arrived in the United Kingdom, British authorities took one look at him and decided he was too young for combat. Instead, he was posted to a Home Defence squadron. Here, he criss-crossed the night skies over London for hours on end, flying a rickety old BE12 in fruitless searches for German zeppelins. He improved his flying, but the work was frustrating and there was no fighting.

Originally, the RFC had planned to keep him in England until his nineteenth birthday, in April, 1918. But so many pilots had been killed during the bloody battles of Vimy Ridge and Passchendaele, that he was rushed to the Front in November 1917. At an age when most boys are still worrying about pimples, Alan McLeod was thrown into combat. He wasn't going as a fighter pilot, however. During his last training flights in England he was ordered to practise bombing runs, photography, artillery spotting and wireless work. Like it or not, he was going to war as a two-seater bomber pilot. Nor was his debut especially auspicious. When McLeod arrived at Two Squadron, near Hesdigneul in northern France, on November 29, 1917, his commanding officer took one look at the teenager and blurted out: "He's a bloody baby! We'd better win the war soon, chaps, because we're running out of men!"[2]

The squadron fought the war in the Armstrong-Withworth, a box-shaped machine that was absolutely massive by First World War standards. Its wing span was forty-three feet, it was more than thirty feet long and it stood eleven feet off the ground. It was also extremely slow, plodding along at between eighty-five and ninety miles per hour. By contrast, the German fighter planes could reach a top speed of 120 miles per hour. Moreover, the ship was a slow climber, needing twenty-three minutes to reach 10,000 feet, and made turns at a tortoise-like rate; looping it was completely out of the question. On the positive side, the "Ack-W," as it was affectionately called by its crew, provided a stable platform for photography and gunnery work. And it was well-armed, carrying a Vickers machine gun, which fired forward through the propeller and was operated by the pilot, and a rear Lewis gun used by the observer.

McLeod's debut was nothing to write home about. He flew on a ten-minute practice flight meant to acquaint him with the district and then crashed on landing, totally demolishing his landing gear. A fuming commanding officer grounded him for a week. He also decided young Alan was too inexperienced to go into combat without one of the best air-gunners in the business, so he assigned him to Lt. Fred Higgins, a six-month veteran of frontline duty. Higgins was a Canadian, from Sherbrooke, Quebec, and he quickly made McLeod feel at home.

The pair flew together for the first time on December 7. They were over enemy territory for two-and-a-half hours in a vain search for a German field battery. This kind of warfare didn't appeal to McLeod. He wanted to do more than direct Allied artillery fire, take photographs and drop bombs. He wanted a transfer to a fighter squadron. When he couldn't get one, he decided to use his lumbering old bomber as a fighter. Whenever his regular assignment was over, he'd head off looking for enemy planes to attack. Higgins, apparently, didn't object. McLeod found what he was looking for six days before Christmas. Or, more accurately, the Germans found him.

McLeod and Higgins were cruising deep behind enemy lines when eight Albatros D-3s jumped them. Not much is known about the dogfight. McLeod's combat report has not been found by historians. But a note in his logbook gives a hint as to what happened. It says, simply that he "scrapped with eight Huns — one spun away."[3] It isn't known whether the German fell to McLeod or Higgins. Probably both deserved equal credit. Two-seaters were no match for fighters, especially not when they were outnumbered eight-to-one. It would have taken a team effort for them to have gotten out of the jam alive, never mind with a victory. A few days later, on December 22, he was not so lucky. His elevator controls were shot away and he was barely able to nurse his crippled plane down from 6,000 feet for an emergency landing behind Allied lines.

But, before the year was out, McLeod became the talk of the Royal Flying Corps. Flying with a Lieutenant Comber, he found himself under attack from three Fokker triplanes. Comber kept up a spirited fire while his nineteen-year old pilot zig-zagged to throw off the aim of the German pilots. Eventually, as they flew closer and closer to the ground, they made their way back over Allied territory. The Germans almost never ventured behind British lines and the three pursuers reluctantly gave up the chase. They began leisurely regrouping for the flight home. McLeod, stealing a glance back over his shoulder, suddenly realized that the enemy fighters had spread out. Moreover, they weren't paying the slightest attention to the retreating Ack-W. Reacting instantly, he swung the big machine around in a wide circle and made straight for the nearest Tripe (a nickname for the triplane). The German was completely unaware of the huge airplane sneaking up behind him. No one would have expected such an outrageous attack. McLeod waited until the pilot's head filled his ring-sight before triggering his gun. The Fokker reared up, hesitated, fell over on one wing and plunged down, completely out of control. Comber, who watched it go down and crash into a million pieces, looked up in astonishment and yelled, "You shot the damn thing down!"[4] Back at the base, the rest of the squadron refused to believe Alan's story. The commanding officer would not grant confirmation, even after Comber backed up his story. Two-seater pilots simply didn't attack single-seaters, never mind shoot them down. And that was that — until a frontline British balloon observer phoned up and reported that he had seen McLeod's exploit.

On January 14, 1918, the young Manitoban added to his growing reputation when he caught an observation balloon dangling 2,000 feet over Lille. He flew twelve miles behind the lines to catch his prey, plunging through a curtain of anti-aircraft fire before pouring 100 rounds into the gasbag, which exploded in a bright orange fireball. McLeod had pressed home his attack to point-blank range. He was so close that he could feel the heat from the blast when the balloon erupted. Balloon-busting was dangerous work. The gasbags (also known as "*drenchens*") were protected by long-range machine guns, Archie cannons and swarms of fighter planes. You had to be quick — and nimble — to attack them with success. In other words, you had to be flying a fighter plane. When word spread that the Canadian had taken one out with an Armstrong-Withworth, he was mentioned in RFC dispatches.

His next exploit was almost as dramatic. McLeod had become annoyed by a certain anti-aircraft battery and decided to take it out. Flying in at treetop level one morning, he caught its crew by surprise, spraying the position with machine-gun fire. Several men fell and the rest ran for cover. Circling back around, he dropped a pair of twenty-pound bombs on the gun, scoring direct hits with both of them. Then he turned and flew home, leaving the German battery a smoking pile of bent steel. By this time, his commander considered him too valuable a man to waste on routine patrols. He gave McLeod a new gunner named Lt. A.W. Hammond, and told him to take on any mission that suited his fancy. Hammond, an Englishman who had already won the Military Cross, was in for the wildest two months of his life. Another two-seater pilot, Arch Whitehouse, recalled years later: "McLeod and Hammond put on a two-man airforce show that had the front ablaze. They spotted for the artillery in the morning and in the afternoon bombed anything in the German areas that moved or looked hostile. Late in the afternoon they became two-seater fighters or trench strafers. Sometimes they combined all three missions and generally came home shot to rags."[5]

Plenty of Targets

The mighty German offensive of March 21 was then in progress, and the two men had plenty of targets. They weren't alone. The sky was filled with Allied and German aircraft. The British were to be found low to the ground, strafing enemy troops. They went at it with such vigour, the German army's official history shows, that one Prussian officer was actually run over by an English plane!

    McLeod wasn't involved in that particular episode, but he was here, there and everywhere. On March 26, for instance, he and Hammond flew three bombing raids. The next morning, despite heavy fog, they were up again. McLeod lost his way in the soup and was forced to land at a neighbouring airfield. He damaged his plane slightly and had to wait around until past noon hour. The rest of the Two Squadron machines had long since returned to base, so McLeod and Hammond continued the mission on their own, directing Allied artillery fire onto unsuspecting German troops. Once that task was completed, McLeod decided to try his luck with a balloon he had spotted in the distance. Using heavy mist as cover, he shot it down with one burst of fire. But the burning gasbag attracted the attention of a nearby Fokker triplane, which made straight for the two-seater. McLeod, never one to run from a good fight, met the German's charge head-on. The two planes rushed at one another with guns blazing. One slug slammed into a centre-section strut, sending up a shower of splinters that just missed McLeod's face. Another ripped into the leather padding that rimmed his cockpit. But the Canadian kept firing back and scored a direct hit on the Fokker's engine. The German climbed above the Armstrong-Withworth, wobbling like a wounded duck, trailing a thick column of black smoke. As it flashed by, Hammond gave it a squirt from his Lewis gun and it fell away, on fire.

McLeod, thought he had pushed his luck far enough and he turned for home. But the Germans weren't about to let him get away. Out of the clouds hurled eight more Fokkers, their bright red noses instantly identifying them as members of Baron von Richthofen's Flying Circus. The Baron, who was less than a month away from his showdown with Roy Brown, was not among them. However, Lt. Hans Kirchstein, one of his top aces, was leading. Kirchstein, a holder of the coveted Ordre Pour le Merit, Germany's top valour award, had scored twenty-seven victories and, on one mission had blasted three British planes out of the air.

The enemy closed in from every direction, with guns firing. McLeod and Hammond found themselves being strafed by sixteen machine guns. The teenage pilot dove sharply to confuse the Germans, while Hammond returned their fire as best he could. One attacker, obviously contemptuous of the old two-seater, came too close and Hammond blew his head off. Kirchstein, enraged by the loss of one of his men, dove under the Ack-W and sprayed its fat belly with two dozen rounds. McLeod felt a stinging sensation in his side, took off a glove, shoved his hand inside his coat and brought it back out again. It was covered in sticky, warm blood. He had been shot three times. Looking back over his shoulder, he saw Hammond slumped in his chair. The Englishman, still alive, had been hit six times. Worse still, Kirchstein's fire had severed several controls and McLeod could no longer take evasive action. Seeing their predicament, another German foolishly flew in, too close, trying to finish them off. Hammond struggled to sit upright and squeezed off another deadly accurate burst. The Fokker literally disintegrated, falling in two before plunging away in flames. Kirchstein was making another pass. He scored a direct hit on the fuel tank and the Ack-W burst into flames. Fire engulfed both cockpits.

McLeod and Hammond seemed to be finished. They had no parachutes and they were still over enemy lines. And it seemed unlikely that they'd be able to get down before the plane turned into a blazing inferno. But Alan McLeod was far from finished. Struggling out of his cockpit, he climbed out onto the lower wing to escape the flames. Clutching a centre-section strut for support, he reached back into the cockpit with his other hand and continued to fly the crippled plane. Hammond was in an equally precarious situation. Fire had burned a hole right through the floor of his cockpit, and his chair had fallen out. To escape the flames, he climbed out onto the fuselage. Another German bored in with guns firing. Two more bullets ripped into McLeod's battered body, but the tenacious youth, still working the controls, side-slipped to give Hammond a clear shot at their tormentor. Firing the Lewis with his good arm, the Englishman shot the Fokker down. That was enough for Kirchstein. He signalled surviving pilots to withdraw. The bomber was obviously doomed, and he wasn't going to lose any more men finishing it off.

McLeod continued to side-slip, fanning the flames away from himself and Hammond. Somehow, he brought the big ship down for a crash landing in no man's land. He pushed his way through the burning debris and pulled his gunner to safety. German soldiers in forward positions were firing at them and McLeod was hit a sixth time. Miraculously, he managed to haul Hammond into a foxhole and the two men lay there until nightfall, when they were rescued by South African troops. They were given morphine to kill the pain and their wounds were patched up. Both men were near death from loss of blood, but they survived the three-mile stretcher ride to a field hospital. McLeod was only there for a few hours before being transferred to a hospital well behind the lines at Amiens. As soon as he was strong enough, he was sent to England for further treatment.

While McLeod was convalescing word came that he had won the Victoria Cross. The citation, which makes fascinating reading, said: "While flying with his observer, attacking hostile formations by bombs and machine gun fire, he was assailed at a height of 5,000 feet by eight enemy triplanes, which dived at him from all directions, firing from their front guns. By skilful manoeuvring he enabled his observer to fire bursts at each machine in turn, shooting three of them down out of control. By this time Lt. McLeod had received five wounds, and while continuing the engagement a bullet penetrated his petrol tank and set the machine on fire.

"He then climbed out to the left bottom plane (wing), controlling his machine from the side of the fuselage, and by sideslipping steeply kept the flames to one side, thus enabling the observer to continue firing until the ground was reached.

"The observer had been wounded six times when the machine crashed in no man's land, and 2nd Lt. McLeod, notwithstanding his own wounds, dragged him away from the burning wreckage at great personal risk from heavy machine gun fire from the enemy's lines. This very gallant pilot was again wounded by a bomb whilst engaged in this act of rescue, but he persevered until he had placed Lt. Hammond in comparative safety, before falling himself from exhaustion and loss of blood."[6] Hammond, who certainly deserved a VC as well, had to settle for a second Military Cross.

McLeod made good progress and his chances for a full recovery looked good. By September he was well enough to go to Buckingham Palace to receive the Empire's highest award from the king. But when he was sent back to Canada that autumn, he contracted Spanish influenza, which was just beginning to sweep the globe, claiming millions of lives. Had he been healthy, he probably would have been able to resist the disease but he was still in a seriously weakened state from his war wounds. He died in a Winnipeg hospital on November 6, 1918, just five days before the fighting ended.

Alan McLeod displayed the fearlessness of youth. His sense of invincibility enabled him to do the unthinkable — to climb out on the wing of a burning plane without a parachute and gamely fly home through a swarm of enemies. Society took advantage of his innocence and courage, filling his mind with tales about the romance of combat and then setting him loose when he was far too young to be in battle. His reckless conduct, from the moment he arrived in France was ample proof that he was too immature to handle important tasks. The Armstrong-Withworth was a bomber and he should not have been trying to use it as a fighter plane. Had he stuck to the jobs assigned to him, it's likely that he would have lived out his natural life span. But the authorities openly encouraged his recklessness, which, at least in the short term, helped the war effort. In the end, his magnificent courage became an inspiration to the whole Royal Air Force. But that is small comfort for a young life so tragically wasted.

FOUR

William George Barker

To all appearances, William George Barker was indestructible. The Dauphin, Manitoba native is celebrated in Canadian folklore as the pilot who won the Victoria Cross by single-handedly taking on fifty German planes and shooting down six of them despite being wounded in both legs and one arm. He was the top-scoring ace of either side on the Italian Front and today, he is probably the only World War One pilot, other than Billy Bishop, whose name would still be recognized by many Canadians. But the whole tragic story of Bill Barker has never been told, because writers have concentrated almost exclusively on his remarkable combat career, glossing over the terrible circumstances of his premature death.

As a boy, young Barker did little schoolwork, spending most of his time hunting birds with a shotgun on the Canadian prairies. He was also an accomplished horseman, so no one in Dauphin was surprised when he left to join the First Canadian Mounted Rifles at the outbreak of war. Barker went overseas in June, 1915, training as a machine gunner at Shorncliffe Military Camp before being sent to the Western Front. Here, he earned a reputation as a crack shot who could take apart and assemble his weapon while blindfolded.

The Mounted Rifles arrived in France to find the war was a hopeless stalemate. The opposing armies had settled into a bitter war of attrition fought largely from trenches. There was no room for horses in this type of fighting, Barker soon found himself slopping about in the mud as an ordinary foot-soldier. He slept in the rain, shared his meals with rats and was always dirty and cold. He was also tired all the time, because the hateful artillery bombardments made it impossible to sleep for long at night. There was nothing glamorous about his situation, and the Germans rubbed it in, erecting a huge sign on the other side of no man's land, about

300 yards away, that asked, in English: "Canadians, where are your horses?"[1] It was a query that irked Barker.

His disillusionment turned to horror when he was thrust into the Second Battle of Ypres only days after he arrived. It was an abominable bloodbath, in which both sides took turns making insane suicide attacks into machine-gun fire. Between charges, they pounded each other with cannon fire or poison gas. And the weather made things even worse. First it started to rain, causing sides of trenches to cave in. The battlefield became a muddy quagmire, in which drowning was a very real danger. After that, winter arrived and frostbite became a serious threat. Amid these hellish conditions, Barker looked up one day and watched a dogfight raging overhead. He watched in utter amazement as a German Fokker Eindekker shot down a British two-seater. Right then and there, he decided the only way out of the trenches was by joining the Royal Flying Corps.

Fighting in the air proved to be even more dangerous than the trenches. After just six days of training as an observer, Barker was sent into combat with a two-seater squadron stationed at Bertangles, in northern France. Overnight, he found himself in the greatest peril of his life. He was posted to Nine Squadron, which was equipped with the outdated BE2c, a slow, sluggish machine with such poor climbing ability that German fighter pilots disdainfully referred to it as "meat on the table." It was, without exaggeration, one of the worst airplanes ever built; so bad, in fact, that the Red Baron, Manfred von Richthofen, single-handedly destroyed sixteen of them.

Barker's squadron flew these sitting ducks into the Battle of the Somme, the bloodiest struggle in human history to that date. It began on July 1, 1916, with a frontal assault that cost the British army 60,000 men in the first half-hour. The battle dragged on for months after that, and the RFC was right in the thick of it, taking pictures of enemy positions, directing artillery fire and conducting bombing raids. Losses were heavy and, before the first month was out, almost every plane in the squadron had been shot down. One of the few survivors was Barker, who not only lived through the maelstrom, but scored his first victory. On July 29, a German Roland dove out of the sun onto the tail of Barker's plane, undoubtedly anticipating a quick, easy kill. But before he could trigger his Spandau gun, Barker caught him in the forehead with one burst from his Lewis, thus becoming one of the few BE2c observers throughout the entire war to record a victory. Two weeks later, he made history, shooting down a second Roland. These exploits, along with some expert troop-strafing, brought him his first mention in dispatches.

Having survived hazardous trench fighting and observation work, Barker longed for a new challenge. He applied for pilot training and was accepted into flight school at the beginning of 1917. Once again, he was a standout, winning his wings after only fifty-five minutes of dual instruction! Posted to Fifteen Squadron in northern France, Barker carried out the same duties as before, but as pilot instead of observer. His plane, the RE8, was slightly better than the BE2c. For one thing, it was faster by about ten miles per hour. For another, it had more guns. In addition to the observer's Lewis, the pilot had a forward-firing Vickers. Despite the increased firepower, it was no match for the new German Albatros and Halberstadt fighters; nevertheless, Barker made the most of what he had, shooting down an enemy plane on March 25, 1917. This victory was as unlikely as his previous exploits with the BE2c.

It should have been clear by now that Barker had the makings of a great fighter pilot. But, for some unknown reason, he was left for several more months on an observation squadron, where he earned a reputation as the best RE8 pilot in France. On April 25, during the height of the Battle of Arras, he was again mentioned in dispatches, this time for directing shellfire onto a trench crowded with an estimated 1,000 German soldiers. The enemy troops, who were preparing to go over the top, were cut to ribbons. Moments later, flying only yards above the heads of German machine gunners, he directed fire onto a pair of long-range cannons, wiping both of them out. Barker's plane was badly shot up, but he won the Military Cross and was promoted to the rank of flight commander. There were several more close calls during this period. Once, he crashed his battle-damaged RE8 on landing, completely demolishing it. Both he and his observer walked away without so much as a scratch. In August 1917 shrapnel from an exploding anti-aircraft shell nicked him on the side of the head, within an inch of his right eye. Blood gushed from the wound so fast that he nearly passed out, but he made it home, was bandaged up and immediately returned to action. His machine, however, was so riddled with slugs that it had to be scrapped. These heroics earned him a second Military Cross.

Barker finally got the break he was seeking when, in September 1917, he was sent back to England to train other pilots. Here, he had his first opportunity to fly the new Sopwith Camel, a 120-mile-per-hour single-seater fighter that could out-turn and out-climb the Albatros, And, like the workhorse of the German air force, it came equipped with two forward-firing machine guns. After eight months of flying an RE8, Barker could hardly believe his luck. He began clamouring for a transfer back to the front as a fighter pilot. But his applications were rejected time and time again. Almost any other pilot would have accepted his fate; many would have been glad to remain in England for the rest of the war. But not Barker. He became so distraught that, after one rejection, he stormed out of his commander's office and proceeded to buzz the airfield in his Camel. Coming in low, with the rotary engine full on, he rattled the windows and dishes in headquarters. He was so low, in fact, that his prop wash blew shingles off the roof! He might well have been court-martialled for this stunt but, instead, he was granted his wish. The Canadian was ordered to report to Twenty-Eight Squadron, which was flying Sopwith Camels on the Western Front.

Having gotten his wish Barker had to prove himself worthy of the task. His chance came on October 20, when three Camel squadrons and a formation of French Spads were assigned to attack the German airfield at Rumbeke. Three of the groups went in low, dropping bombs and spraying the hangars and barracks with bullets. When they departed, Barker's squadron came in behind them, looking for any Albatroses that might try to chase the retreating Allied planes. They found what they were looking for. A brutal dogfight raged for fifteen minutes before Barker settled the issue by shooting the wings off a green-painted German plane.

Four days later he had his first brush with the infamous Gotha bomber — a machine that was being used with great effectiveness against civilian targets in England. The big, twin-engined planes were on their way to bomb London when Barker's squadron intercepted them. No definite kills were scored, but the Canadian sent one of the raiders limping home with a dead engine. Only two days after that, he became an ace, downing two Albatroses in sensational fashion. He was leading six Camels, in the midst of a driving rainstorm, when he spotted a roadway crowded with marching German soldiers. As the Camels swooped down on them, guns chattering, the startled troops stood still for a moment in an eerie, frozen panic. Machine-gun bullets ripped through the column, toppling dozens of men like bowling pins. Thunder clapped all around them and lightning blots flashed across the purple sky. To the grey-clad soldiers, it must have seemed like a scene straight out of hell. All of them might have been massacred where they stood if a flight of Albatroses hadn't come on the scene and dived to the rescue.

The Germans shot down two Camels within moments, and Barker nearly became a third victim. An enemy fighter got on his tail and riddled his fuselage, from the tail section right to the edge of the cockpit. Turning as tightly as possible, Barker held on for dear life as his tilted wing-tips skimmed the tops of a stand of poplar trees. The German followed close behind, firing at every opportunity. Suddenly, Barker had a brainstorm. He knew that his machine was more agile than his adversary's. Maybe he could shake the German off by doing a loop, low to the ground. He wasn't sure that he had enough altitude to pull out before plunging into the mud, but he had to gamble. The German's bullets were whizzing past his head as he yanked savagely on the joystick. The Albatros pilot didn't dare follow him. Barker made his loop in seconds, levelling off less than a yard from the ground and directly behind the German. Still dizzy from the desperate stunt, he squeezed his triggers the moment the enemy's rudder appeared in his sights, sending the Albatros down in a ball of orange flame. A second German dove on his tail and Barker looped again. Within seconds another Albatros lay smouldering on the ground.

The young Canadian was hot! Two days later, he shot down another Albatros — his fourth kill of the month and seventh of the war. This streak convinced his superiors that Barker had the potential to become a top ace, but the fortunes of war dictated that he leave the Western Front. Things were heating up in Italy, and the Allies were losing. A massive offensive by the armies of the Austro-Hungarian Empire, augmented by crack German divisions, had rolled over Italian troops defending Caporetto. Almost 800,000 Italians had been captured in the first few days of fighting, and the whole front was on the verge of collapse. To help stem the tide, the Royal Flying Corps rushed three Camel squadrons, including Barker's, to Italy.

The Italian Front

The Italian Front has been called a "sideshow" by people who weren't there. But the combat, although not generally as large-scale as on the Western Front, was equally deadly. The main difference in the dogfights was that the air forces were smaller. The average formation consisted of only three planes, but, despite the smaller numbers, the fighting still produced several outstanding aces. The top Italian pilot, Major Francesco Baracca, killed thirty-four opponents before being killed himself. Enemy pilots also included several celebrated Austrian, German and Hungarian aces. Perhaps the most dangerous were Huptmann Godwin Brumowski, an Austrian who shot down forty Allied planes before he was killed, and Sgt. Josef Kiss, who had mowed down nineteen opponents when he lost a duel with Billy Barker.

Barker liked the landscape of Italy. The RFC pilots found themselves flying between snow-capped mountains, through vineyard-dotted valleys and above the sparkling blue waters of the Adriatic Sea. The scenery was breathtaking on every patrol. So much so, Barker later told fellow-Canadian ace Tommy Williams, that several pilots were killed because they were so busy looking at the countryside below that they failed to keep a sharp eye out overhead or behind.

Barker scored the first British victory in Italy on November 29, 1917, while leading a flight of four Camels 10,000 feet over the town of Sernaglia-Pieve di Soligo. The formation was jumped by a dozen Albatroses. The Canadian put an end to the battle after twenty minutes of exhaustive fighting by shooting one of the Austrians to shreds. His combat report tells the story: "I dived on one and fired about 50 rounds and he went down in a vertical dive. I followed and as he flattened out at 5,000 feet I got a burst of about 80 rounds at close range. His top wing folded back to the fuselage and later the lower wing came off." Although the Austrians still outnumbered the Camel pilots eleven to four, they gave up and withdrew, perhaps short on ammunition or fuel. In any case, the dogfight clearly demonstrated just how good a pilot

Barker was. Only a highly skilled aviator could have kept out of harm's way — and scored a victory — against such stiff odds.

As on the Western Front, observation balloons played a major role in the air war over Italy. The big gasbags floated high above the battle lines, giving observers dangling below them in wicker baskets a clear view of enemy positions. It was important to shoot them down, but the task was extremely dangerous. Each balloon was protected by long-range machine guns on the ground and fighter planes overhead. Indeed, balloon-busting was one of the most feared missions among pilots on both sides.

Barker, however, quickly established himself as one of the war's top balloon-killers. He reasoned that teamwork was the key to success and he took two wingmen with him on December 3 to tackle his first balloon. The Canadian assigned his men to strafe the machine-gun crews while he went for the balloon. The tactic worked flawlessly. While his wingmen kept the gunners occupied, Barker closed in and sent the gasbag down in flames with one burst. His clever strategy also ensured that he would take out the balloon and be credited with the victory. When a green-and-yellow Albatros tried to interfere, the three Camels swarmed all over it. One of the Allied pilots, Stan Waltho, herded the German into Barker's line of fire. It was over in a flash. Lieutnant Franz Kerrsenbrock, a Jasta 39 pilot, with four victories to his credit, slumped in his seat. His plane crashed on the outskirts of Coneglianc. Not content with the double victory, Barker sailed down on top of an Austrian army staff car and caught it with a sword-thrust of slugs as it rounded a curve on a mountain road. The automobile, with a dead driver at the wheel, flipped over on its back and exploded in flames.

Barker continued his war on balloons with a vengeance. Once, with the help of Steve Hudson of Victoria, British Columbia, he shot five of them down in a single afternoon. (In all, he destroyed nine gasbags before leaving Italy, making him the number one balloon-buster in that theatre of operations.) Hudson and Barker were inseparable after that. They always flew together, one looking out for the other's tail. And they became legends across the front after a Christmas Day raid on an Austrian airfield at Matta. Years later, Captain John Mitchell, another Twenty-Eight Squadron pilot, told what happened. "On X-Mas Day 1917 Barker and a pilot named Hudson decided to do an impromptu raid on Motta aerodrome about ten miles over the lines. They secured a large piece of cardboard and wrote on it 'To the Austrian Flying Corps from the English RFC, wishing you a Merry X-Mas.' They then proceeded to shoot up the hangars and the personnel on the ground."[2]

Christmas was normally a quiet day, with both sides refraining from activity. An unofficial truce was in effect. Therefore the Austrians were angered by the raid, which they saw, with some justification, as an act of treachery. The commander of the Austrian air force was so enraged that he ordered an immediate retaliatory attack on British and Italian airfields on Boxing Day. The move proved fatal to many of his pilots. Most of his men had spent Christmas partying in the mess. Some had gone to bed dead drunk at 7:00 a.m. on Boxing Day, only to be routed out an hour later and sent on their mission of vengeance. As might have been expected under such circumstances, the counter-attack was a colossal failure. The drunken Austrian crews couldn't even maintain proper flying formation. They were scattered all over the sky. Most were spotted long before they reached their targets. Even those who got through did little damage, because they were too hung-over to shoot straight. One pilot was so drunk that he landed on a British runway and fell asleep in his cockpit. RFC pilots who rushed over to capture him thought his plane had been damaged, or that the man was wounded. Instead, they found him slumped over the controls, reeking of alcohol. In all, a dozen raiders were shot down, including one who fell to Barker's guns. If there was a down side for the Allies it was, as one of them noted, that they had to spend most of Boxing Day picking up prisoners.

Billy Barker was by then the leading ace in Italy and he added to his growing reputation on New Year's Day, 1918, when he shot down Lieutenant Koehlschlzky, a German Albatros pilot. Barker was escorting ten RE8s on a bombing sortie when he noticed the two-seaters were being stalked by an Albatros. Looking on from above, he waited until Koehlschlzky was committed to the attack before screaming down on top of him. He caught the German unawares and sent the D-3 tumbling into the side of a mountain. Four days later came word that Barker had won the Distinguished Service Order, the British Empire's second-highest award for valour. He continued increasing his score at a remarkable rate. On February 2, he ambushed eight Austrians, shooting down an

Albatros and an Aviatik two-seater. Captain Mitchell, who knew Barker throughout this period, credited the Canadian's marksmanship, and not his flying ability, for the astonishing string of victories. He thought Barker was a "little ham-fisted on the controls" of a Camel. "Whilst one could not say he was a good pilot, he certainly made up for this in his shooting. I was his deputy leader and probably knew more about him than anyone else. I have seen enemy machines break up in the air or go down in flames long before I realized we were in range."[3]

On the ground, Barker was all business. he didn't drink or smoke, and seldom joined in the good-natured pranks of the others. If he had a girlfriend — either in Canada or Italy — he never talked about her to the others. Those who knew him say he lived only to fly and fight. He was very ambitious and a little vainglorious. Once, after reading a newspaper article about the leading Austrian aces, he wrote the following note and dropped it behind enemy lines: "Major Barker, DSO, MC and the officers under his command present their compliments to Captain Brumowski, 41 Recon. Portobou Hole, Ritter von Fiala Fernbrugg, 51 Pursuit, Gajarine, Capt. Havatil, 3rd Company, and the pilots under their command, and request the pleasure and honour of meeting in the air. In order to save Capt. Brumowski, Ritter von Faila and Capt. Havatil and gentlemen of his party the inconvenience of searching for them, Major Barker and his officers will bomb Gopdigo aerodrome at 10 a.m. daily, weather permitting, for the ensuing two weeks."[4] The Austrians, who were always outnumbered on the Italian Front, could not afford to risk losing any of their top aces in some absurd tournament, and wisely declined the offer. Barker, true to his word, bombed the enemy airfield every morning for two weeks.

Perhaps angered by the refusal of the enemy pilots to go along with his juvenile challenge, Barker decided to take his frustration with the Austrian army one step further. He led his entire squadron down the streets of the town of San Vito al Tagliamento to attack the Austrian army headquarters. The Camels came in low over the Adriatic Sea, their wheels skimming just above the waves, before veering inland at the last moment. The planes were so low as they came up the street that people in second-storey windows were looking down at the Allied pilots. So low that Barker's plane was beneath the telephone wires. So low, in fact, that chips of brick were knocked loose by the wing-tips of planes brushing past buildings. No casualties were inflicted, although several generals were sent scrambling under tables as machine-gun bullets blasted through their windows. The raid was hard on the morale of the Austrian army, and provided a much-needed boost of confidence to the Italians.

The British were so impressed by Barker that they began to rely on him for every difficult mission that came along. He began flying spy sorties on moonless nights. Piloting a tri-motor Italian bomber, he'd go far behind enemy lines, where an agent would parachute into the inky darkness. On one occasion, a spy froze in his cockpit before jumping, so Barker decided to install a trapdoor in the bottom of the plane. On the next mission, when the same spy again hesitated to jump, Barker activated the trap and jettisoned his passenger. The poor fellow landed safely and managed to get back to Allied lines a few weeks later with much valuable information. Barker, who had made it all possible, was granted a Star of Valour by a grateful Italian government.

Enthusiastic Ace

Along with his nocturnal flights, the enthusiastic ace still found time for routine day patrols. On March 18, 1918, he shot down an Albatros. After landing, he had a white stripe painted on the wing struts for each victory he'd scored. A day later, flying 17,000 feet above a valley, he spotted six Albatroses guarding a single Aviatik two-seater. Without hesitation, he attacked, by himself. Within seconds, he found himself in a running fight with two enemy fighters. He sent one down out of control but the other managed to get on his tail, scoring several hits on the Camel's wings and fuselage. Barker rolled desperately out of the torrent of bullets and got in a burst of his own, in the instant that the Albatros flashed past him. The enemy pilot dove for 1,000 feet before pulling up to look back over his shoulder — just in time to see Barker, who had followed him down, open up with both guns. Two hundred rounds rang out, and the Albatros crashed in a cloud of smoke and dust.

By now, Barker had won his third Military Cross, but decorations didn't satisfy his ambitions. He wanted command and expected to get it when the squadron leader was sent back to England for a prolonged rest. Barker was not only the RFC's top ace in Italy and its most decorated pilot, but he was also a flight commander of proven ability. His promotion should have been automatic. But high command, for its own reasons, overlooked him, sending a newcomer in from the United Kingdom to take charge of the squadron. The man in question had no combat experience and Barker was so miffed that he demanded a transfer to another squadron. His wish was granted, and he was posted to Sixty-Six Squadron, which was also stationed in Italy. The only plausible explanation for Barker's being slighted seems to be that he was a colonial officer. Few Canadians were given positions of high authority in the RFC, regardless of how well they did. It wasn't impossible for a man from Canada to get ahead, but it was at least twice as difficult as it was for a Briton.

It didn't take long, however, for him to make his mark with his new companions. Leading two other Camels on April 17, he charged six Albatroses and shot one down. Three others went for him, but he got out of trouble when Stan Stranger, a Montrealer, shot down one of the D-3s in flames. That turned the tide, and Barker shot the wings off another Austrian. The third enemy pilot fled. On May 8, he destroyed an LVG two-seater and, on May 11, added another Albatros. Bill Hilborn of British Columbia and Gerry Birks of Montreal, both members of Barker's flight, each scored during the same dogfight.

The Manitoba ace won his first decoration with his new squadron on May 20, when he scattered a flock of Germans just as they were about to make mincemeat of a formation of French two-seaters. The French Air Force showed its gratitude by bestowing the Croix de Guerre on him. The next day, he destroyed yet another Albatros and, twenty-four hours later, bagged his first Austrian-built Lloyd fighter. Barker got behind the enemy pilot and was about to deliver the deathblow when the man suddenly waved his arms, indicating he wanted to surrender. Showing mercy, Barker signalled him to fly in the direction of the Allied lines. The thought of capturing an enemy plane intact appealed to him. He was just envisioning the reception he'd get back at the squadron when the enemy pilot had a change of heart and made a mad dash to escape. It was the last decision he ever made. Barker was on him quicker than it takes to tell, and this time there was no reprieve. He bore in relentlessly, sending the Lloyd down in flames. Activity was fierce at this stage of the war and Barker scored yet again on May 23, setting an LVG observation plane on fire after a brief scrap.

Barker's greatest victory in Italy — and perhaps of the whole war — came on May 24. Leading another three-man patrol, he encountered six enemy planes led by the Hungarian ace, Josef Kiss. Kiss, flying an outdated Berg fighter, had shot down nineteen British and Italian planes when he met up with Barker. In the rigidly class-conscious Austro-Hungarian air force, a sergeant-pilot could not become an officer, no matter how many planes he shot down. Kiss was from the lower classes, and that was that. Worse still, he was a Hungarian, and the Austrians were the real power in the Empire. It didn't matter that he had been in combat since 1916, that he had been wounded in action or that he was such a courageous pilot that he often offered himself as bait to Allied pilots by flying low while his men waited in ambush in the clouds above. When enemy planes jumped him in such circumstances, he relied on his exceptional flying skills to keep him out of harm's way until his wingmates arrived on the scene.

On this fateful date, May 24, 1918, Kiss and wingman Corporal Kasza, provided the decoy while three other Austrians circled in the sun above. Barker and two of his men walked right into the trap. But when the smoke had cleared, four of the Austrian ships had been downed, and Kiss and Kasza were dead. Barker had got both men. In his combat report, he was full of praise for the vanquished ace, terming him "exceptionally skilful." The Austro-Hungarians apparently agreed, finally deciding to award Kiss a commission — albeit posthumous.

The Austrians had lost one of their top aces, but they weren't about to throw in the towel. As the month of May came to a close, they launched an all-out offensive. The key to victory was to get thousands of troops across the fast-running waters of the Piave River. It was a gamble at that time of year because the waterway had been swollen by spring rains. Nevertheless, the generals ordered pontoon bridges thrown up under cover of darkness and began pouring men across at dawn on May 30. The RFC sent every plane it had in Italy into the air the next morning, in a bid to thwart the attack. More than thirty Camels bombed and strafed the Austrians in a day-long orgy of killing. Barker, one of the few great aces of the war who actually enjoyed strafing, was in his glory, leading six Sopwiths. His men dropped two dozen bombs, scoring seventeen direct hits. Two pontoon bridges, jam-packed with terrified soldiers, collapsed under the explosions and were swept down the raging river. Hundreds of men, laden with battle packs and heavy combat boots, were drowned. Sweeping back for another pass, Barker led a devastating strafing run on a truck convoy and a long column of infantry. Dozens more men died or were wounded before the Canadian turned his attention on an Austrian gun pit, killing the crew with a single burst. By the time he and the rest of the RFC pilots were finished, the enemy offensive lay in ruins.

The war was lost for the Austrians, but their pilots wouldn't concede that fact, and dogfights raged throughout June. Barker took on all comers, destroying a Berg two-seater on June 3 and a pair of fighters six days later. He added Albatros victories on the twenty-first and twenty-fifth, before downing a Berg and an Albatros on July 13. All of this was more than enough to convince the British high command of the previous error of its ways, and Barker was finally promoted to major and made a squadron commander. He was put in charge of 139 Squadron, which was also stationed in Italy. To his disgust, however, he discovered that it was a Bristol two-seater outfit. Barker had no intention of flying a bomber, and, in direct violation of regulations, he brought his Camel with him to his new airfield.

It was a brash move, utterly typical of him. It was also a very good one because, in his fighter, he was able to provide his men with the escort they needed on their raids. He proved that by shooting down an LVG on July 18, two Albatroses on the twentieth and an unidentified black-crossed machine on the twenty-third. For this, he won his second Distinguished Service Order. The citation noted: "Major Barker has frequently led formations against superior numbers of the enemy with conspicuous success." By now, indeed, he had forty victories in Italy to go with the six he had rung up in France a year earlier. The leading enemy ace, Brumowski, also had forty kills but had since died. On September 18, Barker broke the tie. Flying by himself, he attacked nine Albatroses, shooting one down in flames and sending down two others, out of control. He was now the undisputed leading ace in Italy, and no pilot would surpass his record on that front, despite the fact that, when he landed that day, he was greeted by transfer papers.

The British considered Barker much too valuable to risk in combat any longer and ordered him to take up the duties of an instructor at a training school in England. He hated the idea and managed to get himself posted back to the Western Front for a few weeks so he could become familiar with conditions there — and with the new Sopwith Snipe. He couldn't teach rookie pilots about the hot new fighter plane, he argued, if he knew nothing about it himself. So off he went to France for a last go at the enemy. The war was winding down, and Barker knew it was his final chance to experience the excitement — and terror — of battle that he had come to crave.

But, with the Germans in full retreat, there were few opportunities to fight, and by October 27, 1918, when he was ordered to return to England, he had not added a single victory to his total. Deeply disappointed, he lifted his Snipe off the runway at Baizieux Aerodrome and headed home. But Barker had no intention of taking a direct route back to the United Kingdom. He was determined to have one more dogfight. Climbing swiftly to 19,000 feet, he decided to take a route that would carry him perilously close to the battle zone. He intended to fly over the trenches for as long as his fuel allowed, then break off and head to Britain.

Just before 8:30 a.m., he found what he was looking for. A green-and-brown-painted German Rumpler two-seater came into view 2,000 feet above him. The crew was totally absorbed in observation work, taking pictures of Allied positions northeast of Mormal forest. Barker climbed under the Rumpler's looming fat underbelly, closing to within twenty yards before triggering his twin Vickers machine guns. The German ship broke in half, and its two occupants plunged into open space. The gunner was stone-dead and fell like a rock. But the pilot was unhurt and managed to open his parachute.

The Canadian circled in amazement as he watched the enemy aviator descend safely to earth. Parachutes had been available since hostilities began four years earlier, but both sides had refrained from issuing them because the generals had feared that some pilots might bail out rather than bring home damaged machines. Late in the war, however, the German high command had come to its senses and the life-saving devices had been issued.

Barker hadn't seen a parachute jump before, and he watched in fascination as his opponent drifted earthward. He was so taken aback by the scene that he didn't see the Fokker triplane sneaking up on his tail.

The German pilot had Barker cold, and he poured a prolonged burst right into the Snipe's cockpit. One of the bullets tore painfully through his right thigh, ripping apart several muscles as it burrowed deep into his flesh. A steady stream of sticky red blood flowed down his pant leg. Barker kicked the rudder bar and launched the Sopwith into a tight diving turn. It zipped around at an astonishing rate, bringing the German into his gun sights. One burst sent the triplane down in flames.

To his horror, a swarm of enemy fighters converged on him out of nowhere. Allied observers on the ground counted fifty Fokker D-7 biplanes coming in on the Canadian at top speed. One of the most one-sided battles in history was in progress, as Barker, hunched over his guns and decided to fight it out. There was no point in running, in any case; he would merely be exposing his vulnerable tail to 100 German machine guns. It was his last stand, and he knew it. Despite the terror welling up within him, Billy Barker met the air armada head-on, blazing away with both guns. Vickers bullets gutted the engine of the nearest Fokker, sending it plummeting to earth with flames shooting from the fuel tank. One down, forty-nine to go!

He was right in the midst of the Germans by then, and tracers were coming at him from above, below, behind and directly in front. It was almost beautiful to watch the dozens of lines of red bullets streak toward him from all directions. He could hear the terrifying whiplash sound as bullets ripped through his canvas wings and fuselage. Firing back relentlessly, he sent a second D-7 into its death dive. But another hail of slugs smashed into his cockpit, shattering instruments and blasting Barker's left hip-bone to splinters. He passed out at this point, and his plane fell helplessly out of control. The rush of cold air revived Barker, and he pulled up to greet a Fokker rushing for him. Squeezing off a short burst, he watched as the German crashed into the trenches. The ace, despite wounds in both legs, continued to fight with courage and determination, firing whenever he got a black-crossed fighter in his sights. He was a masterful pilot and a crack shot, flying the best Allied plane of the war. But the odds were just too great.

The uneven fight lasted several more minutes, before a Fokker managed to get behind the weaving and bobbing Canadian long enough to shoot him again. This time, an explosive bullet tore off his left elbow. Barker fainted again, and his plane took several more hits. Miraculously, it somehow managed to stay in the air long enough for him to regain his senses. Another of his tormentors was in view and Barker, mad with pain, tried to ram it. He might have been as good as dead but there was no reason why he couldn't take one more German with him. Racing straight for the enemy, he kept both guns wide open as he closed the gap, and the Fokker fell away in a ball of flames before the ace could slam into it with his Snipe.

Fifteen Fokkers then swarmed onto his tail, blasting away with everything they had. A huge plume of black smoke suddenly gushed from the Bentley engine. Barker dived to escape but the Germans were in no mood to let him go — not after he'd just shot six of them down. Eight D-7s followed him down, clinging to his tail and firing at every opportunity. The Snipe and its pilot had been literally shot to pieces, but both man and machine refused to die. Barker, in a tremendous show of stamina, wheeled around and drove off his attackers with several short, sharp bursts. They scattered in every direction and headed for home. An overwhelming force of German fighter planes had been held off by a one-armed pilot with two useless legs! Barker now turned for home, but he was too weak from loss of blood to keep flying. Both his body and the plane gave out at the same time, and the tattered Snipe crashed into the ground just behind the front lines, flipping over on its back before coming to a crumpled rest. When British Tommies got to the scene, they were stunned to find the pilot was still alive. In addition to his bullet wounds, his nose was broken in the crash.

One of the people watching from below, as Barker sent six opponents crashing into the mud, was Canadian general Andy McNaughton. He wrote: "The prolonged roar which greeted the triumph of the British fighter, and which echoed across the battle front, was never matched on any other occasion."[5] Barker, recovering in a hospital bed behind the lines, wrote home that "by jove, I was a foolish boy, but anyhow I taught them a lesson. The only thing that bucks me up is to look back and see them going down in flames."[6]

He was still in hospital when the war ended and word came through that he'd won the Victoria Cross. The citation read: "On the morning of October 27, 1918, this officer observed an enemy two-seater over the Foret de Mormal. He attacked this machine and after a short burst it broke up in the air. At the same time a Fokker triplane attacked him, and he was wounded in the right thigh, but managed, despite this, to shoot down the enemy plane in flames.

"He then found himself in the middle of a large formation of Fokkers, who attacked him from all directions, and was again severely wounded in the left thigh, but succeeded in driving down two of the enemy in a spin.

"He lost consciousness after this and his machine fell out of control. On recovery he found himself once again attacked by a large formation, and singling out one machine he deliberately charged and drove it down in flames.

"During this fight his left elbow was shattered and he again fainted, and on regaining consciousness he found himself still being attacked, but notwithstanding that he was now severely wounded in both legs and his left arm shattered, he dived at the nearest plane and shot it down in flames.

"Being greatly exhausted, he dived out of the fight to regain our lines, but was met by another formation, which attacked and endeavoured to cut him off, but after a hard fight he succeeded in breaking up this formation and reached our lines, where he crashed on landing.

"This combat, in which Major Barker destroyed four machines, three of them in flames (and drove two others down out of control) brought his total successes up to fifty enemy machines destroyed, and is a notable example of the exceptional bravery and disregard of danger which this very gallant officer has always displayed throughout his distinguished career."[7]

For Barker, the war was over, but his terrible suffering was just beginning. His wounds had left him a walking cripple. For an athletic man, being forced to hobble around was an indignity. Those who knew him say he lived in agony for years, with his war injuries never properly healing. He went into the commercial aviation business with his friend and fellow-ace, Billy Bishop, but they both lost their shirts in the venture. Bishop, never one to worry too much about material possessions, wasn't particularly

concerned. But Barker, who as a semi-invalid had few job opportunities, was deeply depressed.

The renowned war hero very nearly created an international
incident when, visiting England as one of Canada's foremost
celebrities, he took the Prince of Wales for a ride over London in
an old two-seater. With the heir to the throne in the rear cockpit,
the one-armed pilot (his left arm was permanently useless) performed reckless stunts right over St. Paul's Cathedral. The king
and queen were furious, and the British Cabinet met to discuss the
escapade. The prince was ordered to confine himself to the
ground, and Barker was told in no uncertain terms that his fool-
hardy behaviour was not appreciated. The prince, incidently, was
thrilled by the ride and corresponded with the Canadian ace for years.

Barker drifted for a time after that, taking up farming before
accepting a job with an aircraft builder. Incredibly, despite his
disability, he was the company's test pilot. As the pain from his
wounds got worse, he fell into a black depression. He confided to
a few old friends that he wished he had died in the clash with the
fifty Fokkers. He joined the Royal Canadian Air Force for a brief
stint but couldn't handle the peacetime atmosphere, in which
politics played a key role in promotions. Before long, he quit.

The end came in March 1930, when he took a plane off the
ground at Uplands airfield near Ottawa. The plane climbed,
stalled, and came racing down, to crash straight into the pavement
with its engine on full. There had been no attempt to pull out.
Those who witnessed the horrific sight were convinced that
Barker had taken his own life. Arch Whitehouse, himself a First
World War ace, said as much years later. He wrote: "There
seemed to be no reason for the crash, and the best that can be said
is that it ended Billy Barker's long agony."[8]

Few men have ever displayed as much bravery as the Manitoba
flyer did the day he held off fifty opponents. Most people faced
with near-certain death would have frozen. But Barker fought
back with a grim determination that was astonishing, even for a
great ace. Few VCs have ever been more deserved than his. And
it should be remembered that, even if he had not flown that day,
he would still have been one of Canada's most celebrated heroes.
As the top gun on the Italian Front, his reputation as an air fighter
of historical importance was assured, even before his epic last
stand. But the lesson to be learned from his untimely death is

perhaps as important as anything we could grasp by studying his life. Some believe he committed suicide to escape the intense agony of war wounds. Others say his plane simply stalled, and, because of his shattered arm, he was unable to regain control in time. Either way, the crash was connected to what had happened to him in his bloody clash with the German Fokkers twelve years earlier. We shouldn't forget the skill and bravery of our most decorated war heroes but if we are to avoid glorifying combat, we should remember too the terrible price so many of them paid for their fame.

FIVE

Bob Leckie

He was a quiet man who appeared to have little interest in wine, women or song. Indeed, those who knew Bob Leckie say he could be a sour individual, totally lacking in love of life. He had enthusiasm for one thing and one thing only — his career. But he was also very probably the greatest combat pilot Canada ever produced. Although few people have even heard of him, Leckie was by far the most successful seaplane flyer of either side in the First World War. He was also the top zeppelin killer, one of only a handful of airmen ever to sink a submarine and the king of the North Sea dogfighters.

Born in Glasgow, Scotland, in 1890, Leckie moved to Canada with his family as a boy. He was, by the time war broke out in 1914, very much a Canadian. In fact, his British squadron mates often complained that they had no idea what he was talking about, because his Canadian accent was much too thick. This posed a serious problem when he became a squadron commander: at least one English pilot has recorded in his memoirs that he could never understand Leckie's orders and simply guessed at the instructions.

Like so many others of his generation, Leckie had a yen for adventure. He was working in a shipping company owned by his uncle in Toronto when the war began. The young man quit at once and enlisted in the Royal Naval Air Service. While he waited to be sent overseas, he spent his own money taking flying lessons from Toronto's Curtiss Flying School. The school closed for the winter before he earned his pilot's licence, but the twenty-four-year-old was still a step ahead of the other recruits when he sailed for England. After a brief stint at a British flight school, Leckie earned his wings and was posted to the big RNAS air base at Great Yarmouth, on the Norfolk coast in southeast England. Here, he was told, his task would be to hunt German submarines, keep an eye out for enemy ships and intercept zeppelins on their way to bomb London.

Zeppelins! The giant airships were the atomic bomb of their era. Air attacks on cities were a new development in the brutal history of warfare and they panicked the population of London. Both sides were convinced that the dirigibles would reduce the British capital to ashes. Indeed, after the first raid, the German newspaper *Leipzig Neueste Nachrichten,* boasted: "England no longer an island! London, the heart which pumps lifeblood into the arteries of the degenerate huckster nation, has been mauled and mutilated with bombs by brave German fighting men in German airships. At last, the long-yearned-for punishment has befallen England, this people of liars, cynics and hypocrites, a punishment for the countless sins of ages past. It is neither blind hatred nor raging anger that inspires our airship heroes, but a religious humility at being chosen the instrument of God's wrath. In that moment when they saw London being consumed in smoke and fire, just as Sodom was burned by fire from heaven to requite the wickedness of its people, they lived through a thousand lives of an immeasurable joy which all who remain at home must envy."[1] The British press was almost as hysterical, branding the German airship crews "despicable brutes and savages" and "craven wretches, contemptible Huns and vandals."[2]

The opposing pilots rose above such hateful propaganda. Leckie was quoted years later as saying the German flyers were incredibly brave individuals carrying out a thankless task. And many of the zeppelin pilots were deeply troubled by the fact that they were dropping bombs on women and children. One of them, Captain Peter Strasser, who was destined to fight Leckie to the death, wrote his mother that "we who strike the enemy where his heart beats have been slandered as baby-killers and murderers of women. Such name-calling is to be expected from enemy quarters. It is maddening to learn, however, that even in Germany there are simple fools and deluded altruists who condemn us. What we do is repugnant to us, too, but necessary. Very necessary. Nowadays there is no such animal as a noncombatant; modern warfare is total warfare. A soldier cannot function at the Front without the factory worker, the farmer and all the other providers behind him at home. You and I, mother, have discussed this subject, and I know you understand what I say. My men are brave and honourable."[3]

For Bob Leckie, however, there would be no immediate clash with a raider. For several months of the campaign, he found himself flying a Short seaplane, a near-useless machine that was poorly armed and with too slow a climbing rate to allow him to get near any zeppelins. The frustration finally ended when Leckie's squadron received the Curtiss H. 12 "Large American" seaplane. It was, in the words of one man who flew it, a "real dandy." Equipped with a pair of 275-hp Rolls-Royce engines, it had a maximum speed of eighty-five miles per hour, carried a crew of five, and bristled with six Lewis machine guns. It also carried two 230-pound bombs, giving it real teeth in the war on the U-boat.

Leckie demonstrated just how effective the Large American could be, on May 4, 1917, after the British intercepted a German radio message that a zeppelin had taken off from its base in East Frisia on the enemy side of the North Sea. Leckie took off at dawn, hoping to catch the raider before it could reach its target. He had been airborne just over an hour when he spotted the airship fifteen miles ahead and 2,000 feet below him. It was absolutely massive. Cigar-shaped, it was longer than two football fields, taller than a three-storey building and powered by three huge engines that carried it through the sky at sixty miles per hour. It was kept aloft by 1.9 million cubic feet of hydrogen. Two dozen men, armed to the teeth with machine guns and 8,800 pounds of bombs, were located in five cars (known as nacelles), two forward, two amidships and one aft. Stamped on its side was a gigantic black cross, outlined in white. Leckie could clearly make out the serial number "L 22" painted on its rudder. Diving under his prey, he came at it from below, using the mist and purple clouds of a stormy morning for cover. When he was less than a half-mile behind it and twenty feet below, his gunners opened up with everything they had. The return fire was fierce, and Leckie dove out of the tracers that were coming right for him. Swinging back around, he was preparing to take another run at the zeppelin, when a bright yellow glow suddenly appeared in the nose of the airship and raced across the length of its body with the swiftness of a brushfire. The L22 rose, as though in agony, for a fraction of a second and then plummeted into the sea. Two of its crewmen were seen falling — or jumping — from the flaming wreckage. Without parachutes, they were as good as dead. The zeppelin itself disappeared beneath the waves within minutes, leaving behind only a great ash stain.

Leckie won the Distinguished Service Cross for this exploit, and, over the next two months, he had five more brushes with zeppelins. Although he shot no more of the huge airships down, he forced several to abandon their missions, and those that continued on in spite of his dogged pursuit did so at higher altitudes, where their bombings would be much less accurate. The Large American didn't have the ceiling for Leckie to follow the Germans when they released ballast and climbed away. The RNAS, to overcome this limitation, stationed two high-flying DH4 two-seaters at Great Yarmouth. These were planes that could go as high as the zeppelins, but the problem was that they weren't seaplanes. If they were forced down on water they would immediately sink because they had no pontoons. The high command, therefore, stipulated that a Large American must escort the DH4s whenever they were aloft over the North Sea. On September 5, 1917, two zeppelins were spotted by Royal Navy ships and a DH4 took off from Great Yarmouth to intercept them, with Leckie and his crew following in their flying boat. The weather was poor, and whitecaps could be seen below. An hour from base, they spotted their prey — the zeppelins "L 44" and "L 46," droning along only 9,000 feet up. Leckie climbed to engage the enemy. At 12,000 feet, with the zeppelins still pulling away, his gunners opened fire but their aim was off. Marksmen on the L44, meanwhile, were shooting back and the Large American sustained minor damage. Both Germans made good their escape, and Leckie suddenly realized that the DH4 was nowhere to be seen. Looking below, he spotted it limping homeward with its engine skipping badly. Either it had been hit in the nose by enemy gunners, or its motor was acting up. In either case, it was rapidly losing altitude and anti-aircraft fire was coming up to greet it from a group of German destroyers and battle cruisers.

As Leckie closed in to inspect the DH4 for damage, his own plane was hit in a wing by shrapnel. The damage wasn't critical, but it did make the machine more difficult to fly. His troubles were minor, however, compared to those of the DH4 pilot. The two-seater's engine had died altogether and the plane was going into the drink. The pilot managed to glide long enough to get well out of the range of the German ships, but he was nowhere near

England when his biplane landed on the water and started to sink. First World War aircraft did not come equipped with rubber rafts, and the two DH4 airmen were doomed to freeze to death unless they were plucked out of the sea very quickly. The waves were rough, however, and any seaplane that landed beside them would be unable to take off again. The odds were good that if Leckie attempted a rescue, he and his four crewmen would drift helplessly out to sea to die slow deaths from starvation and thirst. Nevertheless, he didn't hesitate before landing the big machine on the water. Buffeted by high waves, he masterfully taxied his flying boat up to the sinking DH4 and pulled both men from certain death. Now, however, there were six airmen on the flying boat, and the extra weight would make takeoff difficult, even if seas were to become calm.

Leaking Hull

Pointing his plane toward the U.K., Leckie began to taxi homeward. He was fifty miles away and the hull was leaking from battle damage. He ordered two carrier pigeons set loose with messages tied to their legs that gave his position and plight. (One of the birds was never seen again, and the other arrived at Great Yarmouth three days later.) Water was pouring into the ship and Leckie was forced to head right into the waves — and away from England — to prevent it from capsizing. His five mates, meantime, were kept busy constantly bailing water, using empty fuel cans to do the trick. Eventually, the plane ran out of fuel and they started drifting aimlessly. Night set in and the men were exhausted, but they had to keep bailing or die. Waves slammed into the plane and the wing that had been damaged by enemy fire suddenly broke loose, shifting the weight and forcing one side of the flying boat perilously downward. To cope with the new crisis, each man had to take his turn climbing out on the damaged section to add extra weight. One of the survivors remembered that "one minute we'd be at least 20 feet up in the air, and the next minute down the wing would come with a hell of crash and we'd be buried under water, to be jerked out again, spitting and gasping, half-drowned, to go up like a see-saw and then down again — but still, we managed to stick it out."[4]

When morning came, they were still afloat, but facing a new threat. They had no food or water. Leckie ordered water drained out of the radiators of the engines. It was badly polluted, with a reddish scummy layer of filth, but it was all they had. By noon, they were all deadly ill. Leckie was bleeding internally and spitting blood. Still, the courageous crew hung on, through another hellish night, and a second day. The last two pigeons were set free on the second day. (Again, one took off for parts unknown while the other took its time getting back to Great Yarmouth, arriving twenty-four hours later.) On the third day, the exhausted men were saved by a navy ship that happened by.

Bob Leckie spent a few days in hospital and then went right back into action. Most RNAS airmen stationed in England saw very little combat; in fact, the majority never even saw a German zeppelin or U-boat, but Leckie seemed to attract them like flies. Flying at night, on October 29, 1917, he spotted a submarine periscope on the water. Diving, he unleashed two 100-pound bombs. Both missed, however, and the German made good his escape.

In many ways, the war against the U-boats was even more important than the anti-zeppelin campaign. Hidden under the waves, they encircled the British Isles, torpedoing ships that were trying to reach England. Nearly 40 per cent of Britain's meat and vegetables, half its eggs and margarine, 80 per cent of its cheese, and all of its sugar, was imported. On top of that, most of the nation's war supplies came by boat. The truth was that Germany's submarine fleet was perilously close to winning the war. The subs sank a staggering 2,500 Allied ships in 1917 alone. Only seven of these elusive opponents were sunk by airplanes throughout the entire war, and one of them was destroyed by Leckie. Flying through a blinding rainstorm on February 20, 1918, the Canadian spotted two U-boats on the surface. He zoomed down on top of them at breakneck speed, dropping two bombs. Both hit home, and one of the subs rose out of the water, flipped over on its back and disappeared in a gush of black oil.

The arrival of a new and better plane was welcomed by Leckie's squadron. The souped-up Curtis F2a flying boat had two 350-hp Rolls Royce engines that could keep it tearing through the air at 100 miles per hour for eight hours. It was a good fifteen miles per hour faster than the machine that Leckie was accustomed to, and he put the extra speed to good use on March 18 in a dogfight near the Dutch coast. Spotting two swift Brandenberg seaplanes from the big German air base of Borkum, he immediately attacked. This time, however, Leckie had a real fight on his hands. Both enemy ships had excellent pilots, and one of them peppered his fuel tanks with lead. Two of Leckie's guns had jammed, and his men were running out of ammunition as the battle raged for thirty minutes. Reluctantly, he gave up the pursuit and turned for home when, out of the clouds, three more German fighters came tumbling into the action, guns blazing. Another of his fuel tanks was punctured, but one of Leckie's gunners shot an attacker down in flames and the other two turned tail. The original pair, short on fuel and ammo themselves, also departed. When he landed, Leckie found that his plane was riddled with bullets. About fifty gallons had leaked from his tattered tanks, but, miraculously, no fire had started and no one had been wounded, even though the instrument panel directly in front of his face had been shot to pieces!

On April 1, when the Royal Air Force was created, Leckie was promoted to the rank of squadron commander. He continued, however, to wear his navy uniform. His fellow-pilots remembered him, years later, as a quiet, conservative man who didn't drink or smoke. He loved to read the works of Kipling and gloried in the history of the British Empire. No one could ever remember him joining in the fun in the mess. Some dismissed him as a "dour Scot," but others realized he was simply a shy Canadian. He was also more mature than most of the others and, at age twenty-eight he was a decade older than many of the men under him. Although he could not be described as a popular commander, he was well respected, mainly because he flew as many missions as his men. He shared the risks with them and led by example, searching out an enemy that they seldom ever found.

Almost immediately, Leckie was made a captain as well as a squadron commander, but he ignored the paperwork as much as possible. On April 13, in his first engagement as an RAF officer, he hounded a zeppelin for several minutes before it escaped into a cloud. He searched the vicinity for half an hour but could find nothing. There is no record of an airship attack on England that day, so it seems likely that Leckie's attack caused the enemy commander to turn tail and go back to Germany.

To counter these frequent attacks on their dirigibles, the Germans set up elaborate traps. They began sending out fake radio messages, giving false times and locations of zeppelin flights. Knowing that the Canadian and his men would arrive on the scene, they waited in ambush with swarms of seaplanes. After a few close calls with the black-crossed fighters, Leckie decided to take five flying boats up in a show of force. Normally, the Curtis flew alone, so Leckie was counting on catching the Germans by surprise.

On a clear dawn in early June, he took off and headed for the main enemy seaplane base on the opposite side of the North Sea. Almost at once, however, serious complications arose. One of Leckie's ships developed engine trouble and had to land on the water off the coast of Holland. He flew low and, flashing morse code through a signal lamp, ordered the crew to taxi to shore and destroy their plane before being interned by Dutch authorities. Though Holland was neutral, any combatants who arrived there had to be detained for the duration of hostilities. Suddenly, five Brandenbergs appeared on the horizon. One of them promptly turned and headed back to base to get reinforcements. The other four kept their distance, despite Leckie's attempts to lure them in. The Germans occasionally tried to strafe the flying boat on the water but they were driven off each time by Leckie and his men. Disaster, however, lay just ahead. A rookie pilot, overly anxious for a crack at the opposition, broke formation and attacked the four Germans by himself. He was quickly shot down for his trouble. Then the reinforcements arrived, and Leckie, who had been ready to take on five or six Germans with five flying boats, found himself facing twenty enemy fighter pilots with only three planes of his own. There was only one hope and he seized it. He wheeled his tiny formation around and led it into a suicide charge on the enemy. Leckie tore through the German formation with guns flashing. His three flying boats were equipped with eighteen machine guns, and they caught several Brandenbergs in a withering crossfire. Three enemy planes fell in flames during that first pass. Banking back around, Leckie went at them again. One of his men was hit, however, and had to land on the water. The other two fought gamely on and two more Germans crashed. Fighting was at such close quarters that a German wing-tip clipped the wireless aerial off Leckie's plane.

One of Leckie's men recalled later that "he went hell-for-leather for them and drove clean, slap-bang through the enemy formation, splitting it right up. Everybody seemed to be firing away like blazes, and the air was thick with the smoke from tracer bullets which looked just like the paperstreamers people chuck about at dances. The pilots were sweating blood, following Leckie, who was in and out, all over the place, roaring up the Huns."[5] Even the pilot who had been forced down managed to restart his engine and take off again. Within moments, he was back in the fight and the Germans, having had enough, broke off and fled. One of them made the mistake of taking time out to strafe the first flying boat that had been forced down. It was now almost to shore, and the attack would have resulted in little better than attempted murder, because the men were destined for internment and would be permanently out of the war. In any case, a gunner aboard the crippled British plane scored a direct hit on the incoming German, and he crashed into the sea. Leckie's men returned to base after a six-hour mission in which they lost two flying boats (one to mechanical failure and one to enemy action) and shot down an astounding six planes.

The authorities then gave the Canadian orders not to do any further operational flying. He was to remain at Great Yarmouth as commander, but he was to lead from behind a desk. Bob Leckie had been the most successful Allied seaplane pilot of the war. Only eleven zeppelins had been shot down in four years of combat, and he had had one of them, along with one of the seven subs sunk by aircraft. And he had played a major role in the downing of seven seaplanes. It was a sparkling record, but, Leckie's greatest achievement was still ahead of him.

Final Offensive

In Germany, zeppelin commander Peter Strasser was preparing for a final offensive that he was convinced would gut London and force the British to surrender. He had been put in charge of all navy airships and was determined to show that the big gasbags were still an effective tool. His arsenal included the new L-70, the behemoth of zeppelins. Strasser was brave and fanatical. He sneered at army zeppelin crews who brought along parachutes. He frankly told his men that they must be prepared to die for their country and ordered them to leave their chutes behind so that there would be more weight for bombs. "A crew of twenty-three taking parachutes weighing thirty pounds each," he said, "amounts to 690 pounds, which is a considerable quantity of ammunition to leave behind."[6] When given charge of the L-70, he first proposed an attack on New York City! The airship, he pointed out, had the capacity to cross the Atlantic and return. Such a raid, he argued, would stun the Americans, who smugly believed they were completely safe from attack. Although his plan was rejected, the high command did give him permission to bomb London with the newest lighter-than-air machine.

The L-70 was almost 700 feet long, making it bigger than any battleship on earth. It had four 245-hp engines and was held aloft by 2.2 million cubic feet of hydrogen gas. And it could fly at 23,000 feet, well out of the range of most airplanes. On the evening of August 5, 1918, Strasser took off in the giant ship, leading five zeppelins in a raid on London. The mission was doomed from the start. The wind was much stronger than anticipated and, as a result, the armada of airships arrived over England a good hour ahead of schedule — a disaster, because it brought them over enemy territory while the sun was still up. Worse still, atmospheric conditions had made climbing very difficult. Instead of arriving over England at 23,000 feet, under the cover of darkness, the Germans showed up at 17,000 feet in broad daylight. When they were spotted, every plane at Great Yarmouth was ordered into the air.

One of those to take part in the mad scramble was a British major named Egbert Cadbury, who later founded the famed chocolate company. He was in town that evening, watching his wife perform at a play, when the alarm sounded. Rushing outside, he was stunned to see a zeppelin pass overhead. Jumping into a lorry, he raced back to the air base, arriving just as the last plane — a DH4 — was being wheeled out of one of the hangars. Because the raid was so unexpected, a number of the airmen were away in town and there weren't enough crews to man every plane. The shortage of men gave Bob Leckie his last crack at the enemy: Cadbury asked him to man the rear cockpit, and he instantly agreed. He was in such a rush to get airborne, in fact, that he didn't stop to grab any gloves. It was an oversight that would soon prove to be vitally significant.

The moment Cadbury got over water, he jettisoned his bomb load to lighten the DH4 and tore off after the zeppelins. He climbed to 16,000 feet in ten minutes before spotting three of the raiders a few miles off. The airplane was about twenty miles per hour faster than the airships, and Cadbury gradually overtook them, heading straight for the largest zeppelin, which was leading the fleet. Cadbury concentrated totally on flying, leaving the shooting to Leckie. As he sailed along under the L-70, holding the DH4 steady, the Canadian sharpshooter opened fire. A steady stream of explosive bullets racked the giant ship from stem to stern. A huge hole appeared in the canvas side, and flames spilled out.

Captain Freudenreich, who was in command of the nearby L-63, said later: "I was nearing the coast when we suddenly saw an outbreak of flame on the L-70, amidships or a little aft. Then the whole ship was on fire. One could see flames all over her. It looked like a huge sun. Then she stood up erect and went down like a burning shaft. The whole thing lasted thirty, maybe forty-five seconds. I guessed it had been done by airplanes, so I altered course, ascended to 21,300 feet, crossed the coast later on, and dropped many bombs on a battery which was shooting at me."[7] From his perspective, Cadbury concluded that "another zeppelin has gone to perdition, sent there by a perfectly peaceful, live-and-let-live citizen who harbours no lust for blood or fearful war spirit in his soul. It all happened very quickly and very terribly."[8]

After the hit, the other Germans began climbing frantically away, but Cadbury was after them in a flash. He closed in on the L-65, commanded by Walter Dose, and Leckie opened fire. Again, a bright flash was seen, only this time it was in one of the gondolas, not in the airship's body. Just when it seemed that Leckie was about to destroy his second zeppelin of the night, and his third of the war, his gun jammed. Without his gloves, several of his fingers had frozen in the cold air of the upper sky, making it impossible for him to clear the stoppage. Because the DH4 had already reached its ceiling, Cadbury was unable to bring his forward-firing gun to bear. In fact, his engine was skipping badly, they were over the North Sea, and night was coming. He had no choice but to head for home. The defensive mission had been a spectacular success. The L-70 was not only Germany's biggest zeppelin; her commander was the heart and soul of the airship fleet. Indeed, with the death of Strasser, there were no more airship attacks on England during the last three months of the war.

Despite the fact that he was the only Allied pilot of World War One to shoot down two zeppelins, Leckie was not granted the Victoria Cross. He had to settle for the Distinguished Flying Cross, for downing the L-70, while several British pilots won the VC for destroying a single zeppelin. The Canadian ace was, however, promoted to the rank of major. Leckie remained in the RAF after the war but, when World War Two broke out, he asked to be transferred to the rapidly expanding RCAF. Stationed in Ottawa, he was first an air marshal and then the chief of air staff. In that capacity, he helped organize the highly successful British Commonwealth Air Training Plan. The plan saw literally tens of thousands of pilots from Canada, England, the United States, Australia and New Zealand win their wings at training schools across Canada.

Leckie finally retired in 1947. He died in Ottawa in 1975 at the ripe old age of eighty-five. His main claim to fame is as the man who did the most to defeat the zeppelins in the 1914-18 war. Only twelve of them were shot down in the whole war, and the Toronto pilot got two of them, damaged a third and sent a dozen more running back to Germany. With his destruction of the L-70, he prevented the Germans from launching any further attacks on London during the last three months of the war, thus saving many civilian lives. But Leckie should also be remembered as the man who had the courage to land his seaplane in the middle of wave-tossed seas, with the full knowledge that he wouldn't be able to take off again, in order to save two comrades from drowning. If he wasn't our greatest military aviator of the century, it's clear that he was one of the best Canadian pilots ever to take a warplane into the sky.

SIX

Billy Bishop

Billy Bishop, Canada's most famous — and controversial — war hero, was born on February 8, 1894, in Owen Sound, Ontario. Before his twenty-fifth birthday, he would shoot down seventy-five enemy aircraft, becoming the top Allied ace of both world wars and the first internationally recognized Canadian of the twentieth century. Today, seventy-two years after his last dogfight, he remains by far the most celebrated Canadian ace of them all.

The third son of four children born to Grey County Registrar Will Bishop and his wife, Margaret Louise, Billy came into the world weighing eleven pounds and sporting a full head of blond hair above penetrating blue eyes. Right from the start he was a lad of awesome contradictions. He spoke with a lisp, played the piano and preferred the company of girls, and dressed for school in a suit and tie. Yet, at the same time, he enjoyed hunting and was forever becoming involved in schoolyard fights. He was intelligent and charming, but his school grades were consistently poor. He was a ruffian but not a bully. One oldtimer remembered him as "someone who often went to the rescue of the smaller boys when they were being picked on by the older lads. Billy was in a lot of fights and, although he never started them, he sure finished 'em! He could hold his own in fights with bigger fellows because he didn't show any fear. And because he would attack like a madman. But you shouldn't get the wrong impression. I always found him to be a very good-natured boy. Exceptionally so. He was the class clown at Owen Sound Collegiate you know."[1]

To say Billy hated school is an understatement. He was constantly skipping class to play pool downtown, and his teachers frankly didn't think he'd amount to anything. His grades were barely good enough to allow him to be promoted. Still, he had other strengths that he put to good use. Billy was extremely handsome and he often made money by charging his sister to take out her girlfriends. And he used his charm to lie his way out of trouble whenever he was caught playing hookey.

From an early age, he had a consuming desire to be the best at all he tackled. He soon realized that he could never be a top student, so he refused to apply himself to his books. Likewise, he showed little interest in sports. (He once finished second in a race and promptly gave up on competitive running.) But if he was good at something, he applied himself rigorously until he was the best. A gruesome example of this was hunting. His father presented Billy with a .22 calibre rifle one Christmas and offered him twenty-five cents for every squirrel he bagged. Unbeknownst to the elder Bishop, the lad had phenomenal eyesight and a steady hand. He was soon bringing down a squirrel with every shot and making a small fortune in the process. The local squirrel population was wiped out before he was forced to renege on the deal.

Youngsters often have no concept of danger, but Billy's recklessness was exceptional. When, at age fifteen, he read about airplanes for the first time, he decided to build his own ship. He threw together a crude contraption made of cardboard, wooden crates and strings, and launched it from the third floor of the family home. Some thirty feet off the ground, he sailed a yard or two across the front lawn before plunging into the grass. His sister, Louie, anxiously dug him out of the wreckage, greatly relieved to find him completely unhurt. Billy's only worry was that his parents would find out about his first solo flight. But he had little to fear, because Louie wasn't about to tell. The two were very close. Indeed, her influence had a profound impact on his life in many ways. She was always chiding him to do better, playing an important role in developing his competitive spirit. Perhaps most important, Louie introduced Billy to a good-looking young lady named Margaret Burden. The granddaughter of department-store magnate Timothy Eaton, Margaret lived in Toronto but spent her summers at the family home on Georgian Bay. It was there that she met Louie and, through her, Billy.

He later admitted that he loved Margaret at first glance, although, in customary fashion, he charged Louie five dollars before he would take her friend on a date. Louie's friends were forever asking her to introduce her brother to them and often pleaded with her to convince Billy to ask them out. Billy, ever the opportunist, agreed to do so — but only for a fee. After that first outing, he came straight home and told his amused parents that he was going to marry Miss Burden someday. The Bishops didn't appear the least bit concerned by the bold proclamation, but the Burdens were openly cool to the idea. They had no intention of allowing their daughter to become involved with a middle-class ruffian. Writer Alan Hynd, who interviewed both Billy and Margaret years later, described young Margaret as a "picture of white organdy, with laughing dark eyes and raven hair. Billy was an outdoor boy, and he used to point out to her gaily coloured birds a little girl never saw in the city. She talked about him so much that the two families eventually became acquainted. Fall came and she went away. But she didn't forget and neither did Billy."[2]

Young Bishop had more than just Margaret Burden on his mind as he completed high school. His marks weren't good enough for him to get into university, and he had no idea what he wanted to do with the rest of his life. Unsure of his next step, he applied to and was accepted by the Royal Military College in Kingston. The brass at RMC welcomed Billy with open arms. He was, after all, the younger brother of Worth Bishop, whom they had considered to be the best cadet in the school's history. They were anticipating another hardworking, respectful and talented recruit. But they were in for a rude shock. Billy was a free spirit who had little use for excessive regimentation. He found the dark, austere surroundings and the harsh military discipline hard to take. Before long, his negative attitude was noticed by his superiors, and he was being branded as the worst cadet in RMC history. In truth, it was the school, and not Billy, that was to blame for his misfortune there. It was a place where the commandant quietly winked at the most outrageous behaviour. Senior cadets, for example, were allowed — even encouraged — to mistreat newcomers. Billy was once forced to eat a spider in front of his peers; he was beaten every Friday night, for no apparent reason, and, worst of all, was compelled to kiss a senior cadet every night before retiring. Whenever he sneaked out to visit girls in Kingston, he would return to find that his footlocker had been raided and some of his private possessions were missing. In one letter home, he moaned that "we are the lowest form of military life ... of any life, for that matter."[3]

Deeply depressed, Billy did not apply himself, and failed his first year. He managed a passing grade in year two but his third year was a disaster. One night, along with another cadet, he got drunk, stole a boat and narrowly escaped drowning when the craft capsized. Hauled before the enraged commandant, he was branded a liar and a thief, and was confined to barracks for a month. It was the worst sentence handed out to any cadet in RMC history. Months later, unprepared to write exams, he cheated and was caught. Dismissal was the only course open to the school authorities but, before they could take action, the First World War broke out and Bishop quit to join the Mississauga Horse, a cavalry unit.

Despite his terrible cadet record, Bishop was signed up at once, instantly becoming an officer, with the rank of lieutenant. Such a promotion would have been unthinkable in peacetime, but tens of thousands of young men were pouring into recruiting stations across the country, and there weren't enough officers in the regular army to handle them. Getting into the cavalry was one thing, but staying in it was another matter. Just as had been the case at RMC, Billy chafed at the discipline. He was an inattentive soldier who also seemed to be accident-prone. Once, his mount threw him during a cross-country ride and very nearly trampled him to death. On another occasion, his rifle backfired, almost blinding him. And there were the usual brushes with authority. The most serious incident happened one night when, with a few others, he tried to sneak out of a restaurant without paying.

One of the men with him, Corporal George Stirrett, told what happened: "Some of us got to drinking pretty heavily when we decided to go into town to have supper in the dining room of a local hotel. When we finished, we got the idea that it might be fun to sneak out without paying. It was more for a gag than anything...we weren't out to save money, although Lord knows we never had much.... I guess you could say we were looking for something to break the boredom. So into the bathroom we went, one at a time, trying to squeeze through a very small window. Bish was the last one. He was still out in the dining room flirting with the waitress. She was a good-looking blonde girl and she'd been showing him special treatment all night. We were already outside by the time he comes in (to the washroom). In fact, everybody else had taken off except me.... I was crazy enough to wait for him. Bish tries to get through the window and — without a lie — he got stuck half way out! By this time the manager comes looking for us. He sees Bish dangling half out the window and grabs him by the legs and tried hauling him back in. I'm on the other side pulling for all I'm worth on his arms … it's a small miracle we didn't pull the poor devil limb from limb. Finally, I won the tug-of-war and Bish comes tumbling out, right on top of me. He had a window frame around his waist and one shoe missing. And when he fell on me he twisted my ankle so that I could barely walk. There we were, limping along, both drunk, Bish with a window frame around his waist and one shoe missing — and half the town after us! We only got away because Bish 'borrowed' a car just outside of camp and then snuck into our bunks, freezing wet and banged up."[4] Somehow, Bishop managed to lie his way out of the predicament, convincing the authorities, when they came to arrest him the next morning, that he had been nowhere near the hotel.

Despite his problems, Billy had, as far as the military was concerned, one redeeming quality — his eyesight. He was a crack shot who could pick off targets that other men could barely see. He was so good, in fact, that he was soon placed in charge of the whole machine-gun section.

He completed his training in June, 1915 and boarded a ship in Montreal for the voyage to Europe. The war was still new and exciting to the soldiers and the general population, and the scene at dock-side was almost carnival-like. Billy wrote later: "As we pulled out the crowds cheered and waved like mad. Every whistle within miles blew furiously and our men sang God Save the King and cheered back. It was very impressive."[5]

But the voyage soon became a nightmare. The ship, the *Caledonia*, was a smelly old cattleboat crammed to the gunwales with horses and men. High seas buffeted it, almost from the moment they reached the open waters of the Atlantic. Dozens of soldiers fell sick each day, and scores of horses died below deck. There was a certain foreboding, too, at the knowledge that they'd have to run the gauntlet of German submarines off the coast of Ireland without any escort. And when the U-boats did strike, on June 21, they did so with devastating force. Three ships were sent to a watery grave, taking 300 Canadians to their deaths. Billy, who actually saw one of the raiders on the surface, was badly shaken, writing home to Margaret: "I wonder if I shall ever come home to you."[6]

Sandstorms and Heat

Conditions were even worse when they finally arrived in England, on June 23. The men were shipped to Shorncliffe Cavalry Camp, where they set up tents and horse lines on dusty clay fields. When rain came, as it so often did, the whole place was turned into a filthy quagmire. When it stopped, sandstorms and sizzling heat combined, Billy said, to make the place "unbelievable." On top of all that, reports were now coming in of staggering casualties on the Western Front. Rumours spread like wildfire about insane cavalry charges into the teeth of German machine guns. For Bishop, that was the last straw. He was grimly determined to find a way out. He saw his means of escape one afternoon while slopping about on the horse lines. Sinking up to his knees in mud, he looked overhead just in time to see a tiny Royal Flying Corps airplane appear out of the mist. The machine cut its engine and glided in for a gentle landing in a nearby field. Looking on in wonderment, Billy exclaimed that "It's clean up there! I'll bet you don't get any mud or horseshit on you up there ! If you died, at least it would be a clean death."[7] Bishop applied for admission to the RFC and was accepted as a gunner-observer. He wanted to be a pilot, but accepted the less glamorous job, because it was the only way out of the cavalry. After a brief training period, in which he learned how to take pictures, direct artillery fire and drop bombs, he was posted to 21 Squadron in northern France.

He was out of the trenches, but he found himself performing dreary observation work aboard the RE7, possibly the worst combat aircraft ever built. His pilot, Captain Roger Neville, remembered him as a moody individual who wilted under the restrictions of his machine. "Bish's one object in life was to shoot down enemy aircraft and not just drop bombs or make out artillery reconnaissance reports" he said, sixty-eight years later. The work was indeed tedious and boring, most of the time, but it could also be exceedingly dangerous. Once, Billy was lightly wounded in the head by anti-aircraft fire. On another occasion, the whole squadron was ordered stripped of its guns so the planes could carry more bombs before being sent on a raid twenty miles behind the lines. The scheme was dreamed up by a paper-pusher at headquarters who had never been near the front. Luckily, the defenceless men found the target, bombed it and returned home without being intercepted. Had a flight of Fokkers appeared, the world would never have heard of Billy Bishop.

He survived four months at the front with 21 Squadron, but never even got to fire on an enemy plane. Once, he watched in anger and frustration as a marauding Fokker attacked and shot down a nearby British two-seater. Billy was unable to draw a bead on the skilled German before he flew off. On the ground, he continued to practise his gunnery and, as was the case in the cavalry, he managed to get into one accident after another. The most serious took place when the RE7's engine conked out on takeoff one morning, causing a crash. Billy's knee was badly damaged and he was shipped off to England for treatment. As it turned out, the mishap was one of the luckiest things that ever happened to him. Soon after he left, his squadron was thrown into the bloodbath known as the Battle of the Somme. It raged for months and virtually the whole squadron was wiped out.

While he was in hospital he was befriended by an elderly English noblewoman named Lady St. Helier. She had friends in high places, and with her help, Bishop was soon accepted into flight school for pilot training. There, despite a series of ham-fisted crashlandings, he managed to win his wings and get posted to 60 Squadron — the top British fighter group on the Western Front. The outfit was stationed just behind the lines near Arras, in northern France. It was the hottest theatre of the war, and Bishop arrived just days before the start of the greatest aerial offensive in history. The Canadian Corps was about to storm the seemingly impregnable Vimy Ridge and the RFC ordered every machine into the air in an all-out bid to win total control of the skies over the battlefield.

Day after day, the British ships soared over enemy lines, grimly determined to keep the German air force from witnessing the Canadian build-up around Vimy. But the Allied pilots didn't have the equipment with which to do the job. Bishop found himself flying a Nieuport 17 — a French-built fighter that was slower and less heavily armed than the German Albatros. To make things worse, 60 Squadron was directly across the line from Baron Manfred von Richthofen's dreaded Flying Circus. The Canadian rookie's baptism of fire would be against the highest-scoring aces in the world.

The odds against a newcomer were less than encouraging. Indeed, the life expectancy for a rookie was only eleven days. But despite his slim chances for survival, he was thrown into action within days of his arrival. His first dogfight came on March 25, 1917, and the results were spectacular. Flying at the tail end of a four-man formation led by Squadron Commander Jack Scott, Bishop watched in horror as three Albatroses swept in from the rear. One of them latched onto the major's tail and herded him into a corner. Bishop dove out of nowhere with his Lewis gun pounding. Tracers were seen splashing along the fuselage and the German fighter fell away, apparently out of control. Showing surprising savvy, the untested pilot followed him down to make sure. Moments later, the German pilot pulled up. Just as Bishop had suspected, the man had been faking serious damage. He fired again from point-blank range and the Albatros again plunged away, but this time it thundered right into the ground with a dead airman at the controls. Pulling out, Bishop was stunned to find his engine had died. He had dived too long and too steeply, and it had oiled up. Turning for home, he glided toward the Allied lines, holding out little hope that he would make it back. In a masterful bit of flying, he was able to stretch the glide all the way to no man's land where he made a flawless landing amid the crater-pocked landscape. Scrambling out, under fire from German troops, he made a mad dash to safety and spent the night sleeping in the rain in a British frontline trench.

Indebted to Billy for perhaps saving his life, and impressed by the rookie's performance in his first dogfight, Jack Scott made Bishop a flight commander. It was a critical blunder because, victory or not, Billy was too green to lead men in battle, as he proved five days later, when he led six Nieuports into an ambush. Two of his pilots were killed, and Bishop barely escaped in his damaged ship. Next day, March 31, two more planes under his charge were shot down in flames, but Bishop took partial revenge by blowing the wings off an Albatros. He might not have had the makings of a leader, but he was obviously a great individual fighter pilot. Few veterans had even scored one victory, and Bishop had two kills in his first week of fighting. Noted historian S.F. Wise explained the reasons for his success in the official history of Canada's air force, writing that "he was a first-class shot with the true killer instinct. Like all the great air fighters, Bishop was an expert deflection shot, a skill he maintained by constant practise. His tactics, a subject to which he gave much thought, were built around surprise, which he regarded as the essence of air fighting." Once battle had been joined, Wise continued, "he threw the little Nieuport around with complete abandon and a rare tactical sense."[8]

Bishop won his first gallantry award — the Military Cross — on April 7, 1917, when he pursued an observation balloon right to the ground before setting it on fire. An Albatros tried to intervene, and he shot it down as well. Twenty-four hours later, he was back in action, single-handedly taking on six Germans and shooting down three of them. After that, there was no stopping him, and black-crossed machines began falling like rain before his Lewis gun. By the time the month was out, he was the squadron's leading ace, with seventeen victories to his credit. And the decorations kept coming, too. He won the Distinguished Service Order on the last day of April. The official citation noted: "While in a single-seater he attacked three hostile machines. His courage and determination have set a fine example to others."[9]

It was a virtuoso performance unmatched by any other Allied aviator. Indeed, only the Red Baron did better during what became known as "Bloody April," mowing down twenty-one British pilots. But the Baron was frustrated when he tried to add Bishop to his bag. The two experts shot it out in a classic dogfight on April 30, and both men flew home in badly damaged machines. On the dark side, the rest of 60 Squadron did not match Billy's success. In fact, it was pulverized. Twenty planes were destroyed, representing a casualty rate of 105 per cent in a single month. Thirteen of the eighteen pilots were shot down, along with seven of the men who were called up to replace them. One poor fellow was shot down the very day he arrived. Another disturbing aspect of the carnage was that Billy was beginning to enjoy killing people. He frankly admitted it in letters home, telling Margaret "a bloodthirsty streak" had appeared in him. "You have no idea how bloodthirsty I've become and how much pleasure I get in killing Huns."[10]

In one particularly vile episode, he tried to talk two other pilots into bringing a dead German soldier back to the mess as a kind of grisly trophy. And in the air, he was losing all compassion. At least twice, he strafed downed German airmen. On another occasion, he closed in point-blank and killed the two-seater crew of Fritz Johanntges and Gerd von Rodern after Rodern's rear gun jammed. But he was also very brave. Leading two other pilots, he attacked seven Albatroses, shooting down Burkhard Lehmann in flames and sending another man spinning down out of control. When he went on leave, on May 7, he had twenty-two kills to his credit. Albert Ball, the RFC's top ace, was killed in action the same day, and Billy arrived in London to find himself the Empire's foremost living air hero. He took the town by storm, attending lavish balls and parties in his honour, meeting with members of the Royal Family and dining with a beautiful young actress. His name was splashed around the globe by newspapers that suddenly discovered the new top gun of the Allied air services. The papers exaggerated his exploits, claiming that he had once shot down seven Germans in a single day. Almost overnight, he was the most popular serviceman in the Empire.

Billy returned to the front in late May, a changed man. He had tasted fame and he frankly liked it. His letters home show he was enormously proud of his status as the top RFC ace. Indeed, he was forever comparing his score to those of Ball and the leading French ace, Georges Guynemer, telling anyone who would listen that he intended to surpass them both. He was frustrated, however, to discover that the Arras sector had quieted down. The Germans had moved most of their Jastas further north to take part in the upcoming Ypres offensive. As a result of that, most patrols were now returning to base without so much as seeing an enemy ship. Nevertheless, Billy, flying by himself whenever he pleased, was occasionally able to ambush a German. He shot an Albatros down on May 26, added a Rumpler two-seater on the twenty-seventh and destroyed another Albatros on May 31. That last kill was scored right over a German airfield but no enemy planes rose to help the Albatros pilot. Bishop reasoned that the Germans hadn't been expecting an Allied plane so far behind the lines and were taken totally by surprise. He became convinced that he could probably attack the airfield itself, catching the planes on the ground at dawn and picking the aviators off, one at a time, as they attempted to get airborne. Albert Ball had actually suggested the idea to Bishop, asking the Canadian to accompany him in a morning raid on the Richthofen Circus; but Ball had been killed before they had the chance to carry it out.

Trying Stunts

Bishop was determined to carry out the mission on his next scheduled day off. Even though the Red Baron and his men had left the vicinity, he could try the stunt on another German jasta. Still, he thought it would be wise to bring a wingman along and, with that in mind, he asked his deputy flight leader, Willy Fry, to come along at dawn on June 2. Fry was a courageous airman who might well have accepted had he not been hung over from the previous evening's drunken bash in the mess. He was in such a bad state that he couldn't even get out of bed when Bishop came knocking at his door at 3:00 a.m. Bishop wasn't about to wait another fortnight for his next day off. Taking off by himself, he crossed into German territory and flew towards Cambria with a light drizzle pouring into his open cockpit. Within minutes, he found the airfield he'd been looking for and dove to attack. Closing in, he noticed there was no activity of any kind, nor any sign of men or planes. The place had been abandoned. Deeply disappointed, he milled about for a few minutes, he said later, "...in the hope of coming on some camp or group of troops so as to scatter them. I felt that the danger was nil, as most of the crews of the guns which ordinarily would fire at me would still be asleep, and I might as well give any Huns I could find a good fright." He found nothing, was "in a bad temper," and was about to turn for home when "ahead and slightly to one side of me, I saw the sheds of another aerodrome."[11] Bishop banked sharply and swept down on top of the enemy camp.

Lieutenant Werner Voss, staffel fuhrer of Jasta 5, stepped from his office and surveyed the flight line. The seven ships were almost ready to go; a swarm of mechanics, dressed in wrinkled fatigue uniforms, were already starting some of the motors. The bellow of Mercedes engines echoed off the sides of the brown hangars. Voss's ground crews had put in a long night's work overhauling the planes, some of which had been damaged in skirmishes the previous day, so that they would be ready for the dawn patrol. Now, six fighters were to escort a Rumpler two-seater over the English lines at first light, when the morning sun would be in the eyes of enemy flyers. They'd photograph a position that had aroused the curiosity of the big brass and then dash for home. With luck, it would all be over without having to fight off any of the "Lords," as the Jasta 5 pilots called their RFC counterparts.

The Albatroses were gaily painted; besides their mauve wings and green tails, they sported colourful individual markings. There was von Hipple's bus, which had a silver fuselage embellished with the emblem of a fire-breathing dragon; another plane with a huge lightning streak running down its side; one with sinister crossed bones as its trademark; a ship with an iron fist; an Albatros sporting a clover leaf and still another with a rather innocuous-looking sunburst symbol. This last was flown by young Paul Baumer, an up-and-coming ace affectionately known to his comrades as "Flower Henry." Voss's own Albatros was purple with a white tail. His personal markings included a red heart, outlined in white, and a white swastika framed by a green wreath. (The jasta fuhrer, barely twenty years old, was a Jew whose father owned a Krefeld dye-factory. Needless to say, The swastika was not yet associated with barbarous anti-semitism.) Voss was wearing clothes that immediately told onlookers he intended to lead the mission. During off-duty hours, he often puttered around the airfield in an old grey sweater, with tattered wool socks pulled over his pant legs. But whenever he was going to fly, he wore his finest dress tunic and a clean silk shirt. At his throat was the Pour le Merit, a glittering jewel of a medal that was Germany's highest award for valour. He laughingly told his pilots that, in the event that he was captured, he wanted to look as dashing as possible for the lovely French girls.

Off to one side, a group of pilots, dressed in black leather jackets, had just emerged from a light breakfast in the officers' mess. They sauntered slowly toward the hangars, adjusting scarves, buckling chin straps and chatting in unexcited tones as they walked across the dew-streaked turf. The fresh, lush-green smell of wet pine needles filled the air. A soggy wind-sock lay limp off to one side. Tired mechanics warmly greeted the approaching pilots. They didn't begrudge the airmen the easy life that they led around the base. In fact, they had nothing but respect for these youthful aviators, who, while continuously outnumbered in the air, had scored sensational victories for the fatherland throughout the spring. Jasta 5 didn't get much ink in the national press, but it was one of Germany's top fighter groups. Voss was second only to the Red Baron in victories, with thirty-one Allied planes to his credit. Several of his men were also outstanding pilots. Indeed, in English messes, pilots referred to Jasta 5 as the "Squadron of Aces." It was a well-deserved title considering that it was third among the Imperial Air Service's thirty-six fighter squadrons in officially confirmed victories. The previous April alone, it had destroyed twenty British air crews.

Looking skyward, one of the mechanics noticed that it was already growing brighter. Rain-laden clouds were slowly disappearing. He could pause for a moment to observe this, because his work was completed. Already, some of the more eager pilots were on the line, huddled in small groups as they pored over maps. One of them, doubtlessly an *"ein neuling"* (a rookie), was already in his cockpit. His engine was idling gently. They wouldn't be so quick to be off after a month of experience, veterans often thought, smiling grimly to themselves at such sights.

Jagdstaffel 5's home base of Estourmel was nearly fifteen miles from the front lines — far enough back that on mornings such as this, robins and meadowlarks could occasionally be seen perched on wires connecting the radio-communications shack to Voss's quarters. The mechanic may not have seen anything quite so peaceful this dawn, but certainly what was about to happen must have been the farthest thing from his mind. He didn't hear it, because of the throbbing pulse of the nearby Albatros, but the mechanic sensed it, nevertheless. He must have, because he suddenly looked up just in time to spot a small plane gaining momentum as it plunged through the morning mist toward the airfield. Who could that be, dropping by at this early hour? Pilots from nearby jastas popped in for a visit from time to time, but never at 4:30 a.m. Besides, this fellow, if he was coming in for a landing, was making a terrible approach. As the plane levelled off and pointed its nose at the row of ships parked on the tarmac, the mechanic surely must have frowned. Whoever it was, he was flying much too fast to land, even if he wanted to. Possibly he was going to buzz the place. It wasn't unheard of, friendly rivalries between jagdstaffels, leading to a flyer "bombing" a neighbouring outfit with oranges or rotten eggs. However, such pranks were rare and never, as far as anyone could remember, carried out at dawn.

The craft was close enough now to make out a round blue nose. The only German ship with a circular snout was the Fokker D-5 and, as far as he knew, there were only a few of them on the

Western Front — all stationed across from the French air force. If it was a Fokker pilot, he was a long way from home. One thing was certain — it was a German machine. The British didn't allow anyone except their very top aces to paint the nose, or any other part of their planes, in anything but regulation khaki. Panic! In less time than it takes to tell, all hell broke loose. Pilots and ground crews suddenly scattered in every direction, shoving and pushing one another in a mad stampede for shelter. The startled mechanic, the last one to realize what was coming, heard a dull, crackling sound and saw the unmistakeable pale yellow winking of machine-gun fire coming from the top wing of the approaching plane. Already a siren was wailing. Men shouted and cursed hoarsely as they stumbled into hangars. A few raced over to mounted machine guns.

The mechanic, paralysed at first, watched in fascination as reddish-brown tracer bullets zipped viciously down in a straight line, almost like water from a hose, onto the row of German ships. Possibly he found himself thinking about how a whole night of work was about to be destroyed in a few seconds by a lone raider. This thought may have disturbed him so greatly that he forgot the mortal danger he was in, because he made no effort to escape. Red-hot lead spilled over the last machine and tore off along the ground, kicking up mud and stones as the tracers pursued a group of fleeing men. One fellow, unable to keep up with the rest, ducked his head between his shoulders as Lewis slugs hissed into the mud just behind him. Twisting to escape, he was caught by the menacing stream and fell face-first into a puddle of water.

As the English plane flashed over the rooftops just above their heads, the Germans had a clear view of its silver body, and the blue, white and red roundels that identified it as a Royal Flying Corps machine. It was so close that they could feel the prop wash. Close enough that, if they were looking into the cockpit, they would have caught a glimpse of the pilot, who was smiling. As the Nieuport circled for another pass, airmen and mechanics rushed to the aid of the stricken man. Gently, they carried his shattered body into a hangar. Overhead, Bishop cleared off to one side in order to, in his words, "watch the fun." He wanted to give one of the Germans time to attempt a takeoff. While he waited for someone to accept the bait, he watched the men below him scurrying about, he said, "like rabbits," and recalled "laughing to myself as they did so."[12] He had always enjoyed ground-strafing.

Meanwhile, the rookie in the Albatros frantically tested his controls, checking the response of elevator, aileron and rudder to every motion of the foot-pedals and joystick. The engine was still not sufficiently warmed up, but there was no time for that now. Someone emerged from the safety of a nearby dugout, hurriedly ripped away the wheel chocks, and disappeared. The pilot revved his engine once more and taxied his lightly damaged plane out of the line. With undercarriage creaking and wings bobbing over uneven ground, the German pointed his nose toward the runway and opened the throttle as far as it would go. Water splashed out behind his wheels as the Albatros moved across the moist turf. The machine lurched forward hesitantly, slowly gathering the necessary speed as it rumbled down the field. Normally, the D-3 took off quickly and climbed rapidly, but that was with a warm engine.

At that instant, a pair of machine guns mounted on wagon wheels near the barracks began hammering away. The gunners realized almost immediately that they had the range, because the British fighter suddenly swerved violently to throw off their aim. Bishop, who was executing slow-stall turns at tree-top level, so as to keep the airfield in sight, was a sitting duck. One burst of twelve bullets tore into the fuselage just behind his head. Dodging the fire as best he could, he dropped on the Albatros that was taking off, rocketing in behind it just as its wheels lifted from the runway. One short burst sent it crash-landing into the ground, its prop churning up dirt for a second before shattering into a million pieces. Another Albatros came lumbering down the field, and Bishop darted quickly around to attack it from behind. He fired from 150 yards out, missing the target but so unnerving the enemy pilot that he flew straight into a tree, mangling his wings before belly-flopping with a thud. Neither German had been high off the ground, and both pilots, although badly shaken up, escaped unhurt from their damaged planes.

But the Canadian was due for a shock himself. While he was disposing of his second victim, two other Albatroses had taken off together and were climbing up to greet him. Bishop didn't hesitate, however. Going straight for the nearest man, he began a circling contest, straining mightily to get on the German's tail. For a moment, the enemy had the upper hand and placed five bullets in Bishop's rudder. But seconds later, the tighter-turning Nieuport gave Bishop the advantage, and he got in a clean burst of his own. The stricken Albatros dropped 200 feet and crashed on the edge of the runway. The other Albatros, which had been unaccountably sitting off to one side, now approached, both guns firing. Bishop charged at it head-on, firing a full drum of ninety-nine rounds at it. The German, apparently not a very aggressive fighter, broke off combat and landed. Bishop wasn't about to wait around for any more trouble. He made for the Allied lines as fast as his Nieuport would carry him. Near the trenches, he came under heavy anti-aircraft fire and his ship was damaged by shrapnel. Overhead, he spotted four Albatroses in hot pursuit, but they turned back as soon as he crossed no man's land and entered his own territory. The Germans almost never crossed into British airspace unless they were on a bombing raid or a photo mission.

Victoria Cross

Bishop's astounding one-man show earned him the Victoria Cross, and the distrust of some of his own squadron mates. Several of them believed he had become too ambitious and that he had made up the whole thing. They couldn't know that Allied agents behind the lines had been able to confirm the story, even finding out that the two-seater that never got off the ground had been badly damaged and had to be totally rebuilt. Nor did they realize that French civilians had seen the fight and would confirm its details in interviews with Allied officers later in the war.

There have also been suggestions that some of Bishop's English comrades were put off by the thought of this brash colonial overtaking the record of the beloved Albert Ball. Certainly, relations between the British and the men from the colonies were sometimes strained. German pilot Hans Schroder noticed this hostility shortly after he was taken prisoner. "I was astonished to find this disdain existing not merely between the English, French and American allies, but also between the various component parts of the British Empire," he wrote. "Those English, Scotch, Irish, Canadians, South Africans and Australians detested one another, and made no effort to conceal their feelings from me. How proudly the Englishman spoke those three words: 'I am

British!' And then the disdain in the Englishman's 'these Canadian chaps!'"[13] Whatever the reason, a handful of pilots in the squadron believed Bishop was a charlatan who was padding his record with totally false victory claims. One of them, Willy Fry, was actually sent back to England by Jack Scott after he called Bishop a liar to his face. (Fry returned to the front in 1918 and finished the war with several decorations and ace status.)

Bishop scored six more times before the end of June, but only two kills were witnessed by other Allied pilots. Nevertheless, Scott granted him confirmation for all six. The major, who had personally seen several Bishop kills the previous spring, was willing to give his star pilot the benefit of the doubt in every situation. Bishop, stung by the mistrust of several of his peers, began to seek out the company of animals. He was in some ways a very gentle man who enjoyed playing with rabbits, pigs and dogs. He had four dogs of his own and allowed them to sleep in his hut.

That summer, after Major Scott was invalided back to England with a serious arm wound, Bishop proved he was no fraud. The new commander, Major W.J.C. Kennedy-Cochran-Patrick, was a by-the-book officer who would expect more than just Bishop's word before he would grant victory confirmations. But if Billy's critics expected his kills to suddenly stop coming, they were in for a rude shock. Instead, his score skyrocketed. On July 12, he shot down an Albatros in full view of Sopwith triplane pilot Robert Little and, a few days later, he added two Germans in front of the Bristol fighters of 11 Squadron. When he got two more, on August 5, both were witnessed by Lt. William Molesworth. Captain Keith Caldwell witnessed another conquest that month, and the Bristol crew of Captain Clement and Lieutenant Carter verified one more. Before the summer was out, Bishop had surpassed Albert Ball's record and had fifty victories to his credit. But the victories no longer gave him much satisfaction. He was beginning to recoil from the horrors of war, as his letters clearly indicate. In one, he told Margaret: "I am thoroughly downcast tonight. The Huns got Lloyd today, such a fine fellow too, and one of our best pilots. Sometimes all of this awful fighting makes you wonder if you have a right to call yourself human. My honey, I am so sick of it all, the killing, the war. All I want is home and you."[14]

A terrifying brush with death did nothing to improve his frame of mind. Flying too close to the ground, he was hit in the fuel tanks by German ground fire, and his plane erupted in flames. He was just able to make it back over Allied territory before his ship crashed into a stand of trees. The fire was lapping at his face when a sudden rainstorm came up and saved his life. The experience almost cost him his nerve. He admitted that in a letter to his father, confiding "I find myself shuddering at chances I didn't think about taking six weeks ago."[15] Fortunately, he was ordered home before he could crack. After a visit to Buckingham Palace to receive his Victoria Cross from the king, it was off to Canada to sell war bonds, give speeches and promote enlistments. He also found the time to marry Margaret, keeping a promise he had made to her in 1916. She accepted him despite the fact that he frankly admitted to her that he had kept a French mistress while on the front.

Bishop spent eight months away from the front and, in that time, he was surpassed as top Allied ace by Jimmy McCudden, whose record of kills had soared to fifty-seven. Bishop, now totally rested, forgot about his revulsion for killing and asked to be sent back into action. His ego would not permit him to be number two. He was willing to risk everything to regain his title of ace-of-aces. In some ways he was like a tired old bullfighter who can't live without the acclaim of the crowd.

Given command of 85 Squadron in late May 1918, he prepared for another round of dogfights. His first action took place on May 27, and his combat report tells best what happened. It reads: "While attempting to attack a two-seater at 13,000 feet over Houlhust Forest, I saw ten enemy scouts coming from the southeast so I climbed towards our lines returning twenty-five minutes later at 17,500 feet. In looking for above two-seater I suddenly saw another one 200 feet under me. He saw me at the same moment and turned east. I followed and when he put his nose down I opened fire dead behind from 125 yards range. The observer ceased firing and the machine skidded to the left, in the second burst the left top and then bottom plane(wing) and a little lower the right planes and tail fell off. He fell east of Passchendaele."[16] The kill was witnessed by British anti-aircraft crews, and German records show the crew consisted of pilot Kark Andreison and gunner Lt. Keil. Next day, he ambushed nine Albatroses by himself, shooting down Corporals Siche and Peisker of Jasta 7. He was back in the groove, shooting down seventeen more Germans over the next two weeks to bring his score up to seventy. One of his victims, Paul Billik, an ace with thirty-one victories, escaped with a wound.

The Canadian government was more than impressed and, fearful that the nation's most famous war hero would be killed in action, decided to recall him from the front for good. But before he left, Bishop got in one last patrol, shooting down five planes. Flying alone, he attacked three Pfalz fighters, only to be assailed by two more. It was five against one but the legendary ace quickly shot one down and caused two others to collide. He then turned on the remaining two, shooting one down and driving the other off. He had four kills in as many minutes but still wasn't satisfied. Searching for more prey, he came across an LVG two-seater and sent it crashing in flames into a hillside. Still overcome by blood lust, he swooped down on German troops below, peppering them with lead until his guns ran out of bullets. Then he went home to Canada.

Bishop seemed lost for a time after the war. He travelled across North America, giving lecture tours. At first, there were sellout crowds but, before long, they petered out. One night, only ten people turned out in a hall designed to hold a thousand. After that, he wisely cancelled the rest of his tour. The public was tired of war heroes, and Bishop was perceptive enough to realize it. He lived off his wife's vast income for a time, but he soon became restless and when fellow-ace Billy Barker suggested they set up their own airline, Bishop instantly agreed. They sold shares to prominent businessmen in Toronto and Montreal, using the revenue to purchase three old seaplanes. Although the ships were only designed to hold three passengers, Bishop transported five each time he flew. The flights were from Toronto harbour to the Muskoka cottage country and, except for a few months in the summer, there wasn't enough business to keep them in black ink. Inevitably, they went bankrupt.

Billy next tried his hand at stunt flying, buying an old biplane and performing aerobatics at the Canadian National Exhibition. Once, he dove recklessly toward the grandstand, terrifying thousands of spectators, who stampeded out of their seats in a state of panic. One woman had a miscarriage. That was the end of his career as a showman. Billy and Margaret went to England for a decade after that. She raised their three children and he made a fortune as a salesman for a company that made iron pipe. But he lost it all when the stock market crashed in 1929. Others committed suicide but Billy seemed genuinely unperturbed. Returning to Canada, he accepted a position with an oil company in Montreal and gained a reputation as a top-notch businessman.

When the Second World War broke out, in 1939, Bishop was rushed back into uniform, this time as a figurehead with the rank of air marshal. Put in charge of recruitment, he attacked the job with relish. There was never a more effective propaganda tool. Young people were deeply impressed with his record and they flocked to RCAF recruiting stations after each of his speeches. While the army and navy had trouble coming up with enough men to meet their needs, the air force ended up turning people away. He also helped sell war bonds and served as an inspiration to those already signed up, pinning wings on new pilots and conducting endless inspection tours. The young pilots found him to be a fun-loving fellow, nothing like the stuffed shirts who made up the regular armed forces brass. Indeed, he was occasionally found dead drunk with them late at night. On more than one occasion, inspections had to be called off because Bishop showed up too drunk to stand.

In many ways, Bishop's recruitment effort was his finest hour. His exploits in the First World War had demanded great courage, but the conflict itself was seen by many as a needless exercise that could easily have been avoided had a handful of men of vision been in the halls of power in 1914. But history shows that the 1939-45 war was essential. The Nazis could only be stopped by brute force and Bishop, by helping to make the RCAF one of the strongest air forces in the world, played an honourable role in their defeat. He was old beyond his years and in poor health but he drove himself tirelessly. In a fitting tribute, Minister of Air C.G. Power told the old ace: "Your magnificent record in the First Great War fired the imagination of our Canadian aircrews in this war and has inspired them to deeds of courage to rival your own."[17]

After the Second World War, the joy seemed to go completely out of Bishop's life. He gained weight, drank far too much and went into semi-retirement. During his spare time he read books, took up hobbies and did some travelling. When the Korean War came in 1950, he tried to enlist but was turned down by a government that was wisely trying to limit Canada's role in the Asian conflict. He died in his sleep a few years later, in 1956, at age sixty-two, while on vacation in Florida.

Billy Bishop deserves all of the accolades he received. As a pilot, he was a man of unmatched bravery. In fact, during the darkest days of Royal Flying Corps history, in April, 1917, he was virtually the only Allied flyer who was consistently able to score against the better-equipped and better-trained Germans. Although he was a rebel at heart, he was more scamp than rogue. And he knew when not to cross the invisible line drawn up by authorities. He didn't let them destroy his remarkable spirit but, at the same time, he wasn't a fool who would take on a fight that he couldn't win. A very human person, he was what young people today would term a "party animal." He lived life to the fullest, survived the perils of a thousand ordinary lifetimes, and died peacefully in bed at what, for a man born in the 1890s, would have been considered old age. In other words, for all his faults he was a likeable rascal who beat the odds and became a giant in Canadian history.

World War II
and Korea

SEVEN

George Beurling

They called him "Screwball," "Buzz" and "The Falcon of Malta." But regardless of the many nicknames, George Beurling, Canada's bad-boy air ace, was the greatest Allied fighter pilot of the Second World War. Like Billy Bishop in the First World War, Beurling was a complex, even paradoxical individual. He flew into action with a Bible in his cockpit, but he was most un-Christian to his opponents, sometimes killing them as they floated helplessly to earth below their parachutes. He craved fame but cared nothing for promotions. He loved attention but had little use for intimacy. He was both heroic and pathetic at the same time. And when he died, he was remembered as Canada's most successful — and tragic — combat hero of World War Two. Beurling almost never got into the war in the first place. He was rejected when he applied for admission into the RCAF, despite the fact that he was already one of the best flyers in the world the day that war broke out.

His mother had wanted George to be a doctor. His father hoped the boy would become a commercial artist. But the lad had other ideas. "Ever since I can remember, airplanes and to get up in them into the free sky had been the beginning and end of my thoughts and ambitions," he wrote later.[1] Indeed, George had taken his first flight by age nine. He spent every spare moment at LaSalle Road airport, three miles outside his home of Verdun, Quebec, watching in fascination for hours at a time as airplanes took off and landed. And when he discovered there weren't enough spare moments in the day to satisfy him, he simply played hookey. This, he noted, meant two spankings — one when he got to school and a second when he arrived home at night. But to George, the beatings were more than worth it. When his parents banished him to his room instead of strapping him, the boy spent countless hours building model planes. He then turned around and sold them, using the money to buy flying lessons.

The only interest he showed in reading was to devour books about flight. He especially loved stories about the First World War aces. His father, Fred Beurling, recalled in a 1943 interview: "When George was fourteen or fifteen, I remember when we'd be walking along the street he would suddenly burst out 'Pop, do you know what Rickenbacker did when he had four Jerries on his tail?' Or, 'Remember Richthofen, that big German ace? Do you know what he did when he was outnumbered three to one?' George studied the air battles of the other war and he could describe and argue about the tactics of all the leading flyers. He ate, drank and slept airplanes and especially air fighting."[2] He was so obsessed with flying, in fact, that the other boys in his class would often bully him. No doubt they were motivated by envy because, by flying on a regular basis, George was experiencing a good deal more excitement in his spare time than they were. After he was chased home, his father bought him boxing gloves and taught him how to fight. "I used to get down on the floor and teach him how to box," he recalled. "Soon he was good enough to give me a good fight. I said 'George, I don't want you to look for a fight, but I don't want you to run away.'"[3]

The young enthusiast took the controls of a plane for the first time at age twelve (before that, he had always been a passenger whenever one of the pilots agreed to take him for a ride). He soloed in the mid-winter of 1938 and, from then on, there was no stopping him. Lessons cost the princely sum of ten dollars per hour, but George raised enough to pay for one training lesson per week. For a boy with a one-track mind, this seemed like slow going and he soon became impatient. Anxious to win his wings as quickly as possible, George jumped aboard a boxcar and rode the rails to Gravenhurst, Ontario, where he got a job flying a transport plane into the north country. It was monotonous work, but it racked up more flying hours in his log. After getting his pilot's certificate, he headed west, hoping to obtain a commercial licence in Vancouver. After that, he planned to go to China to fight in the Chinese Air Force against the Japanese.

Beurling did anything that he thought would help him to become a fighter pilot — and every adventure along the way had a profound impact on the course of his life. On his way to the

Pacific, he was drawn irresistibly to an aerial competition in Edmonton. The Quebecer won the event, outperforming a pair of RCAF pilots in the process. He was anything but gracious when he climbed onto the victor's platform to accept the trophy. In a cocky manner, told the stunned crowd that, if this was the best the air force could do, Canada was in a lot of trouble. Later, when the RCAF rejected him, George was convinced that the Edmonton episode was the reason, and he walked around with a chip on his shoulder until the day he died.

Next, Beurling sought out Ernst Udet. The famed World War One German ace, who was doing barnstorming demonstrations across North America at the time, was one of the greatest fighter pilots who ever lived. He had shot down sixty-two Allied planes, making him the top German ace to survive the war. Only his commander and friend, Manfred von Richthofen, had had more victories to his name. Udet taught Beurling how to dogfight. The two tossed their planes around the Western-Canadian sky, looping, rolling and diving for position in a series of mock battles. When he left the old German flyer, George probably knew more about combat flying than any airman in the peacetime RCAF. Ironically, the German ace had taught the Canadian many of the skills he would employ in such deadly fashion against German pilots in the Second World War.

But try as he might, Beurling couldn't get to China. Crossing into the United States with hopes of boarding a ship at Seattle, he was charged with illegal entry and tossed into jail. Sent home, he drifted aimlessly eastward. By this time, war had broken out, and George marched into the nearest air force recruiting station. The RCAF took one look at his poor academic record and sent him packing. Bitterly upset, George decided he'd go to Europe and fight for the Finnish Air Force against the Russians. The Finns, he understood, would take anyone with a pilot's licence. They were fighting a desperate battle with the Communists and they didn't care how a man had done in grade twelve algebra, provided he could fly and shoot. But because he was still only eighteen, the Finnish embassy insisted that he get written permission from his parents. And they refused to give it.

At this stage, just about anyone would have thrown in the towel and joined either the army or navy. But Beurling wasn't just anyone. He was obsessed with the thought of combat flying, and, once he put his mind to something, there was no stopping him. Accordingly, he signed onto a munitions ship and headed to England, determined to jump ship and join the RAF. The crossing was harrowing. Seven ships in the convoy were sunk by German U-boats, but Beurling got through. Once in Glasgow, Scotland, he went to a Royal Air Force office and offered his services, producing his logbook and pilot's licence. The recruiting officer was impressed, but told the young Canadian he couldn't sign up without a birth certificate. Seeing no alternative, Beurling returned to his ship and sailed back across the Atlantic to get the missing document! He had another eventful voyage. On the way home a German torpedo scored a glancing hit on his ship, the *Valparaiso*. His return to the United Kingdom was even more dangerous. The deadly submarines struck again, sinking another member of the convoy. The terrified merchantmen didn't even stop to pluck the survivors out of the icy seas, hoping that navy ships would pick them up.

The British took due note of Beurling's extraordinary tenacity and sent him to a big flight school in northern England. Here, he immediately got into trouble with authorities when he buzzed a control tower, knocking a sentry over the railing with the force of his prop wash. Beurling received a stiff reprimand but, after the terrible losses of the Battle of Britain, the RAF was not about to drum a man out simply for committing a juvenile prank. From flying school, he was sent to Operational Training School, where he had the good fortune to study under ace Ginger Lacey. Lacey was something of a celebrity, not only because he had shot down nearly thirty Germans, but also because he destroyed the Heinkel bomber that had scored a hit on Buckingham Palace during the air raids of 1940. The king had been so impressed that he visited Lacey's fighter squadron. The ace enraged his superiors by ordering the king a beer in the squadron mess.

For Beurling, the war was still seemed very far away, until the day he visited London on leave. He arrived just in time to be caught in a major air strike. As he raced for shelter, the Canadian spotted a little girl, apparently playing with a doll. Bombs were exploding all around her, but she seemed oblivious to the danger. Dashing through the flying shrapnel, Beurling was shocked to see that the girl's arm had been blown off at the shoulder and that she was in shock. Scooping the child up, he rushed her to safety. Not long afterward, he saw a young girl pinned under rubble after the roof of a shelter had caved in from a direct hit. A water main had burst, and water was rapidly filling the room. The girl would have drowned, except that a doctor arrived on the scene and immediately cut off her leg. The two incidents hardened Beurling. He expressed anti-German sentiments in his writings and admitted feeling ashamed that "up to now I'd been thinking of this air war as a great adventure for those who can fly."[4]

Beurling was now in the last stages of training. His performance in air-to-air gunnery tests was remarkable. Flying a Spitfire, he consistently scored direct hits on a target being hauled behind an old Fairey-Battle training plane by a long wire cable. His shooting was so accurate that he occasionally shot the cable off the training plane as well. Ginger Lacey was impressed enough to offer him a commission on the spot, but George turned it down. He distrusted officers, and announced that he preferred to live and work with the sergeant pilots. Posted to 403 Squadron, RAF, Beurling was again offered a promotion. Once again, he rejected it, exhibiting astonishing immaturity.

His commander thought Beurling was either a fool or a man totally without ambition, so he decided to post him to the "tail-end Charlie" position in his flight. What that meant was that George, whom the other pilots had begun calling "Screwball," would bring up the rear. And because the enemy formations almost always tried to attack from behind, he would be the first target in the event of an ambush. Just how dangerous the position was became evident on March 23, 1942, when the squadron participated in a fighter sweep over northern France. Beurling, despite his inexperience, was the first to spot the Focke-Wulf 190s coming down out of the sun on top of them. He radioed "bandits," but the others simply ordered him to maintain radio silence. Moments later, the Germans pounced. George had three of them on his tail and tracer bullets were darting just inches from his cockpit. One of them shot the hood off his engine as he climbed in a rolling move to the right. "I was dead meat until I suddenly got a brainstorm," he recalled later. Dropping his landing gear and wing flaps, he slowed the Spitfire to a crawling speed and all three Germans overshot him.

Back in England, George lit into his flight commander, angrily blasting the man right in front of everyone, moments after the group landed. He might well have been court-martialled for insulting a superior officer, but all he managed to do was pick up a new enemy. Shortly after that, he was transferred to another squadron. Beurling didn't get along much better with his new mates, but he did manage to score his first kill. He was flying 24,000 feet above Calais when five FW-190s attacked him. Once again, he was in the hated tail-end position and took the brunt of the enemy fire. Cannon shells slammed into both his wings, knocking his two cannons out of commission. And for the second time, his cunning saved his life. Pulling back on the joystick, he zoomed straight up into the sun. The Germans followed but lost sight of him in the blinding yellow glare. "They had more speed than I, as they had just pulled out of a dive and they went right past me in the glare, going up,"[5] he said later. As the enemy streaked past him, Beurling lined up the middle machine and let go with his Browning guns, which were still working. The Focke-Wulf exploded in a shattering blast that ripped both wings off and split the fuselage in two. The pilot, Beurling believed, was killed instantly. He expected to be congratulated when he got back to base but, instead, he was chewed out for leaving formation. "Six of us broke formation," he snapped back in open defiance. "Five Jerries and I."[6]

Tail-end Charlie

Despite his victory, he was still the tail-end Charlie two days later, when the squadron was over Calais. Thanks to his incredible eyesight, he again saw the enemy before any of the others. And once again, he was ignored when he shouted out warnings. The others flyers considered him a show-off, and they didn't trust his judgement, despite his victory. They thought that if he had seen anything at all, it must be another Allied formation. Beurling, for his part, wasn't waiting to be peppered with lead again. He peeled out of formation without permission and dove on the incoming Germans, scoring a direct hit on the leader with a perfect deflection shot. The FW-190 went down, trailing thick black smoke and pieces of wreckage before crashing into the sea.

Beurling received another reprimand for disobeying orders, despite the fact that he had clearly been in the right on each of the three missions he'd flown. Some of his superiors, it seems, disliked his rude conduct and were probably more than a little jealous of his flying and shooting ability. In any case, when he asked a few days later for permission to replace a married pilot who didn't want to go to danger-ridden Malta, they instantly agreed to let him go.

His commanding officer on Malta was Laddie Lucas, an Englishman who proved to be a shrewd judge of character. If not for Lucas, it is unlikely that the world would ever have heard of George Beurling. Four decades later, recalling their first meeting, Lucas said, "Beurling was untidy, with a shock of fair, tousled hair above penetrating blue eyes. He smiled a lot and the smile came straight out of those striking eyes. His sallow complexion was in keeping with his part Scandinavian ancestry. He was high strung, brash and outspoken." Lucas suspected that the Canadian wasn't well educated, but added "he was a practical man" who had made a thorough study of flying. "He was a rebel, yes; but I suspected that his rebelliousness came from some mistaken feeling of inferiority. I judged that what Beurling needed most was not to be smacked down but to be encouraged. His ego mattered very much to him and, from what he told me of his treatment in England, a deliberate attempt had been made to assassinate it."[7] Lucas promised to give the Canadian his trust, but warned him that if he abused it, "he would be put on the next aircraft to the Middle East. When I said all this those startling blue eyes peered incredulously at me as if to say that, after all his past experience of human relations, he didn't believe it. He was soon to find out that a basis for confidence and mutual trust did exist. He never once let me down."[8]

Beurling arrived as the seige of Malta was reaching a crescendo. German and Italian planes were pounding the island fortress around the clock, in an all-out bid to blast it into submission. In fact, the day he arrived, a pair of cocky Messerschmitt 109 pilots had raided Takali airfield, coming in just ten feet off the deck before shooting up everything that moved. He got his first taste of action on June 12, when four Spitfires scrambled to intercept a dozen ME-109s. Beurling blew the tail off one of them in a ten-minute fight but — although it is impossible to imagine that the enemy plane could have flown back to base without his rudder — he only received credit for a "probable" kill because no one saw it crash.

There was a brief lull after that as both sides licked their wounds and overhauled their machines. The other pilots at Takali used the time to rest but Beurling spent countless hours working on the principles of deflection shooting. Essentially, what that amounted to was trying to figure out how far to "lead" an enemy plane so that it would fly right into your burst of fire. You had to calculate the speed of your opponent, how fast your bullets would fly, and your angle of fire, all in a split-second, at the same time watching your tail for opponents. It was a tricky business, but Beurling quickly mastered it.

On July 6, he used what he had learned when eight Spitfires rose to meet three Italian Cant bombers escorted by thirty Macchi fighters. Beurling led the charge, diving straight through the fighters before swerving to line up one of the big three-engined Cants. His first burst caught the bomber right in the cockpit, blowing off the pilot's head. Another squirt set an engine on fire. In an extraordinary display of courage, an Italian observer left his gun port and took the pilot's seat, flying the damaged machine back to Sicily where he somehow managed to crash-land it. The plane was written off, although Beurling was not officially credited with a kill. Turning on the Macchis, Beurling executed a lightning turn and fired point-blank at one of the single-seaters. His target went down in flames before the pilot could bail out. Wasting not a moment, he lined up another Macchi and went straight for it. The Italian saw him coming at the last second and dove steeply in a frantic bid to escape. But the Canadian wouldn't let him go, pursuing the Macchi from 20,000 feet all the way down to 5,000 feet. Finally, when the enemy pilot either had to pull up or dive into the sea, Beurling caught him dead to rights with a killing burst. The Macchi exploded "into a million pieces,"[9] Beurling wrote. The luckless pilot's wingmate, whom Beurling had shot down seconds earlier, survived despite cannon wounds in the shoulders, arms and legs and a crash into the sea. Allied doctors cut off his leg, however, and he had an empty pant leg for the rest of his life to remind him of his encounter with Beurling. The day wasn't over for the formidable Canadian. Near sunset, he led four Spitfires into an attack on two Junkers 88s escorted by twenty ME-109s. In the wild dogfight that followed, two Germans dove on Beurling, intending to make short work of the troublesome ace. But he easily outmanoeuvred them, employing tricks he'd learned from Ernst Udet. Circling quickly around, he caught a yellow-nosed fighter with a three-second burst. The volley, which came from an amazing 800-yard range and a nearly impossible angle, hit the German in the fuel tanks and sent him down in flames. In one day, he had destroyed four enemies (although only three were confirmed) and raised his total to five.

Back at Malta, however, the other pilots didn't throw a party for George. Beurling shrugged off the snub, but it was a clear sign of his unpopularity. A fellow-pilot, R.S. Hyndman, knew Beurling well. He told the author in 1989 that "he was a total loner, and irritated many, but I liked him. A wild Errol Flynn he was! But more silent."[10]

Beurling didn't care much for friendship at this stage. He was out to make a name for himself and he'd come to the right place. In a whirling battle on July 8, he shot down an ME-109 and damaged a Junkers. Later, he bagged a second Messerschmitt, but, because it wasn't seen to crash, he was only credited with a "probable." It was an absurd and unfair ruling. The German, after all, had been seen diving away on fire, and several pilots later reported seeing an oil stain on the water, where it had undoubtedly gone in. Beurling continued his success on July 10, using new tactics to bag an ME-109. The ace dove under his victim and then pulled up his nose before raking the German's belly from prop to rudder. That same day he shot down an Italian, separating a Macchi from a formation of seven enemies before dispatching it. Beurling caught his man at the top of a loop and blew his wings off. The pilot managed to bail out, however, and floated down into the sea. Beurling, who was often characterized as a cold-blooded killer, showed compassion on this occasion, giving the man's position to an air/sea rescue team.

When he got back to base, he learned that one of the squadron's more popular pilots, Lt. Chuck Ramsay, had been killed. The next day, another Spitfire pilot went to a watery grave. The squadron, hoping he might be adrift in a life raft, went looking for him. Beurling, who was supposed to be taking part in the rescue attempt, managed to find two Italian planes instead. He shot them both down in just seconds. He had used just two bursts and hit both Macchis in the fuel tanks.

Beurling's marksmanship had now become the stuff of legend. Once, he reported firing five cannon shells into the cockpit of an enemy plane. Allied soldiers who inspected the wreckage on the ground found its cockpit had indeed been hit by exactly five rounds. Spitfire pilot D.J. Dewan, who flew with Beurling, told the author that "he was so successful for many reasons, but the two most important were his eyesight and his knack for deflection shooting. He used to report sightings of aircraft many seconds before others saw them, and he knew whether he hit them in the front, centre or rear of their airplane and he usually used minimum ammunition."[11]

Laddie Lucas credited more than just Beurling's marksmanship and eyesight for his phenomenal success. "He had an instinctive 'feel' for an aircraft," the Englishman said. "He quickly got to know its characteristics and extremes — and the importance of doing so. He wasn't a wild pilot who went in for all sorts of hair-raising manoeuvres, throwing his aircraft all over the sky. Not at all. George Beurling was one of the most accurate pilots I ever saw. A pair of sensitive hands gave his flying a smoothness unusual in a wartime fighter pilot.... This acute sensitivity told him that a Spitfire was only a fine gun platform if it was flown precisely. He therefore set out to make himself the master of the airplane. He never let it fly him." Lucas confirmed that Beurling had "exceptional" eyesight that gave him a clear edge in a dogfight. He was also superb at judging distances. "I never saw Beurling shoot haphazardly at an aircraft which was too far away. He only fired when he thought he could destroy. Two hundred and fifty yards was the distance from which he liked best to fire. A couple of short, hard bursts from there and that was usually it."[12]

But Beurling wasn't the only one who could shoot straight. He got a taste of hot lead on July 14 when three ME-109s and a pair of Italian Reggianes jumped him. He banked away from the Germans, deciding to allow the Italians to have a crack at him instead, figuring they could do less damage. When he got back home he counted twenty machine-gun bullets in his plane. The only reason he hadn't been shot down was that the Reggiane didn't come equipped with cannons. Nine days later, he retaliated by shooting down his first Reggiane, blowing off a wing with a deflection shot. He damaged a German Junkers 88 in the same melee.

The Canadian ace had mixed emotions about his Italian opponents, sometimes lavishing praise on them, at other moments heaping scorn on them. In a 1943 interview, he referred to Italian pilots as "ice cream merchants" and said "the Eyeties are comparatively easy to shoot down. Oh, they're brave enough. In fact, I think they have more courage than the Germans, but their tactics aren't so good. They are very good gliders, but they try to do clever acrobatics and looping. But the Eyeties will stick it even if things are going against them, whereas the Jerries will run."[13]

Regardless of what he thought of them, Beurling, on July 27, administered one of the cruellest blows suffered by the Italian Air Force in World War Two. That morning, the ace pilot Captain Furio Doglio Niclot took off from Sicily with his friend and wingman, Faliero Gelli. The pair had been a thorn in the side of the Malta defenders for months. Niclot had shot down six Spitfires, and Gelli, who always covered his tail, had managed to destroy two. Italian air historian Nicola Malizia, writing in 1982, said that "the outstanding Macchi pilot of 20 Gruppo was Captain Niclot, commander of 151 Squadriglia. He was a courageous and able leader, and his aircraft always carried a distinctive white V on the fuselage which he regarded as a sign of defiance against the English. The RAF had been trying for some time to shoot him down, but without success. One day, after running out of ammunition in a combat, he fought off a Spitfire that was attacking a lone JU-88, which had been damaged over Malta and had become separated from the rest of the formation. Instead of landing at his own base, the pilot of the 88 followed Niclot back to Gela. He wanted to thank his saviour personally and give him a hug."[14]

A Crash Landing

Niclot and Gelli never saw Beurling coming. He picked off Gelli first, hitting his radiator and engine. The Italian managed to crashland on Gozo Island and was taken prisoner. When Gelli was pulled free of his wrecked aircraft his head had swollen to twice its normal size. Only seconds after he wounded Gelli, Beurling killed Niclot. He was about to destroy a third Macchi when he suddenly spotted two ME-109s climbing up to greet him. Seeing richer pickings, he fell on them with guns blazing. The leader, hit in the fuel tanks, went down in a ball of fire. His wingman flew home with holes in his tail and wings. Beurling had destroyed three enemy fighters and damaged one, but he didn't want to stop. Landing only to refuel and reload, he took off again and brazenly attacked four Messerschmitts. His remarkable aim brought down one German in flames, and a second limped home trailing oily black smoke. He probably never made it, judging from the volume of smoke pouring from his engine, but the Canadian received credit only for a "damaged." For this amazing day's work, when he officially destroyed four planes and damaged two others, he won the Distinguished Flying Medal.

He continued to shoot down enemy ships — and to get shot up himself — as what was now known as the "July Blitz" started to wind down. On the twenty-ninth an ME-109 shot the hood off Beurling's Spitfire. But in his excitement the German overhauled the RAF machine and flew out in front of the ace's guns. It was a fatal mistake. A one-second burst shattered the Messerchmitt's cockpit, and the fighter crashed in flames with a dead pilot at the controls. That was enough for Beurling's superiors. They made him an officer on July 30. This time, they didn't offer him a commission. They simply ordered him to accept the promotion. He didn't appear overly impressed, however, and continued to live and eat with the sergeant pilots.

Beurling didn't realize it, but the authorities had had to promote him. The attention of the whole world was now riveted on the seige of Malta, and the stubborn defence of a handful of RAF pilots was making headlines in every Allied nation. Beurling, as the top-scoring ace on the island, was front-page news. Reporters were clamouring for copy about him. And they were beginning to ask embarrassing questions, such as: why was the top gun on Malta still only a sergeant? It wouldn't do to say, "Because he refuses to be promoted." So the powers-that-be rectified the situation by hastily promoting Beurling.

By August, Beurling was exhausted. The intense summer heat of the island, the constant tension of the battle, and a sickness known simply as "the Dog" combined to lay him low. The Dog was caused by the pilots' poor diet. Beurling had lost close to fifty pounds since arriving at Takali, and it was all he could do to drag himself out of bed in the morning. In fact, he was bedridden for a week. But he managed to get into the air on August 15. It was a mistake, because, in his weakened condition, he was no match for the swarms of German fighters hovering over Malta. Fifteen ME-109s jumped him. He had time for only one burst, but it was a killer. One of the Germans dropped like a stone, falling into the sea, but the others shot the Spitfire to pieces. Beurling couldn't bail out because his parachute harness was loose. Had he taken to the silk, he would certainly have ruptured himself. So, with two enemies trailing him, he glided down for a crash landing. He just managed to clear a stone wall before flopping down unceremoniously in a ploughed field. The Dog laid him low for several more days, but he was up with two other pilots on August 23 just in time to intercept a lone JU 88. The German was apparently out on a reconnaissance mission when he lost his escorting fighters. Caught by the three Spitfires, the enemy pilot had no hope of escape. His two comrades both scored hits before Beurling swooped in and shot the 88's right engine off. The bomber crashed in flames and not one of its four crewmen got out. The victory, Beurling's twentieth, is the only one listed in RAF records as a "shared" kill.

That was the end of his scoring for the month, however, as illness again put him on his back. And when he did take to the air, on September 16, his plane was badly damaged by a marauding ME-109. But, a week later, Beurling proved that he hadn't lost his touch when he attacked eighteen German fighters, shooting two to shreds. One was hit in the oxygen bottles and scattered over a wide area. The other fell away, trailing black smoke. A third ME-109 went for him but, seconds later, it was tumbling down in a ball of orange flames.

Then came the October Blitz. The Germans and Italians pulled out all the stops in a last-ditch effort to blast Malta into the sea. Italian historian Nicola Malizia wrote later that "the capacity of the British island to defend itself amazed everyone. Not even the strong German detachments, with their numbers and equipment, seemed to shake its implacable resolve."[15] As the struggle heated up, it became increasingly vicious. Half of Beurling's squadron was shot down in a week. One of the dead pilots, a French-Canadian named Jean Paradis, had been Beurling's only close friend on the island. The two Quebecers had spent many hours swimming and talking. When Paradis died, Beurling allowed himself no further friends.

Both sides were in a hateful mood. George once saw a German pilot slaughtered in his parachute by one of his own men. The ME-109 pilot had mistaken the man in the chute for a Spitfire jockey. Beurling was so shocked, he recounted later, that he nearly vomited in his cockpit. But the atrocities were by no means confined to just the Axis pilots. Malizia said that chivalrous treatment was the exception over Malta. "Several Italian pilots and crews who were shot down over or near the island, and were taken prisoner, told how they had been tortured and maltreated. Moreover, after the invasion of Sicily, there were authenticated stories of brutal acts known to have been committed by British pilots, including the machine-gunning of Italians as they parachuted to safety."[16] Lucas confirmed that one of his men once killed the crew of a JU 88 as they bobbed helplessly in their life raft. But, he noted, the shootings were an act of revenge. Four days earlier, an ME-109 had shot a Spitfire pilot dead as he dangled on the end of his parachute.

Before long, bailing out became just about the most dangerous thing to do. Beurling himself joined in the carnage, collapsing the parachutes of several helpless Italian and German airmen. He justified this monstrous conduct by telling a reporter that, "the way I figure it, he might get down, get back to Germany, and come back to shoot me down."[17] In fact, Axis pilots shot down on or near Malta were almost always taken prisoner. But even if a pilot did manage to land safely, he wasn't always out of danger. One German was set upon by Maltese civilians and promptly beheaded. A local bar owner collected the bloody trophy and stored it in a clay pot that he delighted in showing to customers.

Most of Beurling's victims, however, were shot down in fair combat. He killed two ME-109 pilots on October 9, diving below them before climbing back up to riddle their underbellies. Five days later he scored three more victories, for which he should have been awarded the Victoria Cross. The entire squadron — twelve Spitfires — had been scrambled to intercept a force of fifteen Junkers, escorted by at least eighty Messerschmitts. Beurling, as usual, spotted the enemy first. But he couldn't alert the others, because his radio was dead. So he attacked ninety-five planes by himself! Piling into the Junkers, he damaged one before the fighters were even aware there was a wolf loose in the henhouse. Then he promptly shot down two ME-109s. On his way home he came across one of the Junkers that had been forced out of formation by his original attack and shot it down in flames.

In many ways, the very size of the enemy formation worked in Beurling's favour. All eighty escorting fighters weren't about to leave the bomber unprotected to take on one Spitfire — especially not with eleven other RAF planes hovering overhead. It may have been a classic proof of the maxim that "everyone's responsibility is no-one's job." Moreover, there were so many Germans that many of them wouldn't be able to make sudden moves without risking a collision. Finally, Beurling had the advantage of surprise. He scored quickly and got out in the resulting confusion.

The next day, Beurling flew his last combat mission over Malta. And like so many others before it, it was spectacular. Leading three Spitfires, he took on eight bombers and fifty fighters. Recognizing that the bombers were the main threat to the island — and the easiest targets — he herded one out of formation and sent it down in flames. But a dying rear-gunner scored thirty hits on the Canadian's plane before the JU-88 slammed into the Mediterranean. One of the bullets nicked Beurling's finger and another struck him in the forearm. At that moment, two ME-109s dove on his tail, intent on delivering the *coup de grace*. Ignoring them, with the blood flowing from two wounds, Beurling pressed home an attack on an ME-109 in front of him, damaging it with a burst from 450 yards' range. Only then did he turn on the adversaries behind him. It was almost too late. One of them peppered his tail and wings with cannon shells. The other German shattered the canopy of his cockpit with a well-placed burst. Beurling plunged at 600 miles per hour, managing to lose the two Germans on his tail.

Anyone else would have hightailed it for home to have his wounds treated and his machine repaired. But not Beurling. He spotted an ME-109 below him and just couldn't resist taking a crack at it. Within seconds the black-crossed airplane was in the drink. But Beurling's move caught the attention of more enemy pilots. Several ME-109s dropped on him with guns flashing. A cannon shell sliced off the bottom of his right foot and another grazed his elbow. The controls were shot from his hands and the Spitfire engine suddenly burst into flames. Beurling, wounded four times and with flames licking at his face, slid back his damaged canopy and attempted to bail out. But he was pinned back into his seat by a rush of air as the burning fighter plane spun crazily down out of control. Strangely, he found himself completely calm. "This is it. This is what it's like when you know you're going to die," he thought to himself.[18] Then the will to live welled up inside him, and Beurling pulled himself out of his stupor. Scrambling out of the cockpit, he stood on the starboard wing, trying to work up the courage to jump. The sea was only one thousand feet below. It was now or never! Closing his eyes, he dove over the side. As he plummeted down he found himself laughing hysterically. With only five hundred feet to go, his parachute opened with a painful jerk. Beurling just had time to kick off his heavy boots before he hit the water. Despite his wounds, he managed to inflate his rubber raft and to climb aboard. When the rescue launch reached him, the floor of the raft was covered in blood.

L.G. Head, one of the men who pulled him out of the sea, never forgot the scene. "When we picked him out of the water he was most concerned for a few moments because he was unable to locate a small Bible that he had been given by his mother. He told us that he would not fly without his Bible and was most relieved when we found it and handed it to him. Before we got ashore, he was most adamant that he was going to fly and fight within a few hours, but it was most obvious to us that the wound in his heel in particular would put him out for sometime."[19]

For Beurling, the fighting over Malta was finished, but he faced more danger before returning to England. On the flight back, the Liberator bomber in which he was a passenger crashed into the sea, killing fifteen people, including Canadian ace "Billy the Kid" Williams. Williams was one of five Canadian aces on Malta. Besides Beurling and Williams, the passengers included Wally McLeod of Regina, Malta's second-highest scorer, and Buck McNair, both of whom will be discussed in detail in later chapters. Beurling, who was near a rear door when the plane went into the drink, just managed to get out and, despite being weighed down by a heavy plaster cast on his wounded foot, swam 160 yards to shore.

After a short stay in a British hospital, Beurling was sent home to help sell war bonds and drum up enlistments. But he didn't adjust well to the role of war hero. He was a poor public speaker and quickly became bored by the lack of action. In his hometown, he was openly hostile when a group of girl guides presented him with twenty-nine red roses (one for each of his kills). The gesture had been in extremely poor taste, but the children had meant no harm. When asked by a reporter about the bond sales, he growled that "if I were ever asked to do that again I'd tell them to go to hell or else ask for a commission on the bonds I sold."[20]

Patience Lacking

When it became obvious that he wasn't going to be much of a salesman for the government, he was quietly sent back to England. But the RAF decided not to risk him in combat, opting instead to make him a gunnery instructor. The decision was a mistake, because Beurling didn't have the patience to be a good teacher. He asked for posting to an operational squadron. And when the British continually turned him down, Beurling applied for admission into the Royal Canadian Air Force. Canadian authorities jumped at the chance of landing Beurling. The RCAF was deeply embarrassed by the fact that it had turned down the Quebec pilot years earlier, and was anxious to put the nation's most famous war hero into one of its blue uniforms. And to Beurling's relief, the air force posted him to 403 Squadron, which was engaged in regular combat sorties over northern France.

Compared to Malta, however, the Western Front was a Sunday picnic. The Allies were sending as many as fifty Spitfires into enemy territory at a time. And only one sortie in four was encountering any opposition. Under such circumstances, it was difficult for a lone wolf like Beurling to make his mark. After being accustomed to three dogfights a day, the lack of action drained his spirit. He began breaking formation and going off by himself in search of victims, which left his wingmen exposed to extreme danger. His actions got him in trouble with his superiors. Nevertheless, he soon proved he hadn't lost his touch. On September 24, 1943, he shot down a Focke-Wulf, blowing off one of its wings as it dove on another Spitfire. Three months later he scored again, shooting down another FW-190. "I rolled to starboard and cut into the FW," he said in his combat report. It dove away, but Beurling "turned to follow and took a long range three-second burst from the starboard and I fired another burst for luck. It went straight down in flames and I saw the pilot bale out."[21]

At this point, Beurling had thirty-two kills (one of them shared), but his score would climb no higher. His combat career wasn't ended by a German or Italian pilot, but rather by his own air force. Higher authority decided it could no longer tolerate his outrageous lack of discipline. The RCAF was trying to instill teamwork in its young fighter pilots, and the example of the country's most successful ace ignoring all the rules undermined the air force's effort. Beurling's rebelliousness finally went too far when he flatly refused to stop buzzing the squadron headquarters. Given a direct order to cease the activity, he immediately went out and did it again. Challenged upon landing by his commanding officer, he declared that "you, you can't tell me what to do."[22] That was the end of the line. Any other pilot would have been court-martialled, sent home in disgrace, even spent time in prison. But because Beurling was Canada's most famous fighting man, he was quietly sent home and granted an honourable discharge. He tried to get around the ban by applying to the United States air force, but the trick didn't work this time. The Americans didn't want a rebel either.

George Beurling was lost when peace came in 1945. Canada was tired of war — and war heroes, for that matter. The attention he craved dried up. Worse still, he couldn't get regular work. The airline companies all turned him down, fearful that he would be too wild a pilot for commercial aviation. Eventually, he was reduced to begging on Montreal street corners. Sadly, even his marriage, in 1944, ended in divorce, at least partly because George began flirting with other women while still on his honeymoon. Desperate to recapture the glory years, Beurling decided to join the Israeli Air Force in 1948. But he never made it to the Middle East. The passenger plane he was flying in crashed on takeoff at Rome airport. Sabotage was suspected but never proven.

In the end, George Beurling was destroyed by his love of danger and excitement. He was so obsessed with his role as a swashbuckling air ace that he could never adjust to the life of a normal human being. His life was best summed up by fellow Spitfire pilot Robert Hyndman. Discussing Beurling many decades after the war, he sadly said: "Christ, what a waste!"[23]

Where does George Beurling belong in the annals of history? Was he a Canadian hero or a cold-blooded mercenary? Certainly, he was a man of boundless physical courage, and few have realized just how skillful a pilot he was. His thirty-two confirmed victories made him one of the top-scoring Allied aces of the war. Only a handful of flyers surpassed his record and none of them could match his score of twenty-eight kills in fourteen days over Malta. Beurling's greatest achievement, however, is that he was the only Allied pilot of World War Two who outscored his top Luftwaffe rival in his theatre of battle. In every battle of the war, with the exception of Malta, the leading ace was a German. In many cases, the leading Nazi fighter pilot outperformed the top British, American, French, Russian, Polish or Canadian by a two-to-one margin. In the Battle of Britain, for instance, the leading RAF ace, Eric Lock, scored twenty victories while the number-one German, Helmuth Wick, notched forty-two. In the Battle for France, the Luftwaffe's Wilhelm Balthasar registered twenty-three victories compared to twenty for the French ace of aces. It was the same in the campaign for Denmark and Norway, in the invasion of Poland, in North Africa, over the Russian Front and in the pitched air battles over Germany in the last two years of the war. Only over Malta did the Luftwaffe's best meet his match. Hauptmann Gerhard Michalski's twenty-six victories placed him two behind the campaign's top gun — George Beurling.

Beurling deserves to be admired for that, and for not being a part of the air force establishment. He was a rebel who was refreshingly unafraid of authority. In an age of regimentation, he did things his way. He was a free spirit who rose to the top of his profession, despite the best efforts of his superiors to stop him. It must have been galling to air force generals to admit, both in the First World War with Billy Bishop and in the Second World War with George Beurling, that Canada's leading aces were the mavericks who would not submit to excessive rules and regulations. But Beurling, unlike Bishop, was just too much of a rebel. While Bishop found it difficult to cope with peace, Beurling found it impossible. He just couldn't let go of the exciting life he'd lived during the war years and, in the end, he died a useless and tragic death.

EIGHT

Russ Bannock

Russ Bannock, the cool professional who was Canada's second-highest-scoring ace of World War Two, and the nation's leading night-fighter pilot, probably saved far more lives than he took. The Edmonton, Alberta native was the RCAF's most prolific buzz-bomb destroyer, blasting nineteen of the dreaded German robot-planes out of the sky. And each one of these victories saved a score of civilian lives in London. This achievement alone would have been enough to rank Bannock among Canada's great heroes of the war, but he was also one of the top scorers in the bitter campaign against the Luftwaffe night-fighter pilots, shooting eleven of them down, thereby saving the lives of dozens of Allied bomber crews.

Bannock's thirty aerial victories put him just behind George Beurling on the Canadian ace list but, strangely, his name has been lost to history. He was unknown to the public even during the war and it's safe to say that today, outside of his immediate family and friends, few who know him even realize that he was one of the century's most daring and successful air aces. Bannock specialized in raiding German airfields by himself, roaming far behind enemy lines in his Mosquito twin-engine fighter, picking off Luftwaffe pilots as they landed or took off. His attacks on Nazi bases rivalled Billy Bishop's bold thrust on Estourmel airfield a generation earlier, but, unlike the Ontario ace, he never got much recognition for his feats. What is amazing about Bannock, however, is that he doesn't seem to care about his lack of fame. He was the classic citizen-soldier who performed his duty and, like Roy Brown, simply got on with life.

Russ Bannock was born on November 1, 1919, and the family name was actually Bahnuk. However, his father changed it to the more pronounceable "Bannock" in 1939. It was probably just as well, because Bahnuk was an Austrian name, and Austria became part of Hitler's Third Reich that year. Anyone with a German or Austrian name was likely to find himself subjected to unreasonable suspicion and prejudice when war came a year later. As it was, Russ had two cousins serving in the German air force.

As a boy, he played hockey and baseball, and dreamed of a career in aviation. "I grew up in Edmonton and Edmonton was always known for aviation in those days," he said in a 1989 interview with the author. "I was fascinated by the famous Canadian bush pilots 'Punch' Dickens and 'Wop' May. Wop May is actually the person who gave me my first reference to get into the air force." Bannock planned a career as a flying geologist and, when he finished high school in 1937, "I went up to Yellowknife and got a job (prospecting) with an excavation crew. I came back to Edmonton for three months in the winter of 1938 and got my private pilot's licence, and took a couple of mining courses at the university." By April of the following year, he had his commercial pilot's licence and took a job with Yukon Southern Air Transport, intending all the while to enrol full-time in mining courses at university in September. But September brought the Second World War, and Russ Bannock's life was altered forever. "As the war rolled around, every commercial pilot in Canada received a telegram from the Minister of National Defence, inviting us to become RCAF pilot officers. That was the day war started and I promptly replied 'yes'. Three or four days later, I was sent to Vancouver to learn instrument-flying and aerobatics. I flew the Gypsy Moth, an open-cockpit biplane, and wore leather helmet and glasses. They were fun to fly, but I was sent from there to Trenton Officer School and then to Camp Borden, which was the only service flying school, flying Harvards and Ferry Battles (training planes)."

Bannock, already an experienced pilot, won his air force wings quickly and was posted to No. 112 Squadron, RCAF, which was about to go overseas with the First Canadian Division. But events were moving even faster than his training. "France fell — the Allies pulled out — and I was sent with a few others to become an instructor," in Canada. Today, he admits to being disappointed. "I'd have liked to go overseas." But he agrees the RCAF made a good decision. "I had a little more experience than the others and was needed as a teacher."

For three long years he taught people how to fly, winning promotions to chief instructor and squadron leader. As the war dragged on, he began to fear he would never get a chance to prove himself in combat.

Bannock's big break came in 1943, when he was posted to an operational training unit in Greenwood, Nova Scotia, flying the new Mosquito fighter. After a brief stint there, he was on his way to England, arriving at 418 Squadron, at Holmsley, in southern England, on June 10, 1944. Three days later, without warning, the second Battle of Britain began. The Germans, who were no longer capable of mounting a serious manned challenge to the Allied air forces, had decided to attempt to destroy London with unmanned robot-planes.

The bombardment began on the night of June 13, 1944, when veteran British Auxiliary Coast Guard officer Fred Marsh spotted two strange objects streaking out of the inky heavens at 400 miles per hour. He couldn't hear the drone of airplane propellers and they were coming much too fast to be German bombers. As the cigar-shaped machines with the square wings passed over his observation post at the end of Folkestone Harbour, in southern England, Marsh realized they were also too small to be enemy fighters. Picking up his black telephone, he rang up the nearest Royal Air Force base and reported "two aircraft with lighted cockpits coming in from the French coast in a northwesterly direction."[1] Marsh's warning came too late. Moments after the mystery ships reached land, their engines died. There was an eerie silence that seemed to last for an eternity but actually spanned only fourteen seconds. And then came two gigantic explosions. On the ground, six civilians, mostly women and children, lay dead. Nine others were seriously injured. The casualty toll quickly mounted. Three days later, a single machine demolished a 116-year old church in the centre of London, killing 119 worshippers and maiming 141 others. The devastation shocked the allies and created near-panic in the British capital. Londoners who had only recently brought their children back to the city after several years in the countryside, tearfully packed them off again. Air raid shelters that had been dug in backyard gardens four years earlier were reopened.

The V-1, or buzz-bomb, was dreaded for many reasons. Besides the fact that each one delivered 2,000 pounds of explosives, it had a motor that was automatically turned off just before touchdown. No one was ever sure exactly where it would strike. And there seemed to be an unlimited supply. The Germans used 141 on the town of Croydon Surrey alone, killing 211 people and injuring nearly 2,000. When the smoke cleared, 1,400 homes had been destroyed and 54,000 others damaged. Factory owners were so worried by this new threat that they began posting spotters on roof tops. And the industrialists weren't the only ones in a state of frenzy. Prime Minister Winston Churchill was so incensed that he considered ordering the RAF to retaliate by dropping mustard gas onto German cities. Fortunately, cooler heads prevailed and the idea was dropped. But the fear of these awesome weapons didn't dissipate. Although the rockets had no radar and fell on their targets at random no one believed that — not after a buzz-bomb slammed into the headquarters of General Dwight Eisenhower, supreme commander of the Allied armies.

It was this climate of anger and fear that greeted Russ Bannock when he arrived in the United Kingdom that summer. He'd been trying to get into the air war for five years. Now, he was about to be thrust headlong into the last great challenge facing the Royal Canadian Air Force. It helped that his new squadron flew the powerful Mosquito, the very plane on which he had trained in Nova Scotia. It was a fantastic machine — possibly the best Allied combat aircraft of the war. Equipped with two 1,230-hp Rolls Royce Merlin engines and made of light plywood, it could reach speeds of 400 miles per hour and had a ceiling of 36,000 feet. Moreover, it had an incredible range. Its two-man crew could roam a full 1,200 miles (1,700 if extra fuel tanks were added). That meant it could reach targets all over occupied Europe, as well as deep inside Germany itself. It was being used to attack rail and communications centres across the Reich, to escort RCAF night bombers on their raids into Germany and to tackle the dreaded buzz-bombs.

Bannock's eyes still twinkle when he discusses the Mosquito, much as if he were recalling his first love. "It was one of the fastest piston engine aircraft of World War Two," he says with pride. "It was designed as a high-speed, unarmed bomber but then became a night-fighter. It was fast! Unless the Germans jumped us from above we could always get away from them. They weren't as manoeuvrable as the Spitfire or Hurricane — you wouldn't want to get into a dogfight with an ME-109 — but they had tremendous firepower. If you could get your guns on them you could knock them down." Indeed, the Mosquito seemed the only plane capable of taking on the V-1s. Although unmanned, the robot-planes were extraordinarily dangerous. In fact, one New Zealand squadron lost seventeen planes while attacking them. The reason for that was simple. If you got too close to the rocket to knock it down, the chances were very good that you'd be engulfed in the explosion. And if you didn't get close enough, your shells would bounce harmlessly off the twenty-eight-foot long fuselage, and the buzz-bomb would continue on to the target.

Bannock's first mission took place the night after the first V-1s were spotted by Fred Marsh. Because formation flying was impossible at night, he flew on his own (along with navigator R.R. Bruce) looking for trouble. Not finding any flying bombs about, he searched for German night-fighters. He couldn't find any of them either, but, refusing to give up, he flew over a Nazi airfield at Avord, France. He circled in the dark and waited. Then it happened. A Messerschmitt 110 turned on its navigation lights and started to take off, completely unaware of the danger lurking in the darkness just overhead. Bannock's attention was caught by the green lights on the German machine, and he came roaring down out of the night. The rear-gunner was taken totally by surprise and offered no resistance. Bannock came in swiftly from above and behind and triggered his guns. Four twenty-millimetre cannons roared into life, sending a shower of red projectiles into the Messerschmitt. The plane exploded and crashed back onto the runway, scattering wreckage over a wide area. German anti-air-craft gunners scrambled to their positions but it was too late. The intruder had vanished as quickly as he appeared, leaving behind three dead men. The Albertan's victory was important. German night-fighters were having a field day with British and Canadian bomber crews. Operating under the cover of darkness, they mowed down thousands of four-engine Lancasters while suffering few losses themselves. One German ace, Major Heinz Schnaufer, shot down 121 bombers at night, killing or capturing more than 800 Allied flyers. As a result, Bannock probably saved a score of bomber servicemen every time he shot down a German night-fighter.

But his assistance didn't directly help the civilians in London who were coming under increasing attack from the V-1s. Soon after his first victory, Bannock got a first-hand look at the ordeal they were enduring. "I was in London on leave and I saw one crash just behind our hotel. I went around back and forty people were dead. They terrified people. They came overhead and you could hear them make a putt, putt, putt sound — a pulse jet engine. The engine would stop and nobody knew where they'd hit. The Germans gave them just enough fuel to get to London. They had a two-thousand-pound warhead and they created quite an impact."

At first, 418 squadron had a great deal of difficulty with the buzz-bombs. "They flew over the North Sea at 300 feet, and we couldn't catch them. They were fast. So we learned to patrol at 10,000 feet. We'd get up to 420 or 430 miles per hour in a dive and, as we pulled in behind them, we had forty-five seconds before they'd pull away from us." And, like the New Zealanders, the Canadians initially had trouble keeping their distance. "We lost a couple of aircraft early on because, when they exploded, the whole thing just blew up. They were fuelled with kerosene and hydrogen, and the bomb went off too. It made for a great explosion and, if you flew through the debris, both of your engines would be knocked out."

A Small Target

The Canadian started his private war on the "doodlebugs" on June 19, 1944, catching up with one over the English Channel. Closing in, he noted that "it had a metal fuselage and wooden wings, had a wing span of about 30 feet and was of about the same length, with a big tube engine on the back." It was a small target, but Bannock's marksmanship was accurate and the machine was blasted out of the sky. "I was below it and was able to dive underneath the debris," he recalled, forty-nine years later.

But Bannock was convinced, despite his success, that the best way to deal with the V-1 was to catch it in its lair — on the ground or just after it was being launched. With that in mind, he boldly flew to Abberville on the night of July 3, 1944. He arrived just in time to see German crews sending a whole stream of rockets skyward. Ignoring intense flak, he repeatedly dove on the launching pads, destroying three buzz-bombs in quick succession. It gave him five victories over German flying machines, making him an ace, and, almost overnight, the toast of the RCAF. Three days later, he proved he could score on a regular basis, blasting four of the terrifying machines out of the night skies. Bannock shot down three over the Channel and destroyed a fourth over England. His cannon shells detonated the flying bomb only seconds before it fell into a populated area. Two nights later he shot down two more V-1s. In just three weeks he had destroyed ten rockets, saving dozens — if not hundreds — of lives. Bannock admits today that shooting down the V-1s gave him a lot of satisfaction. "Your job was to shoot things down and they were hard to catch and hard to hit. A couple of times I saw Focke-Wulf 190s that were trying to get us while we concentrated on the V-1s. I saw one and ducked quickly into a cloud."

On July 14, the squadron moved to Hurn, and Bannock marked the occasion by destroying more aircraft. This time, however, both planes were piloted. Flying inside Germany, he chased a night-fighter for seventy miles before shooting it down in flames. Later that night, he launched a surprise thrust on a Luftwaffe airfield, shooting down a fighter as it attempted to land. As skilled a fighter pilot as he was, Bannock was also a sensitive person, who felt there was a difference between destroying a robot-plane and shooting down an airplane, killing people. "There was a lot of emotion to shooting down a German night-fighter," he says. "But all you were trying to do is bring down the machine. A lot of the emotion was getting there and getting back and getting the job done." There was also fear to cope with. "The trouble was you were being shot at from the ground. We took a lot of fire and that gets your adrenalin up." Making the grim task easier was the knowledge that each German night-fighter he destroyed was one less that could prey on the lumbering bombers. The importance of his missions was brought home to him when his brother-in-law, a twenty-year-old Lancaster pilot, was killed in action.

Returning to the rocket bombs, Bannock was here, there and everywhere, seeking out the V-1s with a determination that amazed his squadron mates. He brought down two on July 19, and two more on July 23, then added single kills on July 26 and 27. The squadron moved again, on July 29, to Middle Wallop, but that didn't stop Bannock. He shot down two more buzz-bombs on August 4 and, on August 12 added another to his mounting score.

By then, he noted with pleasure "we had the highest record of all night squadrons in V-1 kills" in either the RAF or the RCAF. And Bannock had destroyed more of them than any other Canadian pilot.

At the same time, his squadron's casualties were very low. "We had a very low mortality rate for the reason that 90 per cent of our pilots were ex-flying instructors like myself. We had averaged 2,000 hours flying each. At a nearby RAF squadron, by way of comparison, they had 400 hours each." He was becoming so experienced, in fact, that the buzz-bomb kills began to look easy. His nineteenth win over a V-1 was a classic. "It didn't take much to disable it," he recalled. "I hit it and it turned back to France." Following, he watched as it fell to earth in German territory and exploded.

The squadron relocated yet again, this time to Hunsdon, where Bannock couldn't find any more buzz-bombs to shoot down. Instead, he strafed several dozen trains and trucks. He didn't keep track of how many he destroyed, but indicated the number was very high. "If we couldn't find any aircraft, we'd go off train hunting or convoy hunting. The Germans moved by night and the lights on their trucks would be dim. But your eyes got used to the dark and you could pick things out. If you hit a train in the boiler, it would let out a hell of a lot of steam." Once he had crossed the flak belt in the Ruhr Valley, Bannock was reluctant to come home with bullets left in his guns. But with twenty-two aerial victories to his credit, Canada's top-scoring night-fighter ace wasn't going to be content with shooting up ground targets. He began stalking German airfields again.

But finding them was difficult, he said, because "the only thing you could pick out at night to give you a pinpoint on where you were was water." He credited his various navigators for much of his success, saying that "it was teamwork, very much so. The navigator ran the radar and tried to pick out targets and that was difficult because, low down, two-thirds of the radar screen" was blocked out by ground images. Flying by "dead reckoning" and guesswork, they patrolled "known German airfields between Hanover and the channel. We'd arrive half an hour ahead of the bombers but, unless we caught their exhaust, you couldn't do much." If he couldn't make out the exhaust flares on night-fighters, the Canadian ace would wait until the bombing raid was over and try to surprise the enemy pilots as they landed. "Quite often, they'd flash their navigation lights on landing to tell their people that a friendly aircraft was coming in. We'd get them on their approach." On the night of August 29, circling above Vaerlose airfield near Copenhagen, he did just that, pouncing on two enemy planes and shooting down a Junkers 88 and an ME-110.

These exploits received the attention they deserved. Four days later it was announced that Bannock had won the Distinguished Flying Cross. He celebrated in typical fashion, launching a single-handed attack on the Luftwaffe airfield at Kitzsingen. "We commenced to prowl around the airfield at about 400 feet and almost immediately observed an aircraft with navigation lights on," Bannock wrote in his combat report. "I did a 180 degree turn to port and followed the aircraft which was climbing steeply over the airfield."[2] Closing in to 125 yards' range, he fired two quick bursts. Both salvos hit home, with Bannock reporting "numerous strikes along the starboard wing and fuselage" before "the starboard engine exploded." The German was lost from view for a moment, and then Bannock's eyes caught sight of a flash on the ground below.

By then, Bannock should have been grounded. He had completed his tour of thirty-five missions and probably needed a rest. But he applied for a second tour and, amazingly, was granted it. "A lot of guys usually got pulled before thirty-five," he concedes today. "And after a tour they took six months' rest, but I was able to talk my way into a second tour without a rest because I'd been an instructor for three years." Returning to the fray as commander of his own squadron, Bannock still found time for operational sorties. Lone-wolf attacks on German airfields provided plenty of opportunity for scoring kills, but they were also extremely dangerous. Bannock was reminded of that on the night of September 27, when he went hunting for Germans at Parrow air base. He arrived just in time to spot six ME-108 trainers taking off. The trainers would be flown by rookie pilots and, better still, might be unarmed. Sensing a rich harvest, the Canadian descended.

Another Victim

The first German fell away in flames without ever knowing what had hit him. Swerving to line up another victim, Bannock fired all four cannons and watched as a second opponent disintegrated. The Messerschmitt, in fact, flew into countless pieces of separating junk and, as luck would have it, one of those flew back at Bannock, striking one of his engines with terrific force.

"I shot down a couple of operational training aircraft but I flew into the debris of one of them," he recounted later. "A piece of it pierced the radiator and very quickly I lost coolant. Then the engine caught fire." If that wasn't enough, an enemy fighter suddenly appeared out of nowhere, guns barking. "I was attacked by an old ME-109 and got a couple of bullet holes in my wing," he stated matter-of-factly. "I pulled away quickly and went down to the treetops. I feathered the burning engine and stayed low." Bannock had never been in a greater jam. His machine was crippled, German fighters were after him and he was hundreds of miles behind enemy lines. Keeping cool, he headed back to England. "That trip was seven hours and fifteen minutes long," he says. "I remember it because we only had endurance for seven hours, but when you only have one engine you use less fuel. And coming home I was slowing the one engine down to use even less. I wasn't too keen on swimming the North Sea." In a masterful display of airmanship, limping along at 190 miles per hour, Bannock made it back, landing with hardly a drop of gasoline left in his one good motor. For this feat he was awarded a second D.F.C.

With the new year, he continued to fly and fight relentlessly. As before, he specialized in single-handed attacks on airfields. And the results continued to be sensational. On January 5, 1945, he caught a Heinkel 111 trying to land at Husum and sent it tumbling into a clump of trees at the edge of the runway, gaining his twenty-eighth win over an enemy flying machine. Bannock was not only bold, but, like all the great Canadian aces, he was very innovative. Once, he caught the Germans by surprise by turning on his own navigation lights as he approached an enemy runway. That convinced the "ack-ack" gunners that he was a returning Luftwaffe pilot, and they held their fire. He shot the place up and made good his escape. Bannock also had a reputation for modesty, never claiming a kill unless he was certain of the victory. All of his kills, he points out, were confirmed by gun cameras in the nose of his Mosquito. Once, when he ambushed a German over Eggebeck airfield, he only claimed a "damaged" opponent. Bannock had seen the German for a second. The enemy pilot had flashed his navigation lights for just a moment before his wheels touched down. But that was enough. The Canadian was all over him, peppering the enemy with lead as he taxied helplessly toward a hangar. It's doubtful if the German plane ever flew again but, because there was no fire or explosion, Bannock did not feel justified in claiming a victory.

When weather hampered his war against the German air force Bannock kept the Nazis on their toes with a series of raids on railroad yards. As soon as the skies cleared, he was back over the air strips. On April 4, he damaged a Focke-Wulf 190 as it landed at Delmenhorst. Later that night, over an airfield, the Germans set a trap for the Mosquito ace. Bannock was about to attack an enemy plane when he sensed danger and stole a glance backward. His finely tuned sixth sense saved him. A second German was bearing down on him. The two adversaries began a bitter dogfight, circling each other for several minutes before Bannock lost sight of the German in the darkness. Determined not to go home empty-handed, he came back later and shot down an enemy plane at treetop level, just before the pilot could touch down. It was his twenty-ninth victory and his tenth over a manned machine. Bannock's last dogfight came April 23, just two weeks before the war in Europe ground to a halt. This time he outfought a black-painted JU-88, pounding it out of the sky with three bursts. The rear-gunner put up a good defence but, as Bannock kept firing, he saw one of the Junkers' four crewmen suddenly bail out. An instant later, the night-fighter burst into flames and crashed. "The JU-88 wasn't as fast or as manoeuvrable as the Mosquito." he says now."If you tangled with them, you could shoot them down. I got a couple of them."

Bannock, who was now a wing commander, was as proud of his men as he was of his own record. "In 406 squadron, when I was CO, we shot down eighty German aircraft and lost only seven of ours, which I think was quite good. And at least two-thirds of our losses were due to ground fire." Although Bannock respected his German opponents, he makes no bones about who had the better pilots during the last year of the war. "We were lucky," he says. "We had quite a lot of experienced pilots. They (the Canadians) were more competent than the German pilots" in 1944 and 1945. "I can only recall one or two aircraft accidents and none fatal. We just didn't suffer a lot of losses (to enemy fire or mishaps)." Besides their vast experience, Bannock's men had high morale, and the atmosphere around the air base was relaxed. "Everybody was pretty light-hearted on operations." Indeed, spirits were kept high by painting cartoon characters on the noses of the Mosquitoes. Bannock joined in the fun, painting the Al Capp character "Hairless Joe" on his machine. Interestingly enough, the German pilots did the same thing, with Mickey Mouse and other Walt Disney characters being favourites.

After the war, Bannock got to meet several German aces and was impressed with them. "I met quite a few of them and they weren't all Nazis at all. They were just doing their jobs and they all thought Goering (Hermann Goering, head of the Luftwaffe) was a horse's ass." One man who particularly impressed him was Lieutenant General Johannes Macky Steinhoff, a 176-kill ace who "had been shot down seven times. Most of his face had been burned off. He was quite a guy." Several German pilots scored more than one hundred victories, far outstripping the leading Allied aces. The main reason for that was that the Luftwaffe made its pilots fly until they were killed — or the war ended. No one could get out of combat, no matter how many missions he had flown. While most Canadian fighter pilots were sent home after flying thirty-five sorties over a period of about six months, a top German ace could fly close to one thousand missions over a six-year span. Many of them were shot down regularly, but they were often able to bail out and return quickly to duty because they fought over their own territory. Famous ace Erich Hartmann, for instance, was shot down sixteen times but was still an active fighter when the war ended. By contrast, even one bail out would have ended Bannock's fighting, because he flew constantly over enemy territory.

On August 17, 1945, word came that Russ Bannock had won the Distinguished Service Order. The citation noted that he had destroyed at least eleven German planes and nineteen buzz-bombs while "causing considerable disruption to the enemy's line of communications. Under this officer's inspiring leadership his squadron has obtained a fine record of success."

Bannock returned home later that year and began a highly successful career as a sales director and test pilot for DeHavilland Canada. Today he lives in Toronto, still flies his own plane and has his own trading and leasing business. His hair is grey and receding a bit, but he is a fit and trim-looking seventy-year-old who vows to keep active as long as he can.

Bannock's record, unfortunately, has been virtually lost to history. His name does not appear on the list of top Canadian aces of World War Two, despite the fact that he was his nation's number two pilot, just behind George Beurling. One of the main reasons he has been overlooked is that writers and historians have not included his victories over the flying bombs when tallying up his score. Because of that, he appears well down the list of aces, if his name is printed at all. Hugh Halliday, in his otherwise brilliant book *The Tumbling Sky,* lists Bannock as the thirtieth top ace with eleven kills. His treatment is even worse at the hands of another writer, who, in publishing a list of the top ten Canadian aces, doesn't list Bannock at all. This outstanding fighter pilot deserves better treatment, even if he is indifferent to his own score today. The fact is that the robot-planes were aircraft. They had to be shot from the sky by pilots possessing good marksmanship and steady nerves. Attacking them could be every bit as dangerous as taking on a manned machine. The RCAF recognized this during the war, decreeing that a buzz-bomb shot down over water was worth one kill while one blasted over land would count as a half-victory. The intention was to provide incentive to pilots to destroy the machines before they got over England.

Almost all of Bannock's V-1s were destroyed over water, but, regardless of where he got them, it seems perfectly obvious to me that each one should be counted as a victory. And because of that, his total should be upgraded from eleven to thirty. It is high time that the remarkable record of this gallant Canadian hero was fully recognized.

NINE

Vernon "Woody" Woodward

Like Russ Bannock, Vernon Crompton "Woody" Woodward was a man overlooked by the propaganda machine in Canada. The Victoria, British Columbia native was the country's third-highest-scoring ace of World War Two, with twenty-five confirmed kills to his credit. He also damaged and probably destroyed at least fourteen other German and Italian machines. At one point, in 1941, he was the nation's leading ace, but his name was known to only a handful of air force officers.

Throughout the war, the Allied governments promoted aces as national heroes, issuing dispatches about their achievements to the press. But you needed more than just a huge tally of kills to become a celebrity. You had to be "good copy," like such dashing figures as Wally McLeod and George Beurling. Woodward, a quiet man of few words, apparently wasn't considered to be "heroic" enough to sell to the public. The fact that he fought in an obscure theatre of war contributed further to his anonymity. While the great battles were being waged in Western Europe, over Malta and in the Pacific, Woodward found himself toiling in Africa and Greece. There were few reporters on the scene and little news made its way to the outside world. Noted British air historian Chaz Bowyer, who interviewed many pilots who knew Woodward personally, described the Canadian as "quiet in manner, almost reserved." Indeed, he "became widely renowned for his cool-headed judgement and invariable calm in all matters including combat, earning for himself the *sobriquet* 'imperturbable Woody' a sincere tribute by his fellow pilots to his 'unflappability,' no matter how fraught the circumstance."[1] In other words, although he was a good man to have on your side in a dogfight, he wouldn't make for much of an interview. The same sort of thing happened in the First World War, when aces like Billy Bishop received a lot of publicity while a hero like Ray Collishaw generated almost none at all.

Woodward was born on December 22, 1916. Victoria was still a small city, close to the wilderness, and young Woody spent much of his spare time hunting. He was very good with a rifle, often bringing down deer at full gallop with a single shot. Strangely enough, however, he was seldom able to hit birds in flight, even with the aid of a shotgun. As he grew into a young man, he lost interest in hunting and, like many others of his extraordinary generation, found himself extremely restless. He'd come though the lean years of the Great Depression and longed for something more out of life. Thirsting for adventure, he turned his attention to the air. Canadians of that era were still captivated by the very concept of flight. Stories of Canada's First World War flying aces, and her 1920s and '30s bush pilots, were the stuff of legend. Woody, like so many others, dreamed of a career in aviation. He was understandably disappointed to learn he couldn't get into the Royal Canadian Air Force because of a lack of formal schooling.

He had a high school diploma, but, at this stage of its history, the RCAF was accepting mostly university graduates for flight training.Woodward couldn't afford to attend a post secondary institution, nor did he want to. He was tired of being cooped up indoors. Undaunted by the RCAF's decision, he sailed for England and signed up with the RAF. The British could sense that war was coming and they were not so picky about who could fly for them. Thus both Woody and Quebec's George Beurling got into action with the British after being turned down by their own air force. The RCAF, to its lasting discredit, rejected two of Canada's top three aces of the war because its bureaucrats decided they didn't have enough paper qualifications to fly and fight. Woodward found that many other young Canadians were taking the same route. In fact, he was one of nineteen Canadians in a class of 124 aspiring fighter pilots. They were all terribly anxious to win their wings, not knowing that, by 1945, more than 100 of them would be dead.

The Victoria native trained on the old Tiger Moth open-cockpit biplane in northern Scotland. He put in about seventy hours on this ancient machine before his flight instructors recommended he become a fighter pilot. Unlike some of Canada's other super aces, who excelled in shooting, not flying, Woodward was a skilled aviator from the start. His superiors, recognizing this, made sure that he was not assigned to a bomber squadron, where his aerobatic abilities would be largely wasted on lumbering behemoths.

Perhaps the planes on which he trained contributed to his flying skills. After the Tiger Moth, he flew the Fury, another highly agile biplane, and then the delightful Audaxes. Such ships were throwbacks to the fighters of the First World War. They were light, fast and responsive to the controls. Old-timers say they were great fun to fly. Pilots couldn't resist looping, barrel-rolling, and twisting and turning all over the sky. By the time Woodward got his wings, he had 120 hours of flying time to his credit, and almost all of them had been logged on biplanes. He was also given the stylish blue RAF uniform, which was denied to cadets until they had successfully soloed. The frugal Royal Air Force was reluctant to spend money on uniforms for men who might not make it as pilots.

After a short stint at gunnery school in the spring of 1939, Woodward was posted, in June, to an operational squadron in Egypt. Officially, 39 Squadron was there to guard the Suez Canal but, in reality, life in North Africa was a lark. Indeed, Woody and his mates lived like kings. He had his own servant, a Sudanese who made his tea, cleaned his barracks and washed his clothes. And during spare hours, the Canadian could visit Cairo, see some of the ancient wonders of Egypt, or lounge about on the beaches and playing fields that surrounded the spacious and comfortable mess. The posting was made even more pleasant because two fellow-Canadians, D.M. Illsley of Nictaux Falls, Nova Scotia, and E.K. Leveille of Winnipeg, Manitoba, were also with the squadron. Illsley was destined to win the Distinguished Flying Cross before being killed in action.

Woodward was flying the open-cockpit Gloster Gladiator, the last biplane fighter ever built. It was out of date the moment it came off the assembly lines in 1937. Germany was already producing the deadly Messerschmitt 109 and Britain was about to churn out Hurricanes and Spitfires. All three were monoplanes with glass-enclosed cockpits, retractable landing gear and modern engines. Each of them could fly fifty miles per hour faster than the Gladiator. About the only thing to be said for the Gladiator was that it had four machine guns — two mounted on the fuselage firing through the propeller and two on the lower wing. In all, the machine could unleash 2,000 rounds — a lot of firepower for a biplane. But it was very clearly a plane of the past, and no one was surprised that when war broke out in September, Woodward and his squadron mates were told to make out their wills. Even more disturbing was the issuing of fireproof identification cards, which the men were told to wear at all times.

As soon as the first shots were fired, the squadron left its cosy base near Cairo and flew off into the desert, in order to be within striking distance of Italian forces in Libya. Woodward had to leave his batman behind. Worse still, he had to learn to cope with intense heat, blinding sandstorms, gales and torrential rains. The weather was as destructive as the enemy, damaging eight planes, including one that was flipped over on its back by high winds. As for the enemy, the Allied pilots were facing formidable odds. There were only seventy-five Gladiators in Egypt and they were up against more than 100 Italian fighter pilots, some of whom had had combat experience in the Spanish Civil War. The Italian air force, unlike Italy's army, had a good reputation. Its pilots had won numerous distance and speed trophies in the 1930s. Many of them, in fact, had a swaggering cockiness about them. They were good and they knew it. They loved fancy aerobatics and, when in combat, they stayed to the bitter end, believing that they were superior to their opponents. The most celebrated among them was France Licchini, who scored five kills in Spain. He quickly shot down two Gladiators, a Blenheim bomber and an RAF flying boat to become the top-scoring Italian pilot in North Africa.

Woodward's first action involved planes on the ground. It came on June 14, 1940 when, with two other RAF flyers, he strafed an Italian airfield, damaging a Ghibli bomber sitting helpless on the tarmac. The plane was so badly shot up that it had to be abandoned when the Italians retreated and, subsequently, it fell into the hands of advancing British Tommies.

Later that day, Woody scored his first aerial victory and had his first brush with death. Along with two other Gladiators, he intercepted a flight of twin-engined Italian Caproni bombers that were attempting to blast a British tank column to pieces. Aiming for the engines, Woodward sent one of them down trailing black smoke. The machine crash-landed smack in the midst of the English tanks and its crew was captured. Return fire from the Italian gunners was accurate, with one machine-gun bullet shattering Woodward's canopy and just missing his head. Undaunted, he turned on an escorting Italian fighter plane, shooting it down out of control. No one saw it crash, however, and he had to be satisfied with a "probable" kill. It was an incredible combat debut. The rookie pilot had knocked out three enemy aircraft, destroying one, damaging a second and probably wrecking a third. His pride in his success was tempered two days later, when an Italian gunner shot down one of his squadron mates. Woody took partial revenge on June 29, when he shot down two Italian Fiat Falcons. It was a scene right out of World War One, with both sides flying biplanes. Woody forced one adversary to land near Fort Capuzzo and sent another crashing into the desert after a long dogfight.

The Italians struck back hard, bombing RAF bases across Egypt. Woody responded to the danger in an imaginative way. Each night at dusk, he flew into the desert, landing on sand flats and sleeping under the wings of his plane. That way, he was never taken by surprise by dawn raiders. The rest of the squadron took similar precautions. Several other pilots also slept in the desert, and crews also set up fake airfields, complete with buildings and planes made of cardboard and wood. The ploy worked, and the Italian air force wasted millions of lire bombing the phoney fields into oblivion. But despite the tricks and precautions, the enemy still managed to catch the Gladiator pilots by surprise from time to time. Once, around noon, Woodward's plane was flipped on its side by a bomb blast just as he was lifting off the runway. Only by a masterful display of flying was he able to recover and zoom for altitude.

The air war was heating up, and the Canadian was right in the thick of it. He shot down three Fiats on July 24, destroying two and probably bagging a third that was seen to fall out of control. However, Woodward lost sight of it, and, because no other Allied pilot saw it crash, the victory could not be confirmed. Next day, he got two more as the Gladiators escorted a group of British Blenheim bombers. One Gladiator pilot was shot down, and Woody himself barely managed to escape when two Italians latched onto his tail and harassed him right to the desert floor. Twisting and turning frantically, he flew so low that his prop wash churned up sand. The Italians, fearful of flying right into the ground, were not willing to perform the hair-raising stunts required to keep him in their sights. Eventually, they abandoned the chase and Woodward lived to fight another day.

For the enemy, it may have been a mistake not to try to finish Woodward off when they had the chance, because only a few days after this encounter, 39 Squadron got the new Hurricane fighter. The arrival of modern warplanes dramatically shifted the balance of air power. This was the eight-gun monoplane that had played such a key role in defeating the Luftwaffe during the Battle of Britain. It had a top speed of 352 miles per hour, although that was reduced to 312 miles per hour when Woody's mechanics installed an air filter to keep out sand. Even with the loss of power, however, it was much superior to the Italian biplanes. But the Italians adapted well, and the air war over the desert was anything but a picnic for the Allies. In a dogfight on October 31, for instance, a dozen planes were shot down. Seven of them bore the white cross of the Italian air force, but the RAF lost five planes. One of the pilots to die in the duel was L.K. Leveille, the Canadian who was a friend of Woodward. Leveille shot down two enemy planes in the melee before being forced to take to the silk. He died a horrible death when his parachute failed to open.

Woodward wasn't in that fight. Indeed, he was having trouble finding enemy planes at this stage of his career. This was not unusual. Often flyers would go through weeks, or even months at a time, without encountering any opposition. Then, just as inexplicably, they would run into hostile aircraft every time they went up, for days on end. He got his first crack at the enemy in his Hurricane on December 9, and he made the most of it, shooting down two Fiats and damaging a third. Ten days later he ambushed a flight of Italian biplanes, shooting two down in flames near Sollum-Bardia. He was up again on Christmas Day, which indicates just how serious the war had become, and his log records one Italian plane as damaged.

That night, Woodward joined in the Christmas activities, eating dinner with officers, pilots and Italian prisoners of war. In keeping with air force tradition, the officers served the enlisted men. Later, after much drinking and eating, another pilot talked Woodward into going along for a joyride aboard a Swordfish two-seater torpedo plane. The flyer, whose name has been lost to history, put the biplane through a number of spine-chilling dives and spins in a deliberate — and successful — attempt to make Woodward vomit.

The Canadian ace closed out the year in dramatic style, shooting down one Italian fighter and damaging another on December 29, and then destroying two Fiats and damaging a pair of tri-motor Spaviero bombers a day later. That gave him a record of five destroyed, one probably destroyed and four damaged in the month of December.

As 1942 dawned, the war in North Africa was finally going in the Allies' favour. An Axis foray into Egypt had ended in humiliation, with 130,000 Italian troops being taken prisoner for the loss of just 600 British and Australian soldiers. But in nearby Greece, things were not going so well. Mussolini had invaded the country in early 1941 and, despite dogged Greek resistance, his legions were beginning to make some headway. Woodward's squadron was packed up and sent in to help the hard-pressed Greek air force stem the tide. Woody now found himself flying out of a ramshackle airfield near Athens that had no control tower, paved runway or permanent buildings. It didn't even have any plumbing, which meant the pilots had to get their drinking water out of a nearby creek. Perhaps it was fortunate that they lived in tents and tar-paper shacks, because the country was subject to earthquakes. One tremor knocked down several buildings at a nearby RAF base, injuring five men. After that, all air force personnel in Greece were ordered to sleep in tents.

Along with a new theatre of war came a new commander, the legendary ace with the unlikely name of Marmaduke Pattle. A South African, Pattle was instantly unpopular with the men, mainly because he ordered everyone to shave and dress properly, but also because they felt one of their own, possibly Woodward, should have been given the post. But Pattle was more than qualified for the task at hand. He'd scored four kills in the 1940 North African campaign and had added twenty more in Greece before Woodward and his squadron mates arrived. The twenty-four confirmed victories made him the top-scoring Allied ace of the war up to that point. Pattle hadn't run up his string of victories by waiting for the enemy to come to him. He was an aggressive commander, and, on March 23, he led ten Hurricanes into a raid on an Axis airfield at Fier. He had given strict instructions to his pilots to strafe the runway and avoid aerial dogfights if at all possible. A force of fifty Fiats tried to intercept them, and both Pattle and Woodward made kills. Although they still had a huge numerical advantage, the Italians quickly withdrew. Perhaps their leader had been killed or maybe they were low on fuel. Possibly the squadron as a whole was not an aggressive one. Some units in every air force were markedly inferior to others — mainly because of poor leadership from the commander. In any case, as soon as they departed, Pattle proceeded to shoot up the airfield, destroying three planes on the ground. Back home, he flew into a rage, blasting his men for not following him into the ground attack.

Possibly they had used up too much ammunition engaging the Fiats. Or maybe they were busy chasing the Italians off. But for whatever reason, they hadn't followed orders and Pattle was almost beside himself with anger. He wasn't particularly impressed with the squadron and he let his men know it in no uncertain terms, thus further alienating himself from them.

What he thought of Woodward isn't known, although he must have been impressed by the Canadian's exploit of April 6, 1942. Woody's guns were being loaded that morning when a flight of four Italian Cant bombers suddenly appeared directly overhead. He took off after them despite the fact that only half of his weapons were operational. Wading into the enemy formation by himself, Woodward aimed for the fuel tanks, which were located on the wings of the big planes. His first burst sent one down on fire. Seconds later a second was an inferno and, moments after that, a third was diving toward the ocean wrapped in flames. Attacking each one out of the sun, he shot holes in the gas tanks and then dove underneath to finish them off from below. He struck so swiftly that the crew of one bomber was still bailing out of the doomed ship when a second Cant caught fire. Return fire from the Italian gunners was heavy, and Woodward's plane was damaged. Still, he was in complete command of the situation. Later, he was quoted as saying that he would have flamed all four had his guns been fully loaded. Almost certainly he was right.

But despite individual heroics, the situation in Greece was looking increasingly hopeless. The Luftwaffe had arrived to help the Italians, giving the Axis 1,300 planes against eighty Allied fighters. And the Germans wasted no time in making their presence felt, shooting down six British ships on April 13. Woody, however, was not intimidated, blowing a green-and-brown Messerschmitt 109 out of the sky. It was his first victory over a German flyer. His victim, who managed to bail out, was one of three Luftwaffe pilots who attacked the Canadian. Despite the odds, Woodward was never in serious trouble, demonstrating vividly just how skilled he had become. His next success, on April 14, was again at the expense of the Germans. Along with a British pilot, he dove to cut off twenty gull-winged Stuka dive-bombers, guarded by a flight of ME-109s. The Nazi fighter pilots appeared to be daydreaming, however, and made no attempt to stop the Hurricanes. Closing in unmolested, Woodward shot one of the slow Stukas down in flames and sent another spinning uncontrollably into the ground. In two clashes with the vaunted Luftwaffe, he had registered three kills.

The Germans, however, were raiding RAF fighter bases around the clock, scoring stunning victories. Once, they blew up a pair of Hurricanes as they attempted to lift off, killing both pilots. Woodward, who said later that his squadron lost more planes on the ground than in dogfights during this period, seemed to lead a charmed life. Whenever the Messerchmitts, Junkers and Stukas came hurtling down on top of him, he always seemed to be standing near a slit trench. When he wasn't hiding in a dugout he was in the air. On April 19, along with Pattle and another Hurricane pilot, he shot down a German Henschel bomber. When a formation of ME-109s attacked them head-on, bent on revenge, they ran straight into the withering fire of two of the RAF's top aces. Pattle killed two Germans and Woodward slew a third. The Germans, however, were firing back, and the other Allied pilot, Francis Holman, crashed into a swamp. The next day, he was found dead in his cockpit. Tragedy struck the squadron again on April 20, this time with a staggering blow felt throughout the Allied nations. More than one hundred German planes attacked Athens that day, opposed only by a handful of Hurricanes. Pattle, as usual, was in top form, shooting down three Germans. He was about to nail a fourth when a German ME-110 two-seater got behind him and sent his machine plunging into Eleusis Bay. The South African, who had forty victories behind his name, was never seen again. No pilot in the British Empire equalled his total throughout the rest of the war.

Despite the loss of the RAF ace-of-aces and four other Hurricanes, the British did manage to shoot down eight Germans that
day, and one of the kills belonged to Woodward. The Canadian
destroyed an ME-110 and damaged three others. By the end of
the day, however, it was obvious that the situation in Greece was
out of control. The squadron was ordered to fly to Crete to defend
the largest of the Greek islands. The Allies had lost on the main-
land and were finally admitting defeat. Woodward was now involved in a desperate last stand against the Luftwaffe. With Pattle
dead, he was the leading Allied ace in the theatre and the others
were looking to him for leadership. He would provide it, although,
in a completely unforeseen turn of events, his next combat was
on the ground.

Scrambling for Cover

Woody awoke on May 20 to a shattering artillery barrage. Shells
rained down on the airfield for more than an hour, forcing the
pilots to scramble for cover. When the deafening salvos finally
ceased, they looked up to see thousands of Germans paratroopers
descending out of the sky. Coming in behind them were enemy
gliders, packed to the brim with storm troops. The Germans had
had enough of bombing. They were going to take RAF airfields
with infantry. Woodward took in a colourful — almost beautiful
— scene as the assault unfolded. The paratroopers floated down
in red, white and green chutes, straight out of an azure-blue sky.
A Luftwaffe transport plane, flown by a man of exceptional
audacity, set down right on the field. A side door popped open
and, as Woodward looked on in astonishment, a machine-gun
crew raced down a ramp aboard a motorcycle equipped with a
sidecar!

The RAF pilots may have been momentarily mesmerized by
the sight but they soon regained their composure and took up rifles
and machine guns. At first, the Germans were sitting ducks.
Woodward estimated later that seventy per cent of them were
picked off as they dangled helplessly on their parachutes. But the
ones who reached the ground alive immediately raised hell. German paratroopers were among the toughest and bravest soldiers
in the world, and the survivors were in an ugly mood when they
reached earth."So many landed alive in the first 10 minutes that

our half mile to the New Zealand positions is two hours crawling on our bellies, dashing across a space to the next cover, never knowing from which direction the next Tommy gun will bark,"[2] Woodward wrote later.

Over the next several days, the German and Allies attacked and counter-attacked, and the airfield changed hands several times. In the end, however, overwhelming numbers prevailed and the RAF contingent was forced into the hills. Woody Woodward, at that time Canada's leading air ace with twenty-three kills to his credit, found himself in the mountains of Crete, armed with a German bren-gun, fighting as a guerilla soldier. And the combat was barbarous. The Germans rounded up British prisoners of war and used them as shields for their attacks up the hillsides. Woodward and his mates had to hold their fire until the enemy was almost on top of them so as not to hit any of their own men. The danger was further increased because both the German paratroopers and the RAF men wore blue uniforms. Not surprisingly, several men on both sides were killed by "friendly" fire.

On a number of occasions native New Zealand Maori soldiers attacked the Germans. The Maoris were fierce fighters, but the German soldiers stood their ground and eventually won the day. Woodward came face-to-face with a Nazi paratrooper before he, like the rest of the Allied fighting men, was forced to retreat. He was eating lunch during a lull in the battle when a German popped his head up over a hedge only yards away. The two men looked at one another in astonishment for a long moment. Then, without a word, the German turned on his heels and ran off. Woodward burst into uncontrolled laughter and it was several minutes before he recovered enough to give chase. By that time the man was long gone, which may have been just as well for both of them. There was nothing funny, however, about Woody's escape from Crete. Leading 100 men on an eighteen-mile march through enemy lines in the dead of night, he was twice intercepted by the Germans. Both times he and his men escaped by making as much noise as possible, convincing the enemy that they were facing a large force. During daylight hours, the tiny band of men hid in caves. Eventually, they reached a cliff and climbed down 500 feet to the beaches before loading onto an Australian destroyer. Even then, their ordeal wasn't over. Stuka dive-bombers came screaming down on them in an hour-long attack. Several bombs just missed the ship. More by luck than skill, the Aussie crew was able to evade the hail of bombs and make its way to safety.

Woodward arrived in Egypt to learn he had won the Distinguished Flying Cross. He was pleased with the news but far happier to be able to resume combat in the air. His first time back in a plane, on June 17, he shot down an Italian fighter. A few weeks later, he closed out his combat career, chasing a German Junkers 88 bomber down to the deck before sending it slamming into the desert. Two of the four crewmen crawled out of the burning wreck, but both died of wounds in an Allied hospital.

Woody, who now had at least twenty-five confirmed victories to go with several probables and a handful of damaged planes, received a second DFC and a posting to a Rhodesian training school. There he served as a flight instructor, a task he sometimes found more dangerous than combat itself. Rookie pilots appeared to be attempting to ram him all the time. One actually succeeded, chewing off part of Woody's tail with his propeller. Somehow, the ace managed to put his crippled plane down safely. His continual requests for a transfer back into combat were finally heeded and he was sent back to North Africa. Although he was now a squadron leader, there was little to do, because the Axis was in full retreat. Woody's men occupied themselves flying as escorts for convoy ships. The skies were empty of Italian and German planes.

When the war ended, Woodward found he was virtually unknown outside his hometown. He was the third-highest-scoring Canadian ace, behind only George Beurling and Russ Bannock, but, like Bannock, he was a man few of his fellow-countrymen had ever heard of. Woody was determined to remain in the military, but, like so many Canadians, he felt there was more of a future in the RAF than the RCAF, mainly because Canada traditionally maintains a small peacetime armed forces. He retired in 1963, with more than 3,300 hours in his logbook. Moving to Australia, he operated a charter airline business for many years before coming back to Canada to retire in Victoria.

Vernon Woodward was one of the great unsung heroes of World War Two. His twenty-five confirmed kills not only placed him third on the Canadian ace list, but also ranked him as the twelfth-best fighter pilot in the whole British Commonwealth. He fought in the theatres of war that got the least amount of attention and, consequently, his story has been all but lost. But Woodward's heroic struggle against vastly superior enemy formations over North Africa and Greece was as inspiring as anything accomplished by the Allied flyers who engaged the Axis forces on the Western Front or over Malta. By single-handedly wiping out the equivalent of two German and Italian squadrons, he played a crucial role in turning the tide in a little-known but vital theatre of war.

TEN

Buck McNair

Buck McNair was perhaps the most courageous fighter pilot Canada produced in World War Two. His wing commander, famed British ace Johnnie Johnson, described him simply as "tough." Practically blinded in a dogfight, he returned to action with limited vision and continued to mow down opponents. A hard-nosed, no-nonsense individual who looked remarkably like James Dean, he could be as demanding of his own men as he was with the enemy. Once, disgusted by a pilot's timid performance, he got on the radio and threatened to shoot the man down! He believed in teamwork and, when given the opportunity to take legendary ace "Screwball" Beurling into his ranks, rejected it. Beurling was a loner, and McNair wanted nothing to do with him. But if he could be hard on his men, he was an absolute terror to the Germans. McNair was a determined foe. He once survived several hours in the frigid water of the English Channel and then rushed right back into combat. Shot down a second time, he overcame severe burns and blurred vision and carried on. By the time he was finished, he was one of the top-scoring Canadian pilots of the war.

Robert Wendell McNair was born on May 15, 1919, in Springfield, Nova Scotia, only a few miles from the Bay of Fundy. His childhood was spent in the Annapolis Valley and, later, in North Battleford, Saskatchewan, where his family moved in search of work during the Great Depression. Unlike many of the great aces, he was a good student, and completed high school in 1937. McNair was working for the provincial ministry of natural resources when the war started. He quit at once and joined the Royal Canadian Air Force. After attending training schools in Toronto, Windsor and Kingston, he was posted to 411 Squadron in June 1941. Unlike many pilots of the First World War, who had only a few weeks of preparation before being sent into combat, McNair was in uniform for two years before he saw his first enemy plane. His experience demontrates how much better training Second World War pilots received than those in the 1914-18 conflict. Although the Allies were on the defensive, and needed every man they could get, the leaders of the RCAF weren't about to send helpless recruits to be slaughtered, as had happened in the RFC a generation before.

McNair was introduced to the air war on September 27, 1941, when he was assigned to escort eleven English Blenheim bombers on a strike against the railway yards at Amiens and a power plant near Mazingarble. A flight of Messerschmitts tried to intercept the convoy and a ballet of death was on. The Nova Scotian handled his Spitfire well in his first dogfight, sliding in behind an ME-109 and scoring hits on it with a two-second burst. He saw pieces of metal fly from the wings of his opponent before the German flipped over on his back and dove out of harm's way. The Canadian peeled over on one wing, straining to keep the German in his sights but, before he could line the black-crossed machine up for another squirt, a second ME-109 came darting out of a cloud with guns blazing. McNair took wild evasive action himself and managed to shake off the German. Back in England, he was told that other pilots had seen his tracers hacking up the Messerschmitt, and he was credited with a "damaged." It wasn't the most spectacular start in history, but it was far more than most rookies accomplished.

But McNair was anything but satisfied, writing later "I should have shot it down."[1] He took his frustrations out on the next German he encountered. Flying over Boulogne on October 13, he spotted seven ME-109s circling a man in a rubber raft offshore. Despite the odds, the Spitfire pilot kicked his rudder and dove straight into the enemy group. McNairs's audacity paid off. He caught the Germans napping and sent an ME-109 down on fire with two short bursts. The other six turned on him and several more Germans dropped out of the sun overhead. One of them placed a stream of bullets into McNair's engine, causing his fighter to wobble uncontrollably across the sky. Another enemy fighter took advantage of his plight, coming up behind the crippled plane and sending a fusillade of fire into its tail and wings. Smoke filled the cockpit, stinging McNair's eyes. The German was certain he'd scored a kill and turned his attention to another plane. It was a fatal mistake. Despite the flames ripping through his cockpit, McNair banked over on one wing and shot down the ME-109 with his one good gun. The Spitfire was now wrapped in flames and rapidly losing altitude. With less than 500 feet to spare, he bailed out. The parachute jammed in its harness, opening only seconds before he hit the icy waters of the channel. Luckily, he was rescued within fifteen minutes by a seaplane that had been called in to pluck McNair's first victim out of the drink.

   Although he had been shot down, McNair's two victories impressed the RCAF brass. The Allies were looking for good fighter pilots to send to the besieged island of Malta. Getting there wasn't easy, because the Germans and Italians commanded the Mediterranean Sea. Only a handful of flyers could come in at a time, taking off from the deck of the aircraft carrier *Eagle*. It was extremely hazardous, mainly because the Spitfire was never designed to be a carrier fighter, but also because of incredible navigational obstacles. Malta was a tiny dot of an island, difficult to spot from the air. If the Allied pilots weren't exact in their calculations, they could easily miss it. And with barely enough fuel to make the 700-mile trip, there was precious little margin for error. In fact, thirty-seven British Hurricanes had gone down in a single day when they all lost their way, ran out of fuel, and crashed into the sea. None of the pilots was ever heard from again. The Canadian took off from the wave-tossed deck of the Eagle on March 2, 1942, leading seventeen Spitfires into the air. His plane rolled across the flight deck at a tortoise pace, virtually falling off the edge of the ship, and plunged toward the green waters. Resisting the temptation to immediately pull up, he gathered more speed before raising his nose, which was just yards from the surface when he finally zoomed for altitude.

   Malta was a hot theatre of war and it didn't take McNair long to find the action that he craved. On March 18 he damaged a Messerschmitt and the next day he sent one of the square-winged German fighters down in flames for his third confirmed kill. The Axis air forces were stepping up their assaults on Malta just as McNair arrived. They were determined to invade the island and, to do that they had to enforce a strict blockade. That meant sinking ships in order to prevent food, fuel, ammunition and reinforcements, from getting through to the garrison. So when a group of British ships approached Malta on March 26, more than one hundred enemy planes rose to attack them. McNair and every other Allied pilot on the island scrambled to provide air cover, and the biggest dogfight Malta had yet seen was underway. The Canadian somehow got through a cloud of enemy fighters, and, ripping into a formation of Junkers 88 bombers, shot one down in flames and sent two more back to Sicily seriously damaged. When he landed, there wasn't a round left in any of his eight guns.

From then on, McNair was in almost constant combat, and his score climbed steadily. On April 20, he soared to 17,000 feet, with five other Spitfires in tow, before dropping out of the sun onto a group of JU-88s and ME-109s. One burst sent a German fighter slamming headlong into the sea. Then, turning his attention on the bombers, he damaged a Junkers with a volley from long range. The Nova Scotian was now officially an ace, with five destroyed aircraft behind his name — and he was out for more blood. He found rare easy pickings four days later, as he headed off a flight of Stuka dive-bombers. These were slow, plodding machines, and McNair caught one of them cold, shooting part of its tail off. But a formation of ME-109s roared to the rescue, and he was forced to break off before he could destroy the gull-winged ship. McNair, although outnumbered, damaged two of the Messerschmitts and drove the rest off. Spotting a bomber, he chased it halfway back to Sicily, scoring several hits. But the German rear-gunner knew his stuff and kept McNair at bay until, low on gasoline, he was forced to break off and return to base. The Canadian finished the day with four "damaged" Germans to his credit. Although none of them would be counted in his kill total, it is likely that some of them were so badly shot up that they had to be written off when they got home.

May came, and the Axis pilots stepped up their aerial bombardment. They had dropped 7,000 tons of explosives on Malta in April and intended to surpass that performance in the coming weeks. Dogfights were frequent and bloody, and the Canadian ace shot down two Messerschmitts, although only one was officially accepted as destroyed. The other went into the books as a probable kill, although several pilots had seen it on fire in the air and watched its pilot preparing to bail out. Because the man hadn't been seen to jump and, in the heat of battle, no one had seen the crash, confirmation was not granted. Nevertheless, McNair now had six confirmed kills to his credit, and if he was upset with the stringent scoring system, he was pleased when he received word that he had won his first medal — the Distinguished Flying Cross. The citation read: "This officer is a skilful and courageous pilot. He invariably presses home his attack with the greatest determination irrespective of odds. He has destroyed at least five and damaged seven enemy aircraft (the citation was written before his sixth kill). Four of these he damaged in one combat."[2] The decoration was followed by a promotion to the rank of flying officer and, not long after that, to flight lieutenant. McNair shot down a Messerschmitt on June 10 to gain his last aerial victory on Malta. His final combat over the island followed a few days later, when he strafed an Italian warship, killing several sailors on deck.

A Notorious Loner

Later that month, a young Canadian pilot with the reputation of a rebel showed up on Malta. "Screwball" Beurling reported to McNair's squadron fresh from combat over northern France. McNair was not impressed with Beurling, whom he considered to be a dangerous troublemaker. He believed explicitly in team fighting and Beurling was a notorious loner. When asked by higher authority for his opinion, McNair recommended that Beurling be sent packing. Fortunately, his suggestion was rejected. The troublesome newcomer went on to become the top scoring ace over Malta.

McNair flew only one sortie with the newcomer before he himself was posted out. The whole squadron was taken temporarily off operations so that mechanics could catch up on long overdue maintenance work on the worn out Spitfires. While they were grounded, McNair was sent back to England on a two-week leave. He was then posted back to his original squadron, 411, which was operating over France. McNair had an uncanny ability to arrive at a new theatre of war just as something big was in the works. He showed up just in time to take part in the Canadian raid on the French seaport of Dieppe. The attack was a disaster for Canada. German defenders knew the Canadians were coming and they smashed the invasion on the beaches of the coastal town. When it was over, nearly 1,000 Canadian soldiers had been killed, wounded or captured. German losses were less than one hundred. In the air, too, things went badly for the Allies. McNair's squadron alone lost three pilots. But for McNair personally, Dieppe was a success. Flying over the beaches, providing air cover, he managed to intercept and shoot down a Focke-Wulf 190 before it could strafe Canadian soldiers pouring ashore. However, because no one else saw it crash, he received credit only for a probable kill. Later, over the same area, he damaged another FW-190.

McNair, who by then was suffering from battle fatigue, was given leave and returned to Canada. Unlike Beurling and Wally McLeod, his arrival went completely unnoticed in the national press. Perhaps it was just as well, because he was badly in need of some peace and quiet. He stayed in Canada for six months, selling war bonds much of the time, before being ordered to take command of an air training school on the Prairies. Furious, he demanded to be sent back into combat and, in January, 1943, his wish was granted. McNair was given command of 416 Squadron, RCAF, replacing Foss Boulton, the ace from Coleman, Alberta who had been shot down over enemy territory. He had no sooner settled in, however, when he was transferred to 421 Squadron, whose commander had just been shot down. Such was the life to which McNair was clamouring to return.

Despite his long absence from the cockpit, McNair proved his skills hadn't diminished, shooting down an FW-190 in his first dogfight in nearly a year. On June 20, 1943, he was leading a whole wing of Spitfires in escort of a formation of American heavy bombers on their way to Germany when the Luftwaffe attacked. The Canadian met the enemy charge head-on, firing at two FW-190s without result. Spinning around, he got onto the tail of one of them, sending a burst of cannon shells right into the pilot's seat. Moments later, the machine fell away on fire, shedding pieces of wreckage and undercarriage as it went. The stricken fighter crashed into a hillside, and if the pilot hadn't been killed outright by McNair's shells, he surely died in the resulting crash and explosion. Another German was shot down by one of McNair's men, but the Germans clearly won the battle, blasting five Spitfires out of the sky.

Two weeks later, on July 6, McNair destroyed an ME-109. He would have added yet another kill to his score on July 9, but his windshield frosted over in a high-altitude scrap, making it impossible for him to finish off an opponent he had damaged. The next day, flying much lower, he knocked a Messerschmitt out of the air after laying a careful ambush. McNair used half his squadron as the bait, having them fly low while he waited in the sun overhead with the rest of his men. It was a trick as old as aerial combat, but the Germans fell for it. When a group of ME-109s walked into the trap, McNair and his wingmen came catapulting down on top of them. McNair, who was leading the assault, drew first blood, and the Canadians coming behind him also scored, sending two more Germans down in flames.

McNair had done exceptionally well since returning to action, but he couldn't escape unscathed forever. A few days later his luck changed, when his engine mysteriously died over enemy lines. Whether it had been hit by anti-aircraft fire, or simply suffered a malfunction, he did not know. All he knew for certain was that it was on fire. He tried to coax the wounded bird back to England but, over the Channel, it gave up the ghost, falling hopelessly out of control. His decision to try to make it home was very nearly fatal. He had trouble getting out of the cockpit because of the intense heat. Flames burned his hands and face, and it was only with superhuman effort that he managed to break free. Once out, he was unable to get his fire-damaged parachute to properly open. Indeed, it was only just partly activated yards above the water. McNair was in the drink, and in serious trouble. He was only ten miles from enemy-occupied France and he was too weak from his burns and his jarring splashdown into the channel to get into his raft. Fortunately, one of his wingmen circled overhead until a rescue seaplane showed up and made a rough landing in choppy seas. Had the wingman gone home — and his fuel was dangerously low — it is highly doubtful that McNair would ever have been seen again. As it was, he was chilled to the bone from a long wait in the water. The ace was hospitalized for several weeks but, somehow, he was able to hide the fact that his eyes had been damaged in the fire. He even talked wing commander Johnny Johnson into keeping his post as squadron commander open until he could return to duty. While he was recovering he received some good news in the form of a Distinguished Flying Cross. The citation said: "This officer is a skilful and determined fighter whose record, achievement, and personal example are worthy of high praise."[3]

McNair returned to action despite badly blurred vision and shot down an ME-109 on the last day of August. He added an FW-190

a week later. Unable to see long distances, he closed in to point-
blank range before triggering his guns. His men, unaware of his
eye troubles, mistook McNair's tactics and word spread throughout the RCAF that he had become overly aggressive. Buck
McNair and his men were indeed on a streak. The squadron, which
had been dubbed the "Red Indians" by British pilots, accounted
for several Germans without loss over the coming weeks. McNair
himself next scored on October 3, pouncing on a Focke-Wulf four
miles above Antwerp. The enemy went down in flames, but, at
the moment of victory, Buck's engine suddenly caught fire and
he spun down out of control. The whole squadron broke off
combat and followed him anxiously down. Somehow, McNair
was able to pull out, extinguish the fire and glide thirty miles
homeward. It was the longest glide on record but it wasn't enough
to get him back to England. Luck, however, was on his side. The
damaged engine sputtered back to life on its own and he flew the
rest of the way back to base without incident.

McNair was then named a wing commander and placed in
charge of 126 Airfield. Only twenty-four years old, he was in
command of more than seventy Spitfire pilots. On October 7, he
received another DFC. The citation said that his "outstanding
ability has proven an inspiration to the squadron he commands.
He completed a large number of sorties and has destroyed fifteen
and damaged many other enemy aircraft. His keenness has been
outstanding."[4] McNair lived up to the high words of praise, continuing to fly throughout the winter of 1944-45, despite the fact
that his eyesight was getting weaker. He found little opportunity
to score, however, adding only one more German to his tally. The
Luftwaffe was all but finished, and it was becoming rare to encounter any black-crossed machines during daylight hours. Perhaps it was just as well, because his vision became so impaired
that he could no longer hide it from those around him. In truth, he
was endangering his own life — and the lives of his men — by
his dogged determination. Eventually, the authorities caught on to
him and he was officially grounded. He remained in the air force,
but was confined to a desk.

If Buck was hurt by the turn of events, his spirits must have
been picked up when he won the Distinguished Service Order, the
Commonwealth's second-highest decoration. The citation noted:
"Since being awarded a second bar to the Distinguished Flying

Cross Wing Commander McNair has completed many further operational sorties and destroyed another enemy aircraft, bringing his total victories to at least sixteen enemy aircraft destroyed and many others damaged. As officer commanding his Wing he has been responsible for supervising intensive training in tactics. The results achieved have been most satisfactory. The Wing, under his leadership, destroyed at least thirteen enemy aircraft. Throughout, Wing Commander McNair has set a magnificent example by his fine fighting spirit, courage and devotion to duty both in the air and on the ground. He has inspired his pilots with confidence and enthusiasm."[5] The French government also recognized his courage, bestowing the Legion of Honour and the Croix de Guerre on the Canadian, giving him a total of six medals. This made him one of the most-decorated servicemen in Canada's million-member armed forces. And with sixteen confirmed kills, he was one of the country's leading acess.

Amazingly, McNair had one more brush with aerial death — and won another bravery award — eight years after the end of the war. He was on board a passenger plane flying into Vancouver when the machine crashed on landing, severely injuring his back. Despite excruciating pain, and the fact that he was soaked in jet fuel, Buck ignored the threat of fire and led the evacuation of people on board. His cool head helped everyone get out alive. And like a true hero, he didn't leave the wreck until the last person had escaped. For his gallantry, McNair was granted the Queen's Commendation for Brave Conduct. He stayed in the RCAF, and was made a group captain, commanding a NATO squadron in West Germany until 1961. By 1965, however, McNair had contracted leukemia and his duties were restricted. Nevertheless, he battled the disease with the same determination with which he had tackled the Luftwaffe, remaining on active duty until the end. When it came, in 1971, at age 52, the plucky ace was in London, still working for the air force. Perhaps fittingly, he is buried in an English cemetery alongside Canadian flyers killed in action a generation before.

McNair is included in this book not so much for his score — although sixteen victories was impressive, to be sure. However, there were other Canadian pilots in both world wars who surpassed his total but have not been included. McNair is outstanding because he displayed more raw courage than any of them. He demonstrated it time and again. Shot down over the English Channel, he went right back into action. Sent down in flames and half-blinded in a subsequent dogfight, he still refused to give up combat flying. Even as a civilian, he demonstrated his great courage and coolness in a crisis. He could be unforgiving of those who didn't give their best, but he never asked his men to do anything that he himself wouldn't be willing to try. And no fighting man could ever ask more from a leader.

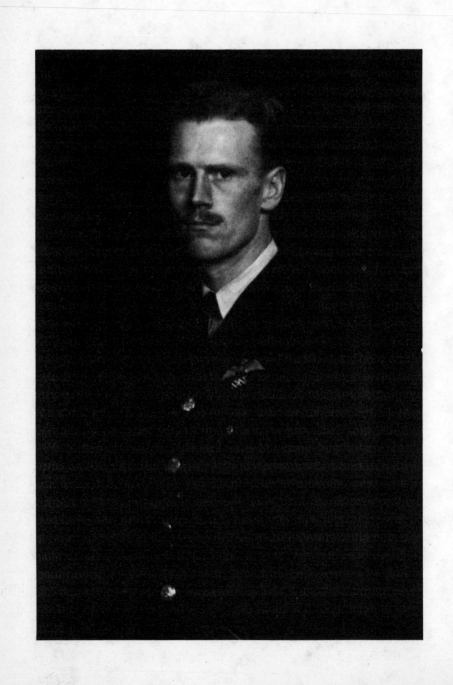

ELEVEN

Wally McLeod

Wally McLeod, the second most famous Canadian fighter pilot of the Second World War, was also Canada's least personable ace, remembered by his contemporaries as a "cold-blooded killer"[1] out to make a name for himself. To the Regina, Saskatchewan native, the war was one big sporting event, staged for his personal gratification. He was a fierce competitor, and the skies over Malta and western Europe were his playing fields. If he ever felt remorse over the taking of human life, he never revealed it to anyone. He cared nothing for grand strategy either, and never expressed any interest in who was winning the war. Instead, obsessed with getting to the top, he concentrated on the ace list. He gave no more thought to downing German and Italian pilots than a hockey player would give to scoring another goal; indeed, when he shot down a man, he would whoop for joy like an athlete celebrating a victory.

At the top of his game, with a chest full of medals, the "Eagle of Malta" — as he was known in the press — returned to Canada to train other flyers. Despite his pre-war training as a teacher, however, he was a despondent and ineffective instructor whose paramount objective was to return to the front. He was, after all, still only second on the ace list, behind George Beurling. And when he couldn't get his way, he took to heavy drinking. Finally, he was able to wrangle his way back into combat, where he continued to rack up kills and take foolish risks in a desperate bid to catch Beurling. It was a dangerous game he was playing, but he paid no heed to those who urged him to be more careful. McLeod vowed not to quit until he was number one — or dead.

Henry Wallace McLeod was born in Regina, Saskatchewan, a week before Christmas, 1915. His father, James, was a native of Brooklyn, Nova Scotia, and a graduate of Acadia University in Wolfville. At a time when few Canadians had completed high school, the elder McLeod was a graduate of both university and law school. But he had to go out west to find work, eventually settling in Regina. Young Wally didn't have a happy childhood. His mother died of Spanish influenza in 1918, when he was only three years old, and her loss had a profound impact on him. Indeed, there are those who attribute his bitterness to the death of his mother. Unlike his father, Wally proved to be a poor student. He enjoyed sports and usually ignored his studies in favour of the playing field or the hockey rink. But, he was by no means a slow learner, always managing a passing grade by last-minute cramming before exams.

He completed high school but didn't have the marks, the money or the inclination to go to university. Instead, in a bizarre move, the poor student decided to become a teacher. He trained at the Regina Normal School, but the Great Depression was in full swing and Saskatchewan was especially hard-hit. He was unable to find a job, and became even more cynical about life. Wally decided that if no one would hire him, he would create his own work. His scheme was imaginative. He travelled all over the Prairies, showing Hollywood films in school gyms, church basements and town halls. Before long, he was something of a legend from Alberta to Manitoba. Whole communities looked forward to his visits. People needed an escape from the hard times, and McLeod was providing it. It wasn't much of a career, however, and lack of success weighed heavily on the young man. When war broke out in 1939, it was almost a relief to Wally. He sold his projector and enlisted in the RCAF. A day after Hitler's armies rolled into Poland, Wally McLeod became an aircraftsman second class.

He trained in Brandon, Manitoba, Saskatoon, Saskatchewan, and at elementary flight school in Prince Albert, Saskatchewan. Promoted to leading aircraftsman, he was sent to Camp Borden, Ontario, in January 1940. His training indicates just how thorough the RCAF was in those days. After attending five different schools in three provinces, McLeod still wasn't finished with instruction. When he arrived in England later that year, he was posted to a combat-training outfit. By the time he was posted to an operational squadron, McLeod was a highly trained professional. He led his class in gunnery drills, and also did well in aerial dogfighting and formation-flying.

His first posting was to the RCAF's 132 Squadron in southern England. He flew two combat missions over France during the summer of 1941, and came under fire from German anti-aircraft gunners, but saw no sign of the Luftwaffe. Later, he was transferred to 485 Squadron but his experiences over hostile territory remained relatively uneventful. Shipped out to 602 "Glasgow" Squadron, he found more action. During his first dogfight, McLeod shot down a Messerschmitt 109. Details of the battle have been lost and most histories of the RCAF make no mention of it. But noted historian E.C. Baker confirms the victory in his book, *Fighter Aces of the RAF*. McLeod's history with his next outfit, 411 squadron, is almost as little known. Records show that he took part in six duels, damaging two ME-109s and a Focke-Wulf 190. Again, however, no details of the engagements have survived.

On April 15, 1942, Wally was promoted to the rank of flying officer and assigned to the United States navy aircraft carrier *Wasp* on its way to the island of Malta. Malta was called a "fighter pilot's paradise" and "hell on earth."[2] Both descriptions were correct. It was the only piece of real estate in the entire Mediterranean still in Allied hands. From its remote flying fields, pilots could badger Axis shipping on its way to North Africa to reinforce General Erwin Rommel's Afrika Korps. The garrison was a thorn in the side of the Germans and Italians and they were determined to take it out. But before they could invade, they had to win control of the skies. And to do that they launched an around-the-clock blitz that made the Battle of Britain seem almost tame by comparison. For a man hoping to live through the war, a posting to Malta was pure hell. But for someone out to make a reputation for himself, it was a golden opportunity.

McLeod, however, almost never made it to Malta. Taking off from the deck of the Wasp, he radioed the island for directions. Moments later, a German speaking perfect English gave him co-ordinates that, had he followed them, would have taken him straight to Italy, where he would have spent the rest of the war in a prisoner of war camp. The Canadian recognized the deception and continued on his course, depending on his compass to guide him. This was a trick used by both sides — sometimes with lethal results. On one occasion, a Malta radio operator, speaking fluent German, ordered an ME-109 pilot to attack a formation of Luftwaffe planes. The German shot down two of his own countrymen.

McLeod got his first taste of action over the besieged island on June 4. It was very nearly his last. Attacking an Italian tri-motor Cant bomber, he scored several hits, seriously damaging his opponent. One of its three engines was on fire and a second was sputtering badly. The lumbering machine slowed to a crawl and was unable to take evasive action. Finishing if off should have been easy, but McLeod made a fundamental error. He became so absorbed in the task at hand that he didn't keep a close watch behind. An Italian Macchi fighter pilot zoomed onto his tail and put a dozen holes into his Spitfire. The Macchi was a fast and handy machine but, fortunately for McLeod, it was also poorly armed, being equipped with only two low-calibre machine guns. Had it carried cannons, McLeod's career might have ended then and there. As it was, he was barely able to coax his damaged fighter back to base. As he flew home McLeod got a glimpse of the fate he had so narrowly escaped. He watched as another Canadian shot down a Macchi. The pilot was thrown free of his exploding machine, but his parachute was on fire and the Italian plunged three miles to his death.

The bombardment was now in full swing, and there were more than enough targets for a pilot out to make a name for himself. On one mission, in fact, McLeod and his squadron encountered 100 enemy aircraft. His second dogfight over the island was another close call. McLeod was attacking a German Junkers 88 bomber when two Italian Macchi fighters approached him from above and behind. They had the Canadian in the classic pincer squeeze, but he kept his cool and got out of the jam like a seasoned veteran. Slowing down to almost stalling speed, he watched as the two enemy pilots overshot his Spitfire and dashed out in front of his guns. The tables were turned, and he flung himself at the nearest Macchi like an uncoiling cobra. McLeod's aim was off, but one of the enemy, in his hurry to escape, dove right into the sea. "He went into the drink from sheer fright,"[3] McLeod wrote later. The other Macchi pilot kept his head and managed to escape in his damaged ship.

Wally's aim was improving but he was hardly the nemesis of the Italian air force at this time. That dubious honour belonged to one of its own cooks, who put a whole squadron out of action!

Sergeant Luigi Valcano turned the trick quite by accident. He bought some fish in a Sicilian open-air market and planned a gourmet meal for the long-suffering pilots of 360 Squadriglia. But when he got back to the mess, he was mortified to discover there was no cooking oil. Valcano improvised by using airplane motor oil! No one noticed the difference at the dinner table. Indeed, several pilots complimented him on his cooking. But, next morning, the entire squadron reported sick with severe stomach cramps and diarrhoea. All operations over Malta had to be scrubbed for twenty-four hours. Except for that incident, the Italians lived and ate much better than the RCAF defenders on Malta. Albertan Peter "Cowboy" Blanchford proved that when he shot down an Italian bomber and then inspected the wreckage. Inside, he found two hampers absolutely stuffed with wine, cheeses, cakes, king-sized loaves of homemade bread, sausages and a smorgasbord of fruits. And that was just what the airmen had brought along for lunch on the long flight to Malta! On the embattled island, by the way of contrast, McLeod was greeted every night by a plate of corned beef, a few dates and olives, and a skimpy ration of carrots dipped in revolting cod liver oil. And there was precious little of this fare, because the Axis naval blockage was slowly starving the island to death.

The Italians deserved their comforts. All the pilots were volunteers and considered themselves to be professionals. Many seemed to enjoy mixing it up with the Spitfires and, if their planes had been better armed, they might well have turned the tide. They were so good that some German bomber crews were quoted as saying they preferred to be escorted by Macchis than Messerschmitts. Certainly, the Canadians on Malta respected their Italian adversaries. McLeod, like fellow-ace George Beurling, thought the Germans employed better tactics but that the Italians had more staying power when a fight got hot. The Luftwaffe, he discovered, would only accept combat when it had a clear advantage. On July 23, an Italian pilot shot several holes through McLeod's oil pump, forcing him to make an emergency landing. The Canadian admitted that he would have been killed if his opponent had had cannons at his disposal.

Back in Action

McLeod was back in action the next day. This time, the opposition was provided by the Luftwaffe, and he was more successful. After a prolonged engagement, he got in a killing burst on an ME-109. Although the German's canopy was shot off and fire was seen in the cockpit, he only received credit for a probable kill. The desk-bound intelligence officers who bestowed victory confirmations may have denied McLeod on that occasion, but they had no choice but to grant him a "destroyed" on August 10, when he closed to within seventy-five yards of a Messerschmitt before blasting it to pieces. He was so close that chunks of the exploding German plane embedded themselves in his Spitfire. The enemy pilot was hurled free by the blast and floated down below his parachute, landing on the water. McLeod flew low and noticed that the German was making no effort to inflate his rubber raft. Assuming it must be defective, he tossed his own dinghy overboard. The German waved his thanks but made no attempt to climb aboard McLeod's raft either. Wally learned the reason when he got back to base. One of the Canadian's cannon shells had ripped straight through the man's chest, exiting out his back. He died in a rescue launch before reaching shore. Although it was fruitless, Wally's act of compassion, so rare for him, created something of a sensation in the Allied press. One newspaper reported that he had "extended the hand of friendship to a vanquished foe."[4]

In eighteen months of war, McLeod had scored only three confirmed kills, one probable and several damaged. The main reason for his slow start was his poor marksmanship. Pilots who flew with him say he would get into a favourable position only to blow a sure kill with sloppy shooting. It happened to him twice on August 13, when he could only damage a pair of German planes on which he had the drop. His superiors were, nevertheless, impressed with his leadership abilities, and made him a flight lieutenant on August 28. The promotion seems to have given Wally new confidence, because he responded twenty-four hours later by shooting down an ME-109 and damaging two Junkers. He had been spraying the twin-engine bombers with lead when the Messerschmitt attacked from behind, knocking out all but one of his guns. But the German fighter pilot failed to take into account that McLeod had slowed in order to keep the slower

JU-88s in range. In his haste, the ME-109 flyer overshot the Spitfire and McLeod made him pay for the miscalculation by taking his life with twelve rounds from the one gun still in operation.

McLeod's scoring slowed for a time after this, partly because his limited rations seriously weakened him. On a couple of occasions he was so weak from hunger that ground crews found him unconscious in the sweltering heat of his cockpit just before takeoff. He was feeling better by September 26, 1942, partly because the hottest days of summer were over, and also because fresh food had arrived. He responded by winning his first decoration. Leading three other Spitfire pilots into an assault on twenty ME-109s, he shot down one Nazi plane and drove off the rest. This accomplishment officially made him an ace, and he was awarded a much-deserved Distinguished Flying Cross.

In October, the Axis air forces threw 300 warplanes against fewer than one hundred Malta defenders. But despite the odds, the Allies, led by five Canadian aces, won the battle. During the first nineteen days of the month, the Germans and Italians lost seventy planes. The Allies, on the other hand, wrote off only thirty Spitfires. The score was even more one-sided than it sounds, because every Axis airman shot down was either killed or captured. Allied pilots, on the other hand, often returned to their squadron the same day that they were shot down. This was possible if they weren't wounded or too badly shaken up. In fact, seventeen of the thirty Spitfire pilots shot down lived to fight another day.

McLeod was instrumental in holding off the enemy. On October 11, he shot down a pair of Junkers 88s. A gunner aboard one of the doomed German bombers riddled McLeod's machine with twenty rounds. The Spitfire was barely responsive to the controls but Wally stayed in the fight, shooting down an ME-109 and damaging another before withdrawing. In one combat, he had increased his total of confirmed victories from five to eight. His marksmanship was improving and his victories increased dramatically. He bagged another Messerschmitt on October 12, and added a Macchi and a JU-88 the next day. Two more enemy planes were damaged by his shooting. In three days, the Canadian flyer had destroyed six Axis planes and damaged three others.

With his increasing success came greater ambition. He had twelve victories to his credit, and, when Beurling was shot down and wounded over Malta on October 14, Wally began to dream about replacing the Quebec pilot as Canada's top ace. He was a long way from Beurling's thirty victories but he moved a step closer on October 16, when he shot down an ME-109. He killed a Macchi pilot a few days after that, gaining his thirteenth conquest over Malta and his fourteenth overall. After that, however, the siege lifted and McLeod flew back to England for a much-deserved rest. He spent a few weeks there before being granted home leave. Back in Canada, McLeod was surprised to find himself a national hero. His October scoring spree had made him his country's third-highest ace and, because Woody Woodward fought in a theatre that received almost no publicity, he was completely unknown, even among most RCAF personnel. Therefore, when McLeod reached Regina, he was hailed as Canada's number two ace and was toasted from coast to coast as the "Eagle of Malta." McLeod took to the publicity like a duck to water and soon became a tiresome braggart and a heavy drinker. He foundered as an instructor and soon found himself in trouble with the authorities. He was placed on probation for sixty days and flatly told that he wouldn't be allowed back in action unless he kept his nose clean. The threat worked and, two months later, Wally was on his way back to England as commander of 443 Squadron.

His wing leader was Johnnie Johnson, the leading British ace. He recalled the Canadian as "a tall, alert, cool-eyed man of almost thirty. He moved about the room with a restlessness which I came to know well during the following months. Wally had a reputation of being a deadly shot and very fast on the draw. 'A killer, if there ever was one,' I thought. 'I'm pleased he's with me and not on the other side. He might be inclined to stick his neck out too far so I'll watch him'"[5]

McLeod and Johnson flew together for the first time on April 19, 1944, when a German Dornier 17 bomber was spotted near Brussels. Johnson was leading and should have led the attack. However, out of the corner of his eye he noted that McLeod was so anxious to get the kill that he was about to break formation and go after the twin-engined machine himself. More to make the move legal than anything else, the Englishman turned on his radio and said, "It's yours Wally. Let's see how you do it." McLeod peeled out of formation and dove for his adversary. Johnson told what happened next: "It was all over in a flash. There was no tearing pursuit. No twisting and weaving as the bomber tried to escape. It was a classic example of fine shooting with a master of the craft in the Spitfire. Wally nailed his victim with the first burst, and the Dornier pulled up steeply so that we saw it in plain view, hung for a moment in the air, and then fell on its side and crashed with a sheet of flame near the back gardens of a row of cottages."[6] The crew had bailed out but they were much too low to the ground and died hideous deaths when their parachutes failed to open.

Johnson was impressed, but he lost his patience with the Canadian ace a few days later. In the midst of a wild dogfight, McLeod lost his wingman and found he was unable to jettison his portable fuel tank. That made the Spitfire far less agile but, instead of heading for base, he took off alone after a retreating Focke-Wulf 190. The rest of the wing wisely headed home. On the way back Johnson heard someone say over the radio, "Take that, you bastard!" He recalled that, "although the voice was faint, the intonation was quite definitely Canadian, and I was quite sure it was Wally's voice." Johnson said later, "I was certain that McLeod had singled out an opponent and chased him towards the frontier of Germany itself. By this time I knew sufficient of the character of the man to know that once he had his teeth into a Hun, he would never let go until one or the other had been vanquished."[7] Eventually, McLeod returned to base, reporting that he had shot down the FW-190, for his sixteenth victory. But he didn't get the warm reception he had anticipated. Johnson said: "I calculated that he had been airborne for almost three hours, and this was stretching a Spitfire 9's endurance to a very fine point. He grinned sheepishly as he clambered out of his cockpit."[8] The Englishman angrily blasted McLeod and then called a squadron meeting to hammer home the importance of teamwork.

If the Regina native was looking for action, he found plenty of it in June, when the Allied armies invaded France, opening the long-awaited second front. Canadian troops led the way, penetrating seven miles inland the first day. And in the air, the RCAF was also in the forefront, with McLeod its top gun. He opened his scoring for the month eight days after the first troops stormed ashore, shooting down a Dornier that was attempting to bomb the invasion fleet. Two days later, he shot the tail off a Messerschmitt 109 and, on June 23, scored his most impressive kills of the war, destroying a pair of FW-190s. Johnson, who was in the thick of the fight with the Focke-Wulfs, was amazed to learn that McLeod had downed both victims with a total of fifty-two cannon shells — twenty-six from each gun. "Each carried a total of 120 rounds, so that Wally had used only about one-tenth of his ammunition. It was a remarkable display of both flying and shooting skill and, as far as I know, the performance was never equalled."[9]

McLeod became obsessed with his score. He chased an FW-190 halfway across France on July 20, only giving up when the harried German pilot took to his parachute. It was his twenty-first kill, and he hadn't even scored a hit on his opponent. He tormented another Luftwaffe pilot ten days later, chasing him into the treetops for half an hour before finishing him off.

Canadian fighter pilot Don Walz, who lives today in Moose Jaw, Saskatchewan, was one of those who knew McLeod at this time. He recalled that, once the ace got on a German's tail, "he'd trail it to Berlin — or until he got him." McLeod was "always a fighter pilot" but, despite that "he was very good with the squadron. He mixed well and I dont know of anybody who disliked him at all."[10] In many ways, Wally's relationship with his peers was similar to Billy Bishop's experience with 60 Squadron in the First World War War. Although many pilots were put off by his casual attitude to killing and his constant grasping at glory, most were willing to admit McLeod was fun-loving when off duty.

Few enemy planes were even seen in August, as the Germans saved their strength to beat back massive American bombing raids on their homeland. U.S. fighter pilots, equipped with two long-range fuel tanks, were getting all the action over Germany, while the RCAF conducted fruitless patrols over France. Frustrated, the Canadians loaded bombs under their Spitfires and took their anger out on the German army. But that didn't satisfy McLeod, who wanted aircraft victories to his credit. Looking at the bombs in disgust, he told Johnson that "if we'd get two decent long-range tanks to hang under the wings, instead of those things (the bombs) we could go to Berlin with the Yanks and get stuck into some real fighting."[11]

When his wing was taken off operations for a few days rest, McLeod was almost beside himself. Johnson recalled: "Wally was desperately keen to get into the air again and continually badgered me for news of our next move. He found it hard to relax and made no secret of the fact he was out to increase his score. Officially, he was recognized as the top-scoring fighter pilot of the RCAF. Although Screwball Beurling had destroyed a greater number of enemy aircraft, most of his victories were attained while he was serving in the Royal Air Force. This was a very fine point of distinction and simply meant that Wally was the top scorer of the RCAF, but Beurling held the record for Canadian pilots. Wally intended to settle this untidy matter once and for all simply by passing George's total."[12]

It was in such a frame of mind that the Saskatchewan pilot sailed into the air on September 27, 1944. Over Holland, he led a dozen Spitfires into an attack on nine ME-109s. Five of the Germans were shot down, but McLeod hadn't bagged any himself. Frustrated, he climbed after a Messerschmitt, giving it the advantage of height. Johnson, who had tangled with that particular German pilot earlier in the fight, shouted: "Watch that brute, Wally. He knows the form."[13] McLeod paid no heed and continued after the enemy. The German fell on him with guns blazing. Wally McLeod's Spitfire tumbled out of the sky and crashed into the ground near the German border. The Eagle of Malta was dead.

McLeod's sad death was a good example of what could happen to even an experienced ace if he wasn't careful. It could be said that his excessive overconfidence and ambition cost him his life. Certainly that is the portrait Johnson painted of the Canadian in his autobiography, *Wing Leader*.

In many ways, McLeod was a hard, ruthless character. Johnson tells us the Saskatchewan pilot was "a killer, if ever there was one." And both the British ace and Don Walz have testified that McLeod would never break off combat until a decision had been reached, no matter how dangerous the circumstances. He was also a glory seeker, who openly announced his intention to become the top Canadian ace. Canadian author Arthur Thurston has speculated that Wally's loss of his mother at an early age had left him with a bitter edge and this is probably correct. Once he became a famous ace he felt as if he had a role in life for the first time, and his attempts to get to the top were in many ways admirable. He was a somebody, and, naturally enough, he wanted more. He realized the status of Canadian ace-of-aces would give him a place in history and he was out to obtain it.

McLeod overcame great odds to become a high-scoring pilot. He was a poor shot in the beginning but drove himself relentlessly until he was one of the RCAF's most deadly aerial marksmen. For all his personal faults, he was a very brave man and a splendid flyer who helped turn the tide in favour of the Allies in the crucial siege of Malta. Because the Nazis lost that battle, they were eventually turfed out of the oil-rich Middle East. It was a major victory, which helped the democracies win the war, and Wally McLeod was one of the handful of people who made it possible.

TWELVE

Omer Levesque

Korea has been called Canada's forgotten war. The 1950-53 conflict cost relatively few Canadian lives, produced no household names and enjoyed little popular support. Within years of its conclusion, the war had virtually faded from public memory. In fact, while it raged, the United Nations would not even admit it was a war. Governments preferred to call it a United Nations "police action." Before long, with the influence of Hollywood, most people viewed it as an American-Chinese confrontation. Few realized that Canada had participated at all. And because of this, the nation has for nearly forty years ignored its last great fighter ace. His name was Omer Levesque, and he was unique, for several reasons. First, he was a French-Canadian, and most of Canada's combat air heroes had been English. Second, he was the first Allied fighter pilot of World War Two to destroy one of the legendary Focke-Wulf 190 fighter planes. He also survived three years in a Nazi prisoner of war camp, returned to the RCAF and became the first Canadian to enter the Korean war. There, as the first of his countrymen ever to fly the fabled F-86 Sabre jet, he became Canada's first — and last — jet ace.

Levesque had been interested in the military as a boy, but when he grew older, the Montreal native shied away from the air force. It was an all-English organization and young Omer didn't speak the language well enough. Instead, he contented himself with enlisting in a militia unit in Mont Joli. There, he did well, rising quickly to the rank of lieutenant with Les Fusiliers du St. Laurent. "I was actually in the army at the beginning of the war," he explained in a 1989 interview with the author. "I was in the non-permanent militia and going to Ottawa University. I'd been playing hockey against the air force at Rockcliffe and that's what got me interested in flying. And because Ottawa was the first bilingual school in the country, it helped me to understand English well enough to get through the Air Force training." When he transferred to the RCAF, he had to accept a demotion, falling back to the lowly rank of aircraftsman second class. "I had to lose my officer's status but it was worth it because, after Dunkirk, the situation looked pretty hopeless" for the army.

The war wasn't popular in Quebec, and his decision to enlist made him something of an outsider with many of his friends. "I don't know why," he says of Quebec's lack of support for the conflict. "It seemed distant to most people." But Levesque, like most great fighter pilots, was a bit of a rebel. He did things his way, not worrying too much about what others thought. Sent to Camp Borden, in Ontario, he had no difficulty fitting in with the mostly English-Canadian RCAF personnel. "I got along well, I didn't feel any resentment toward me whatsoever because I was French. In fact, it was just the opposite." He quickly won the respect of his colleagues — and his wings — on April 1, 1941. Levesque was given a two-week leave and shipped immediately to England. His logbook shows he had 160 hours flying time to his credit. High seas and German U-boats made the voyage miserable. "There were eighty or ninety ships in the convoy to Iceland, and it was a terrible time to be at sea," he says. "We spent five days there and then moved on to Scotland, throwing depth charges on a few occasions, but we made it!"

Once in the United Kingdom the twenty-one-year-old wasn't thrown straight into combat. Instead, he learned how to fly the Hurricane, putting in sixty-five hours on the fabled workhorse of the Battle of Britain. "There were Poles and Czechs, but most were Canadians," he recalled. From there, he was posted to RCAF 401 Squadron, which had distinguished itself in the Battle of Britain. This was a veteran outfit and, better still, it was equipped with the famous Spitfire. "We'd heard so much about it and it really was beautiful — unexpectedly beautiful — to fly. It was so smooth and responding to the engine. The weight of the aircraft wasn't all that much. It had tin wings and the Hurricane had had very heavy (wooden) wings." It was also better-armed, coming with two cannons and four machine guns. The older "Hurri's" had six machine guns.

Flying out of Biggin Hill, Levesque entered the worst phase of the war for Allied fighter pilots. The German pilots were top-notch and they were fighting over their own territory. "Most new pilots bought it after two or three sweeps (missions over northern France). Once we nearly lost the whole squadron, losing nine pilots in one sweep. We were just about decimated. In the Battle of Britain you could bail out and be home the same day, but over France you were a prisoner. And the Germans were so powerful and cocky in those days. They'd sometimes chase us right back over the channel. They were wiping us out." Distressing as the losses were, they also meant swift promotions for the survivors. "I was told, 'Even if you don't want to be an officer, you have to be, because we can't have an NCO leading a flight.'"

The only reason the Canadians could hold their own against the more experienced Germans was that the Spitfire was marginally superior to the ME-109. But on November 22, 1941, Levesque and the rest of the Commonwealth got a shock. Those crack German fighter pilots showed up over the battlefield in a deadly new warplane. A whole wing of Spitfires had taken off from Biggin Hill, crossing the channel at Dover. They eventually climbed over four miles up, keeping radio silence until, without warning, someone shouted over the intercom: "Bandits!" Levesque looked up just in time to see a band of single-seaters with round yellow noses come hurling down out of the sun right on top of him. He could make out huge radial engines that looked nothing like the snouts of the old ME-109s. Even from a distance, he knew these machines were more agile than the Messerschmitts. They were also faster, more heavily armoured and came equipped with four cannons, two machine guns and rockets. The Germans flashed across the sky at 400 miles per hour, guns winking. Levesque could make out light blue underbellies, with grey-and-green wings. They came in with incredible speed and violence. One of the nimble fighters was right inside the Spitfire formation before anyone could react. A split-second later, it was gone and the lead Spit was a ball of raging orange flame. "I was flying number two to Hank Sprangue, who was shot down just in front of me," he remembered decades later. "He was a good pilot with one probable kill to his credit." The Montrealer turned sharply to his right and was relieved to see Sprangue's parachute open. The RCAF had just been introduced to the FW-190.

Levesque wasn't about to wait around to see what else the German plane could do. "I made a complete circle, saw an enemy aircraft and climbed toward it, getting on its tail. I got in a pretty

good shot…. all of a sudden, smoke came out the full length of
its fuselage. I got him in the fuel tanks but the sealant prevented
a fire. He wasn't finished and dove away, turning to keep from
me. But I stayed right with him all the way down from 22,000
feet. He went straight down and I kept firing at him, using up just
about all of my 120 rounds of cannon fire." The two men were
locked in a desperate, falling circle. Holding on for dear life, the
German turned his damaged plane ever tighter in a bid to get home
alive. Levesque followed close behind, hanging tenaciously to his
opponent's tail even as the G-forces pinned him against his seat
and pushed his mouth open inside his oxygen mask. The turns
were so tight that some of the rivets popped out of the Spitfire's
wings. But the Canadian held like grim death to the German's
swastika-decorated rudder, matching the enemy pilot's every
manoeuvre. Once, as they circled tightly, the ground spinning
crazily below them, the two men were so close that Levesque
could look right into the terrified eyes of his adversary. Finally,
he got a clear shot and let go with everything he had. The Spitfire
shuddered briefly as it spat out machine-gun and cannon fire.
Chunks flew off the Focke-Wulf and the crippled machine suddenly burst into flames. It nosed over on one wing and trailing
smoke, thundered into the ground. "I didn't see a chute,"
Levesque said. "I was pretty close to the ground and barely got
out and pulled up in time myself."

For Omer, there was no time to celebrate his first kill. He was
now separated from his squadron mates, dangerously close to
earth and rapidly running out of fuel. And more Germans were
scrambling from the nearby fighter base at St. Omer — the home
of several top Nazi aces. Looking up, he spotted another formation
of FW-190s. They were thirsting for revenge and the Quebecer
was an easy target. A more experienced pilot pilot might have run
for it, but not the rookie. He broke every rule of aerial dogfighting,
deciding to attack a superior force from below. The bold move
caught the Germans by surprise. Levesque's guns clawed down a
second FW-190, and the others scattered.

Back in England, he was told that another RCAF pilot had seen
his first victory, but that the second was listed only as a probable.
He felt no remorse about the man he'd killed. "It was so imper-
sonal. It didn't bother you…you thought more about the aircraft
than the man. You didn't think in terms of somebody being in it.

It was like shooting at a mechanical target in the circus." But more important than his personal feelings was the information he had about the new German fighter. Air force officials pumped him for details about the Focke-Wulf, even going so far as to have him draw a picture of it. Omer had always been good in art class and he produced an amazingly accurate likeness of the fighter. His outline was immediately reproduced and distributed to pilots all over England.

Levesque didn't get another crack at the enemy for several months, because winter weather severely restricted flying on both sides of the channel. And when he did get back in action, he found himself pitted against German sailors. He was loafing about in a London restaurant one afternoon when he was unexpectedly re-called to base. Moments later, he was winging his way toward France, leading a trio of Spitfires. One of his wingmen developed engine trouble and had to return to Biggin Hill, but Levesque and the other man continued on. In the overcast skies, it was difficult to see for any distance, so the two Canadians dove to within a few thousand feet of the choppy waves. Out of the mist in front of them a German convoy appeared, almost ghostlike. Without hes-itation, Levesque led his wingman into the attack. "We didn't have any bombs but with our cannons we could do a lot of damage," he said. "We tried to hit the chimneys, where we could blow the boilers." He pressed home his attack, showering a pro-longed burst into the nearest enemy ship. The Germans were firing back, both from the deck of the destroyer and from nearby shore batteries. Both Spitfires were bracketed by exploding black puffballs. Several rounds exploded into the water just under their wings, sending up a mountain of spray. Levesque found himself thinking absurdly that, only a few hours before, he had been having lunch in London. "It was a crazy war!" he said.[1] The German gunners, fortunately, couldn't get a bead on the two Canadians as they streaked in. The Spitfires raked the destroyer from bow to stern, then raced for home.

Commissioned as a flying officer in February, 1942, Omer now found himself being sent out over the channel on a regular basis to look for the German navy. On February 12, he led a whole squadron into combat after word arrived that three Nazi cruisers — the *Prinz Eugen*, *Gneisenau* and *Schainhorst* — were attempt-ing to sneak through the channel on their way to Germany. The mighty warships were escorted by several destroyers and a swarm of fighters. And the breakout was intentionally staged during foul weather, to avoid detection by the Royal Navy. The British navy was caught totally off guard. The Germans were almost home free when they were spotted. It was too late for ships to intercept them, but aircraft could still do the trick. Unfortunately, the first wave of Allied planes on the scene were the old Swordfish biplanes. These torpedo-firing machines didn't stand a chance against modern fighters, and not one of them returned. Levesque, meanwhile, was flying alone. Visibility was so poor that formation flying had become impossible. Collision with friendly aircraft was such a real possibility that the squadron had split up, leaving each man on his own.

Levesque was zipping in and out of the clouds looking for the German fleet when it suddenly found him. Anti-aircraft bursts began exploding all around his canopy, rocking the Spitfire violently upward. Looking down, he had no trouble spotting the enemy fleet. "You could see a tremendous amount of smoke from those ships," he remembered. And the flak crews were firing everything they had at anything they saw — whether it was an Allied or German airplane. Just ahead in the murk, Levesque caught sight of a Messerschmitt 109 dodging its own ack-ack. The German was so busy trying to avoid being shot down by his own countrymen that he never saw the Spitfire creeping up behind him. Levesque was still several hundred yards off when he triggered his guns. Normally, he would have closed in for a better shot, but, in the gloom, he knew it would be easy to see his bright-yellow tracers streaking into his opponent. Slugs tore into the square-winged fighter's cockpit. The pilot crumpled in his seat and the ME-109 keeled over, crashing straight into the sea.

A Wild Dogfight

But there was more to come. Levesque suddenly found himself in the midst of a wild dogfight. "We got mixed up with a whole bunch of aircraft and we were only 300 to 400 feet above the ships. Those huge ships were firing at us and big balls were coming up from them. At the same time, German fighters were all over the place. We were really going crazy, skirting in and out of clouds in a fight that lasted twenty to twenty-five minutes." He popped out of one cloud just in time to see an FW-190 directly in front of him. Without thinking, he lined it up in his sights and fired. A second German pilot went to a watery grave. A third adversary appeared out of nowhere: the sky had become a veritable shooting gallery. "Dogfights were like that," he recalls. "One moment, the sky would be filled with planes and the next moment there wouldn't be any, and you'd have no idea where they'd gone." Levesque squeezed his control-column trigger a third time. His aim was true, and a third man went down in flames.

He had scored three kills in one fight and was just thinking of the celebration he would have that night in the mess when something went very, very wrong. Cannon shells exploded in his engine. A quick look in his rearview mirror showed an FW-190 sitting on his tail. More shells slammed into his wings, and his radio went dead. A gauge in front of him showed that the temperature of his engine was rising uncontrollably. Flames began whipping from the cowling. Levesque veered out of the hail of bullets, dousing the fire in his motor by activating an automatic extinguisher. Another look behind showed that the German was moving in for another pass. He turned sharply to the right, throwing off his pursuer's aim. There wasn't a plane in existence that could turn as tightly to the right as the Spitfire and, within seconds, the Focke-Wulf roared right by him. Levesque was now on the German's tail He opened fire. Nothing happened. His guns were out of ammo! He nursed the Spitfire around and headed for England, trailing columns of black smoke. The enemy pilot was either out of ammunition himself, or had lost sight of the crippled RCAF fighter, because he made no further attempt to kill Levesque. But the Canadian's problems were far from over. There was no hope of making it back to base, and, with a dead radio, he couldn't even call for help. When more flak began exploding around him, he wisely decided to ditch into the channel. It was out of the question to bail out because he was much too low. He hadn't enough altitude to be sure that his parachute would open.

The doomed fighter came roaring down at several hundred miles per hour, its anxious pilot aware that the fabled Irish ace, Paddy Finucane, had drowned while ditching into the same body of water. "Very few Spitfire pilots ever escaped" before the machine sank, he remembers. Levesque pulled back his canopy, brought up his nose and smacked into a twelve-foot wave. The

fighter began sinking at once. Levesque, who was stunned at the
moment of impact, recovered to find himself being sucked under
the waves. "I woke up. I felt good — it was like a dream. I thought
to myself, 'If I come back from this, there's nothing to dying,'"
he told an interviewer thirty-six years later.[2] The Spitfire was now
underwater, and Levesque was still struggling to free himself from
his safety belt. His parachute harness was caught on a hunk of
jagged metal. But he somehow stayed calm and broke free. Looking up, he could see a trail of bubbles "floating up towards the
surface — the light filtering down was a deep bottle-green. Finally, I got loose and started swimming. Then I noticed I was
bleeding — from hitting my head in the crash."[3] He popped to the
surface, gasping desperately for air, only to be struck in the face
by a powerful wave. His eyes were stung by salt water and he was
dizzy and disoriented. Soon, he was suffering from the brutal cold.
But at least the low temperatures helped slow the bleeding. It was
little consolation, however, because Omer Levesque was half an
hour from freezing to death, and he knew it. That is, if he didn't
drown first. Again and again, king-sized waves rolled over him,
making it almost impossible to breathe. His life jacket was so poor
that it barely kept him afloat. And his rubber raft refused to inflate.
"I knew it was just about the end but it didn't bother me," he
recalled. "At the time I was very cool. I guess I didn't know what
I was doing. It was like being in the bottom of a pool." One of his
gloves was missing, and the numbing cold had all but drained him.
Within minutes, he felt himself nodding off into a peaceful sleep
from which he felt he would never awake. He was only vaguely
aware of hands grabbing him. In a state of shock, he found himself
being put in a net and hauled up the side of a ship. But he passed
out before determining whether it was reality or just a final dream.

When he awoke, several hours later, the Quebecer found himself in the dark hold of a vessel, lying in a cot. His knee had been
bandaged, his head felt better and he could make out voices in the
background. He wasn't sure what language they were speaking
but he was certain of one thing — it wasn't English or French. He
vaguely hoped they were Norwegians. But, as his eyes slowly
adjusted to the dark surroundings, they focussed on a painting in
the doorway. He recognized the man in the picture at once. It was
Adolf Hitler. "I thought, 'For Cripes sake, it's a German ship!'"
The enemy sailors treated him well enough, but Levesque's ordeal

was just beginning. He was packed off to Stalag 3, near Berlin, where he began three years of captivity. There were times when he despaired that he would ever be a free man again. But he avoids discussion about his experiences. "No need to talk about the prison camp," he says.[4] An artistic man, Levesque spent as much time as possible drawing pictures of planes, the camp, cartoons and combat scenes. He was in the camp in March, 1944, when the famed "Great Escape" took place. Prisoners tunnelled under the wire and made a mad dash to freedom. Levesque wasn't one of those chosen by the escape committee for the breakout and, for his sake, it was just as well. Of seventy-six men who broke out, all but a handful were rounded up by the Gestapo. Fifty-three were then killed by the Nazis. Several had been friends of Levesque.

For Levesque, an active individual all his life, the boredom of camp life was even worse than the poor food and grim conditions. But all this changed in February, 1945. With the Russian army closing in, the prisoners were packed up in the middle of the night and marched westward at gunpoint. They stopped just outside Berlin and were put back behind barbed wire. But the end was approaching and it came suddenly, with Russian tanks charging into the camp one night with guns firing. "They came in at three in the morning, blowing trees over," he recalls. Within days, Levesque was back across the Elbe River, where he met up with American troops. "That was the first time in three years that I saw white bread. Our diet hadn't been too good. Few of our Red Cross parcels ever got through to us."

Despite the hard years, Levesque was still very much in love with flying — and with the Royal Canadian Air Force. He was proud of his service to his country. His four confirmed victories had left him one kill short of the coveted title of fighter ace, and although it didn't look like he'd get a chance to notch his fifth victory now, it was still a very good record. Levesque was given a leave of absence from the RCAF to study at McGill University in Montreal, eventually graduating with a B.A. in political science and economics. By 1947, he was back at the controls of a fighter plane, flying with Canada's first jet squadron — the Blue Devils, demonstration team. He quickly gained a reputation as a top test pilot, setting a speed record of more than 645 miles per hour while flying a Vampire jet from Montreal to Ottawa in just eight-and-a-half minutes.

In June, 1950, just one month before war broke out in Korea,
Levesque was posted to the United States as part of an RCAF/USAF
exchange program. "They wanted to send me to England to fly
Meteors with the RAF, but I didn't want to fly that bloody old
plane. I wanted to go to the States where they had the new planes."
Indeed they did. Within days of arriving in the United States,
Levesque was introduced to the new F-86 Sabre jet. For Omer,
accustomed to the much slower Vampire, the sleek Sabre, with its
swept-back wings was frightening. He'd never flown anything as
fast or smooth in his life. "It was like being on a bucking bronco
— I didn't ride it, I just hung on!"[5] But once he got used to the
fantastic speed (it was 200 miles per hour faster than the Spitfire)
he found it a delight to fly. "It had lots of power and could turn
around on a dime. When you pull back you get a whole lot of air
— the stabilizer doesn't fight the elevator. This made the aircraft
tremendous." He also noted it had almost no vibration — and that
it was armed with six fifty-calibre machine guns.

While Levesque was learning how to master the Sabre, the Cold
War was heating up in Korea, half a world away. Communist
forces from the northern half of the country invaded the south on
June 25, 1950, sending 90,000 troops crashing down on 15,000
South Korean soldiers. The heavily outnumbered defenders were
easily hurled back. Within days, the United States, which was
pledged by treaty to defend the south, had intervened militarily.
China, an ally of the north, soon followed suit and a superpower
confrontation was underway.

At first, the Americans underestimated their enemies. They
held their Sabres back thinking they could defeat the Communist
air forces with a few F-80 Shooting Star fighters and a handful of
World War Two vintage B-29 Superfortress bombers. They were
in for a rude shock. In October, swarms of Russian-built MIG-15
jet fighters appeared over the battlefield. They were fast, high-per-
formance planes armed with three cannons. And they made an
immediate impact, shooting down five of the giant four-engine
B-29s and seriously damaging several others in just a few days.
The Shooting Stars proved no match for them in dogfights. The
appearance of the MIGs changed things overnight. Air superiority
had been lost and, in a bid to regain it, President Harry Truman
ordered the 334th Fighter Interceptor Squadron to the war zone,
along with its Sabres and the Canadian exchange pilot, Omer

Levesque. Thus did Levesque become the first Canadian fighter pilot in Korea. Others would soon follow. Canada entered the war along with several other United Nations countries, and the call went out for volunteers. Prime Minister Louis St. Laurent, who was anxious to keep the nation's commitment to a bare minimum, refused to dispatch RCAF fighter squadrons. However, he did agree to allow a handful of Canadian pilots to serve in United States air force squadrons.

A Small Wonder

The Canadians in Korea proved to be among the best pilots there. Looking at their records, it is small wonder. Among them was Doug Lindsay, of Moose Jaw, Saskatchewan., who had shot down several Germans over Europe. He would take up where he left off in World War Two, shooting down two MIGs and damaging three more. Another, John MacKay, had shot down eleven Germans. Indeed, he was one of the few fighter pilots in history ever to have tackled an enemy jet at that time. He had helped shoot down a Nazi Messerschmitt 262, the twin-engine turbo fighter that Hitler had introduced in the last months of the war. In addition to that kill, he had damaged a trio of German Arado AR 234 jet bombers. MacKay proved he hadn't lost his knack for bagging jets when he got to Korea, destroying a MIG on June 30, 1953, and becoming the last Canadian in history to score an aerial victory. Another World War Two ace on the scene was Bob Davidson, who had the unique distinction of being the only Canadian fighter pilot to score victories over airmen from all three Axis powers. He had downed two Germans, two Italians and two Japanese pilots. Now he was hoping to add a pair of Chinese MIGs to his total. The Canadian fighter pilots were an average age of twenty-eight and had each flown approximately eighteen missions in World War Two. They were more mature than when they had flown in the Second World War. Indeed, most of them gave away the two bottles of Old Mathuse whisky issued to them by the Americans, having long since learned that a man with a hangover was at a serious disadvantage in a dogfight.

For those interested in the pleasures of the flesh, the airfields were surrounded by houses of prostitution. The buildings were off limits to all personnel, but, as Ernie Glover of Niagara Falls,

Ontario found out, the regulation was blatantly ignored by some men. He saw that for himself when a Sabre lost power coming in for a landing and ploughed through a row of forty-six of the houses of ill repute. "Nobody was hurt at all, but suddenly there were fifteen or twenty guys in various states of undress bailing out of these houses and running like the devil. The whole thing was hilarious, particularly because every one of those places was strictly off limits."[6]

When Levesque arrived on the scene, most of the UN pilots were wearing white silk scarves and brown leather helmets. Pilots only switched to the moulded plastic helmets when directly ordered to do so. The MIG jockeys, interestingly enough, also wore leather headgear. And perhaps appropriately, they were often seen sporting red silk scarves.

In battle, the Communists enjoyed every advantage. They hovered around the Yalu River, which separated North Korea from China, looking for easy targets. When attacked, they fled across the Yalu where, for political reasons, the Canadians and Americans were forbidden to follow. Claude LaFrance, a young pilot from Montreal, recalled that "the F-86 pilots were operating at a disadvantage in many ways. Firstly, we were fighting our war near the Yalu River, some 200 nautical miles behind enemy lines while, of course, the enemy was over his own backyard; this meant that we had no radar assistance, but the enemy did — it also meant that we had to fight relatively heavy, with a fuel reserve for a flight back home. Secondly, the enemy could fly into Manchuria, a sanctuary we were not supposed to violate, although, flying without navigation aids and often above cloud, I suppose we did so from time to time. Thirdly, and most importantly, the MIG-15 had a higher ceiling than did the F-86." LaFrance found that last point the most significant. While the Sabres flew at 45,000 feet, the MIGs often operated 10,000 feet higher. "This meant that the enemy could decide whether or not to engage" and would only do so if he thought he had a clear advantage. "We, however, could only wait and seek to strike a good compromise: appearing to be sufficiently vulnerable to entice the enemy to engage while avoiding suicide."[7]

Such handicaps prevented Levesque from having immediate success in Korea. He flew fifty missions without scoring a kill. Four months after arriving in the war zone, he finally got his big chance. It was March 30, 1951, and he was flying with two squadrons of Sabres as they escorted a group of B-29s towards a bombing attack on enemy bridges over the Yalu. Two formations of white-painted MIGs with red stars on their wings dropped on them from above, their cannons tossing out bright-orange tracer shells that seemed to lazily arc across the sky toward the Sabres. Levesque and an American pilot, Ed Fletcher, dropped their auxiliary fuel tanks and turned tightly to face a pair of MIGs boring in from the left. The speed of the battle was like nothing the Quebecer had experienced over Europe. The MIGs were there one moment and gone the next. Turning on the afterburners, Levesque took off in hot pursuit.

The enemy pilot closest to him pulled up into the sun, hoping to lose Levesque in its blinding glare. But the Canadian was wearing sunglasses and was easily able to keep his opponent in sight. Besides that, in the extreme cold of the upper altitudes in which they were fighting, the jets gave off a clear condensation trail that revealed their positions to both friend and foe. Levesque held the Sabre steady, closed to within 1,500 yards and let go with all six machine guns. "I got in a really nice deflection shot but with those six guns firing you lost 30 to 40 knots of speed, which was a hell of a lot! I aimed again and fired another burst and, all of a sudden, the flaps came down on the MIG. He kept on turning and I followed him down." Levesque was "partially blacking out" but he clung to the MIG, realizing its flaps had been lowered because his fire had shattered its hydraulic system. Firing again, he raked the ship from nose to tail and watched as it rolled end over end, crashing into the hills below. A flash of red flame and hot white smoke marked the spot where it had gone in.

Levesque pulled up to find another MIG on his tail. Standing the Sabre on its rudder, he climbed straight into the sun. The enemy pilot followed but apparently wasn't wearing sunglasses, because he soon lost sight of the Canadian and flew off in the direction of China. But Levesque was still in mortal danger. "I went right through the B-29 formation and they all shot at me! Thank God they missed. I waggled my wings and they stopped firing, but lots of shells had just missed me." Levelling off, the Canadian found his flying suit was soaked from his own sweat. And his fuel was nearly exhausted. He climbed to 40,000 feet, where the F-86 got better mileage and headed home, arriving back at Suwon airfield with only a few drops left in his tanks. It had taken nine years and two wars, but Omer Levesque, after countless narrow escapes, was finally an ace!

He flew twenty more missions after that, encountering MIGs on a few occasions but scoring no further kills. When the war ended, he was Canada's last ace. No Canadian downed five MIGs in Korea, although Ernie Glover destroyed three and damaged three more. Overall, Levesque and his countrymen forged an impressive record. In many ways, it was even more outstanding than the accomplishments of the Canadians who flew only in the world wars. A mere eighteen Canadian fighter pilots saw action in Korea, but, despite the most difficult circumstances, they managed to collectively shoot down or damage twenty MIGs. Not one of them was lost to an enemy jet. In fact, the only casualty was Andy MacKenzie of Montreal, who was accidentally shot down by his American wingman. MacKenzie, who survived two years in a Chinese prison camp, had been a Second World War ace with eight Germans to his credit.

Levesque is especially proud of the record. "We achieved absolute air superiority in Korea," he says of the UN pilots, "It was just classic. The Chinese said afterwards that they would have gone over us like a steamroller if it hadn't been for the Allied air force." Levesque stayed in the RCAF until 1965 and was with a Canadian delegation that visited Vietnam in 1960. He met President Ho Chi Minh and General Vo Nguyen Giap, the legendary North Vietnamese military leader, during a visit to Hanoi. He stayed in aviation after his retirement from the air force, serving on the Air Transport committee in Ottawa until he retired in 1987. Today, he lives in his native Quebec.

Levesque's story is important because it helps debunk the myth that French-Canadians couldn't — or wouldn't — fight in Canada's wars. It's true that many Quebecers saw the world wars as European conflicts in which Canada should not have been involved, but many fought in all three branches of the Canadian armed forces, winning their share of honours, including Victoria Cross citations. In the air, there were French-Canadians in all three of Canada's wars. One of Billy Bishop's squadron mates in 1917 was a Major Milot, a French-Canadian who was killed in action. The best friend of George Beurling was Jean Paradis of Quebec, who died in a Spitfire over Malta. A French-Canadian named

Richard Audet shot down five German planes in his first dogfight, becoming one of the few pilots in history to become an ace in one combat. He added six more victories before giving his life for Canada. Over Korea, both Levesque and fellow-Quebecer Claude LaFrance were MIG killers.

But Levesque showed a special brand of courage. Many good men had their spirits broken by Nazi captivity. Few would have been willing to go back into action years later, again flying over enemy territory. Levesque, however, volunteered for Korea, despite the fact that he knew all of his combat missions would be over the other side of the lines. Levesque, who had lost three years of his life to captivity, nevertheless was willing to risk capture or death a second time. And just like the first, he emerged triumphant. Buck McNair may have shown the most physical courage in the face of agonizing wounds, but Levesque was perhaps the Canadian pilot with the most mental toughness. And that kind of bravery may be the rarest of all.

Conclusion

Were Canada's air aces dashing heroes or bloodthirsty madmen? That's a question most often ignored by those who write glowing accounts of the exploits of the great fighter pilots. To answer it, we need to understand the role of the single-seater aviator. While bomber crews were charged with striking unseen targets many miles below them, and reconnaissance airmen took spy photographs of enemy positions or directed the artillery fire, fighter pilots were expected to win air superiority. In other words, their job was to shoot down enemy planes, pure and simple. It was a task that did not change throughout all the wars of this century. And to achieve their goals, unlike the bombers, they had to be extremely aggressive. They not only saw their prey, they closed in point-blank to knock it down. If they were successful, they could sweep the skies of enemy planes and turn the tide of the whole war. A good example of this was the 1940 Battle of Britain, where a handful of RAF fighter pilots stopped Hitler from invading England. The Nazi armies had the Allies reeling but they couldn't conquer the United Kingdom, because the Luftwaffe was unable to command the air above the beaches.

Air power played an insignificant role in World War One, mainly because the machines were too small to cause large-scale destruction. But by 1939, bomber fleets could destroy whole cities, if they could get through the protective screen of opposing fighter planes.

In London today, countless historic buildings and monuments are still with us because of the skill and courage of a few air aces. The Germans made an all-out effort to blast London off the map but gave up when their aircraft losses became unacceptably high. In Germany, a few years later, a thousand years of history was lost because the Luftwaffe fighter pilots failed in their bid to protect that country's great cities from Allied bombers. Air power also turned the tide in North Africa. The Axis powers had to knock Malta out of the fight in order to control the shipping lanes in the Mediterranean Sea. They couldn't do it, because of a few fighter pilots who refused to be beaten, despite overwhelming odds against them. Aircraft played a key role over the battlefields as well. Because the Allies had complete control of the sky by 1944, the German army only dared to take offensive actions during bad weather. They launched their famous Battle of the Bulge attack, for instance, in the midst of a blinding December snowstorm, when they knew the Allied air forces would be grounded for several days. And they made remarkable progress until the skies cleared and the Canadian, British and American airmen were able to get back into action. Nowhere was the importance of air power better demonstrated than in Korea, where the badly outnumbered United Nations troops were able to fight the Chinese to a standstill because they had air superiority. And that supremacy was gained by Allied fighter pilots who outscored the MIGs by an astounding fourteen-to-one ratio.

There's no doubt that fighter aces shaped history. It's also obvious that it took a special brand of courage to be an ace, mainly because they fought alone. A bomber was manned by anywhere from two to ten men, and there is courage in numbers. Fighters were almost all single-seat machines, and to operate them also required special skill. Bombers were multi-engined aircraft loaded down with tons of explosives. They were incapable of fancy aerobatics, so you didn't have to be an especially great pilot to fly one. Fighter jockeys, on the other hand, depended on their ability to toss their little machines all over the sky in lightning moves, not just to score kills, but to stay alive. All of this is not to denigrate the bomber crews. Theirs was a dangerous and thankless task. They took very heavy losses and received almost no glory. Indeed, they were often unfairly painted as murderers of civilians. But the fact remains that they didn't require the very special qualities that a great ace had to possess.

Yet, there was more to being a top gun than skill and courage. If we examine their lives, we find many common threads. First of all, almost to a man, they were nonconformists who did things their own way. Some, like Bishop, Beurling and Barker, were out-and-out rebels, who sometimes came close to courtmartial. Others, like Levesque, showed their rebel streak simply by being in an air force that was not especially popular with their peers. As a French-Canadian in the mostly English RCAF, he was one of very few, but he ignored mainstream opinion in Quebec and did what he wanted to do. All of them had adventurous spirits. Collishaw ran away to sea as a schoolboy. Beurling, while still a teenager, made a serious attempt to get to China. Bannock was prospecting in Yellowknife at age eighteen. Woodward was already in the Middle East when war came. Even Roy Brown, a mild-mannered fellow on the surface, left home as a youngster to take flying lessons with the Wright brothers. Although that sounds relatively tame, it should be remembered that flight was in its infancy then, and airplanes were far more dangerous, even, than the untrustworthy crates being flown a few years later in World War One. When Brown's parents heard the news that he was going to Ohio, it would have been as big a shock as a mother and father hearing today that their teen was leaving on a space-shuttle mission.

They were also very enterprising individuals with a "can-do" attitude. When Wally McLeod couldn't find work, he created his own job, showing films across Western Canada during the hard days of the Dirty Thirties. Few seemed to enjoy working for others, and in peacetime Bishop, Barker, Brown and Woodward all owned their own companies, while Bannock was the president of a major firm. Even those who remained in the air force, like Leckie and Collishaw, quickly rose to positions of command. All of them appear to have been of above average intelligence. Bannock was taking university courses in an era when few people completed high school. Buck McNair was also a good student. Many of the others were too restless to excel in class but they all seemed to have a certain natural cleverness. Most of them enjoyed the outdoors, hunting and contact sport, although there were a few notable exceptions. It's safe to say they were mostly high-spirited, aggressive boys. But none of them were mean-tempered bullies. While the aces made their mark through the use of brute force, none was ever in trouble with the law at any time in their lives. They came from middle-class, hardworking backgrounds and there wasn't a thug among them.

What was it, then, that gave them the ability to cut down other human beings so casually? Some, like Bannock and Levesque, seemed to have been motivated by patriotism. Collishaw, on the other hand, thought many Canadians had been duped by propaganda into fighting a European race war. Most were bothered by the killing and concentrated on shooting down airplanes rather than pilots. They ignored the human aspect as much as possible, thinking of their victims as machines to be put out of commission. Others were motivated by self-preservation, realizing it was "kill or be killed." A few, like Bishop and Beurling, came to enjoy the killing, and, interestingly enough, they became the top-scoring Canadian aces of the world wars. Although there's no denying that some got caught up in the excitement of battle, it's important to remember that they were just boys, set loose by society and told to kill. When they were successful, they were showered with fame and glory. Each time the top aces scored a victory, they received another headline. It's small wonder, then, that some of them came to enjoy their trade. If anyone is to be condemned, however, it should be the statesmen who started the wars and not the junior officers sent off to fight them.

It should be remembered, also, that some were motivated by revenge. They'd seen their friends slaughtered and were having their own lives threatened on a daily basis. Some reacted with genuine anger and struck back hard at every opportunity. Beurling, for one, could be very cruel, but he was caught up in desperate circumstances.

If we admire the aces it shouldn't be because they were good at shooting down enemy planes, no matter how important that task may have been. If they are to be revered, it should be for their bravery. They were willing to put their lives at risk, two and three times a day, whenever society asked them to do so. Most showed extraordinary tenacity. Bishop, Beurling, Collishaw, McNair and Levesque were all shot down but had the courage to return to battle. Barker and Alan McLeod kept fighting gallantly after receiving grievous wounds. Woodward carried on even after losing his plane and being forced to fight in the hills as a foot soldier. Bannock barely made it back to base in his damaged plane, then went right back into the fray. Wally McLeod did the same thing over Malta. Leckie had the courage to land his plane on the water when he knew he couldn't take off again, in order to rescue others. And even after that harrowing experience, he shunned a comfortable desk job.

What is the future of the fighter pilot? None at all, it is to be hoped. Weapons have become so dangerous that warfare is no longer a viable way to settle differences between nations. Indiscriminate mass killing began to be used toward the end of the Second World War and continued in Vietnam, where the B-52 bomber pilot played a much more important role than the fighter aces. Flying in massive eight-engine ships loaded with hundreds of tons of explosives, they hovered at the very edge of the stratosphere, raining mass death on those far below.

Since that time, even more vile weapons have appeared. Today, unmanned cruise missiles can deliver a nuclear bomb from West Germany to Moscow in about six minutes. By the time the incoming projectile was detected it would be too late to get a fighter off the ground to try to intercept it. If there is to be war in the future between the superpowers, the "heroes" will be faceless people in concrete bunkers, pressing buttons to destroy targets thousands of miles away. There will be no role for the brave young pilot in a leather helmet, with a scarf flying rakishly in the wind.

It's obvious to all but the most deceived of fools that we must eliminate war or disappear as a species. There are signs in the world today that that fact is slowly sinking in. The more thoughtful leaders, like Russia's Mikhail Gorbachev, are reducing troop levels — and tensions — in Europe. If this mood prevails, the fighter pilot, and all other warriors, may fade into history.

With a little luck, Canada's great air aces will be remembered as the last of a gallant breed, taking their place in folklore alongside the knights of the round table. We shouldn't forget them, because they played a colourful and important role in our history. But we should also hope that we've seen the last of them.

Ace Lists

The following is the most comprehensive list of Canadian aces ever published. It differs in several important respects from those published elsewhere, including as it does the balloon victories of World War One pilots, the buzz-bomb kills of Second World War aviators and machines destroyed on the ground. As well, it counts shared victories of World War Two aces as whole kills. Many Canadian writers, for instance, credit George Beurling with thirty-one-and-one-third victories but this list gives him thirty-two. The change was made so that Canadians can better compare the records of their leading aces to those of other nations. The British, for example, always credit their famous airman, Johnny Johnson, with thirty-eight kills, despite the fact that seven of those victories were shared with other pilots. Likewise, the First World War balloons are usually counted in the scores of pilots from other nations, but, for some strange reason, seldom mentioned in the tallies of Canada's aces. Buzz-bomb victories were considered equal to airplane conquests during the 1939-45 war, but most writers have since arbitrarily decided that they shouldn't count. I can see no justification for this line of thinking, so I have reinstated these victories. Likewise, I have counted enemy machines destroyed on the ground, reasoning that it made very little difference whether you destroyed an aircraft on the runway or in the sky, provided that it was knocked out of action. Because of these changes, many of the scores presented here will be slightly higher than those published elsewhere.

Dan McCaffery

Canada's Top Ten First World War Aces

Name;	Home;	Score
Billy Bishop;	Owen Sound, Ontario;	75
Ray Collishaw;	Nanaimo, British Columbia;	68
Don MacLaren;	Vancouver, British Columbia;	54
William Barker;	Dauphin, Manitoba;	53
George McElroy;	Windsor, Ontario;	46
Fred McCall;	Vernon, British Columbia;	37
Bill Claxton;	Gladstone, Manitoba;	36
Stuart Fall;	Hillbank, British Columbia;	34
Alfred Atkey;	Toronto, Ontario;	33
Albert Carter;	Pointe de Bute, New Brunswick;	31

Canada's Top Ten World War Two Aces

George Beurling;	Verdun, Quebec;	32
Russ Bannock;	Edmonton, Alberta;	30
Woody Woodward;	Victoria, British Columbia;	25
Wally McLeod;	Regina, Saskatchewan;	22
John Caine;	Toronto, Ontario;	20
George Keefer;	Charlottetown, P.E.I.;	18
Jim Edwards;	Nokomis, Saskatchewan;	17
Bill Klersy;	Brantford, Ontario;	17
Bill McKnight;	Edmonton, Alberta;	17
Earl Boal;	Weyburn, Saskatchewan;	17

Canada's Korean War MIG Killers

Name;	Home;	Destroyed;Damaged
Ernie Glover;	Niagara Falls, Ontario;	3;3
Doug Lindsay;	Moose Jaw, Saskatchewan;	2;3
Omer Levesque;	Montreal, Quebec;	1;0
Claude LeFrance;	Quebec;	1;0
Larry Spurr;	Middleton, Nova Scotia;	1;0
John MacKay;	Cloverdale, B.C.;	1;0
Bruce Fleming;	Montreal, Quebec;	0;2
Andy Lamros;	Ottawa, Ontario;	0;2
G.H. Nichols;	Dresden, Ontario;	0;1

Alberta Aces

Name;	War;	Home;	Score
Russ Bannock;	WW2;	Edmonton;	30
John Caine;	WW2;	Edmonton;	20
Bill McKnight;	WW2;	Edmonton;	17
Rod Phibbs;	WW2;	Strome;	16
Don Laubman;	WW2;	Provost;	15
Wop May;	WW1;	Edmonton;	13
Alfred Carter;	WW1;	Calgary;	13
Ross Gray;	WW2;	Edmonton;	12
Don Gordon;	WW2;	Edmonton;	12
Richard Audet;	WW2;	Lethbridge;	12
Jim Walker;	WW2;	Claresholm;	11
John Manuel;	WW1;	Edmonton;	10
Stan Puffer;	WW1;	Lacombe;	9
Dallas Schmidt;	WW2;	Wetaskiwan;	9
George Keith;	WW2;	Cardston;	9
Rayne Schultz;	WW2;	Bashaw;	8
Hazel Wallace;	WW1;	Lethbridge;	7
Emile Lussier;	WW1;	Medicine Hat;	7
George Bodard;	WW2;	Lethbridge;	6
James E. Walker;	WW2;	Claresholm;	10
James A. Walker;	WW2;	Gleichen;	6
Peter Blatchford;	WW2;	Edmonton;	6
Lionel Gaunce;	WW2;	Lethbridge;	6
Foss Boulton;	WW2;	Coleman;	5
Walter Kirkwood;	WW2;	Vegreville;	5
Esli Lapp;	WW2;	Redcliffe;	5
Ben Plumer;	WW2;	Bassano;	5
Don Reid;	WW2;	Lacombe;	5
Gord Wonnacott;	WW2;	Edmonton;	5
Forgrave Smith;	WW2;	Edmonton;	5
Jacob Wyman;	WW2;	Sexsmith;	5
W.J. Gillespie;	WW1;	Dayland;	5
Dave Dack;	WW2;	Calgary;	5

Atlantic Canada Aces

Name;	War;	Home;	Score
Nick Carter;	WW1;	Point de Bute, N.B.;	31
George Keefer;	WW2;	Charlottetown, P.E.I.;	18
Buck McNair;	WW2;	Springfield, N.S.;	16
George Hill;	WW2;	Pictou, N.S.;	14
Joe White;	WW1;	Halifax, N.S.;	13
Frank Soden;	WW1;	Peticodiac, N.B.;	9
Hugh Trainor;	WW2;	Charlottetown, P.E.I.;	9
Bill Rogers;	WW1;	Alberton, P.E.I.;	8
Bill Chisholm;	WW2;	Berwick, N.S.;	7
Gord Troke;	WW2;	Sydney, N.S.;	7
Bob Hayward;	WW2;	St. John's Nfld;	6
Don Kimball;	WW2;	Oromocto, N.B.;	6
Sid Ford;	WW2;	Liverpool, N.S.;	6
Leo Fownes;	WW2;	Baddeck, N.S.;	5
Bill Matheson;	WW1;	New Glasgow, N.S.;	5
Ralph Britten;	WW2;	Depcousse, N.S.;	5

British Columbia Aces

Name;	War;	Home;	Score
Ray Collishaw;	Russia/WW1;	Nanaimo;	70
Don McLaren;	WW1;	Vancouver;	54
Fred McCall;	WW1;	Vernon;	37
Stuart Fall;	WW1;	Hillbank;	34
Woody Woodward;	WW2;	Victoria;	25
Colin Finlayson;	WW2;	Victoria;	17
Noel Gibbons;	WW2;	Vancouver;	16
Charles Hickey;	WW1;	Parksville;	16
John McElroy;	WW2;	Kamloops;	14
Robert Barton;	WW2;	Kamloops;	13
Robert Kipp;	WW2;	Kamloops;	13
Albert Godfrey;	WW1;	Vancouver;	13
John McKay;	Korea/ WW2;	Cloverdale;	12
John White;	WW1;	Vancouver;	12
Howard Cleveland;	WW2;	Vancouver;	10
Homer Cochrane;	WW2;	Vernon;	9
John Williams;	WW2;	Kamloops;	9

Name	War	Home	Score
George Thompson;	WW1;	Celistal;	9
Bill Brown;	WW1;	Victoria;	8
Ernest Hoy;	WW1;	Vancouver;	8
Guy Moore;	WW1;	Vancouver;	8
Phil Brook;	WW2;	Salmon Arm;	8
Robert Buckham;	WW2;	Golden;	7
Art Cochrane;	WW2;	Vernon;	7
Mervin Sims;	WW2;	Vancouver;	7
John Latta;	WW2;	Vancouver;	7
Noel Stansfeld;	WW2;	Vancouver;	7
William MacDonald;	WW1;	Vancouver;	7
Bob Davidson;	WW2;	Vancouver;	6
Vernal Shail;	WW2;	New Westminster;	6
James Whalen;	WW2;	Vancouver;	6
John De Poncier;	WW1;	Vancouver;	6
Bill Hilborn;	WW1;	Alexandra;	6
Harold Hudson;	WW1;	Victoria;	6
Claude Wilson;	WW1;	Vancouver;	6
Harold Crawford;	WW2;	Revelstoke;	5
John Neil;	WW2;	Nanaimo;	5
Jackson Sheppard;	WW2;	Vancouver;	5
Carl Clement;	WW1;	Vancouver;	5
Emerson Smith;	WW1;	Victoria;	5
Roy McConnel;	WW1;	Victoria;	5
Joe Hallonquist;	WW1;	Mission City;	5
James Glen;	WW1;	Enderby;	5

Manitoba Aces

Name;	War;	Home;	Score
William Barker;	WW1;	Dauphin;	53
Bill Claxton;	WW1;	Gladstone;	36
John Kent;	WW2;	Winnipeg;	13
Fred Brown;	WW1;	Winnipeg;	11
Roger Delhaye;	WW1;	Brandon;	9
John Sharman;	WW1;	Oak Lake;	9
John Greene;	WW1;	Winnipeg;	8
James Smith;	WW2;	Winnipeg;	8
Mark Brown;	WW2;	Portage la Prairie;	8
Dave Forsyth;	WW2;	Winnipeg;	8

Geoff Northcott;	WW2;	Minnedosa;	8
Gerald Racine;	WW2;	St. Boniface;	7
Malcolm McLeod;	WW1;	Winnipeg;	7
William Stephenson;	WW1;	Winnipeg;	7
Lorne Cameron;	WW2;	Roland;	6
Wilbert Dodd;	WW2;	Rennie;	6
Harry Fenwick;	WW2;	Transcona;	6
Bill Atkinson;	WW2;	Minnedosa;	6
George Robinson;	WW2;	Transcona;	6
John Francis;	WW2;	Winnipeg;	6
Allen Angus;	WW2;	McCreary;	5
Colin Matheson;	WW2;	Winnipeg;	5

Ontario Aces

Name;	War;	Home;	Score
Billy Bishop;	WW1;	Owen Sound;	75
George McElroy;	WW1;	Windsor;	46
Alfred Atkey;	WW1;	Toronto;	33
Andy McKeever;	WW1;	Listowel;	30
Art Whealy;	WW1;	Toronto;	27
Frank Quigley;	WW1;	Toronto;	25
Reg Hoidge;	WW1;	Toronto;	25
Stan Rosevear;	WW1;	Thunder Bay;	23
Hank Burden;	WW1;	Toronto;	22
Bill Alexander;	WW1;	Toronto;	20
Ellis Reid;	WW1;	Toronto;	18
Bill Klersy;	WW2;	Brantford;	17
Don MacFadyen;	WW2;	Toronto;	17
Dave Fairbanks;	WW2;	Toronto;	16
P.S. Turner;	WW2;	Toronto;	16
Roy Brown;	WW1;	Carleton Place;	13
Ken Conn;	WW1;	Almonte;	13
Wilfred Curtis;	WW1;	Toronto;	13
Art Fairclough;	WW1;	Toronto;	13
George Johnson;	WW1;	Woodstock;	13
John Turnbull;	WW2;	St. Thomas;	13
Irving Kennedy;	WW2;	Cumberland;	13
Tommy Williams;	WW1;	Woodstock;	12
Stearne Edwards;	WW1;	Carleton Place;	12

George Howson;	WW1;	Port Perry;	12
Alex Stewart;	WW2;	Toronto;	12
Robert Dodds;	WW1;	Hamilton;	11
Jack Sorsoleil;	WW1;	Toronto;	11
Lloyd Schwab;	WW2;	Niagara Falls;	11
Albert Houle;	WW2;	Massey;	11
Bill Harrison;	WW1;	Toronto;	10
Roy Manzer;	WW1;	Oshawa;	10
Bill Hubbard;	WW1;	Toronto;	10
Hiram Davison;	WW1;	Forbar;	10
Alan Aikman;	WW2;	Toronto;	10
John Draper;	WW2;	Toronto;	10
Colin Evans;	WW2;	Hamilton;	10
Hilliard Bell;	WW1;	Toronto;	9
Gord Irving;	WW1;	Toronto;	9
Bill Irwin;	WW1;	Ripley;	9
Mansell James;	WW1;	Watford;	9
Alex Shook;	WW1;	Tioga;	9
George Bulmer;	WW1;	Toronto;	9
Ed Leslie;	WW1;	Smiths Falls;	9
George Johnson;	WW2;	Hamilton;	9
Jim Lindsay; Korea;	WW2;	Arnprior;	9
Gord Raphael;	WW2;	Toronto;	9
James Sharples;	WW2;	Toronto;	9
Harry MacDonald;	WW2;	Toronto;	8
Warren Peglar;	WW2;	Toronto;	8
Robert Smith;	WW2;	London;	8
James Ballantyne;	WW2;	Toronto;	8
Bruce Ingalls;	WW2;	Danville;	8
Dave Jamieson;	WW2;	Toronto;	8
Stan Cotterill;	WW2;	Beamsville;	8
John Boyle;	WW2;	Toronto;	8
Fred Armstong;	WW1;	Toronto;	8
Lloyd Breadner;	WW1;	Toronto;	8
James Foreman;	WW1;	Kirkfield;	8
Ken Junor;	WW1;	Toronto;	8
Ron Keirstead;	WW1;	Toronto;	8
J.F. Larson;	WW1;	Waltham;	8
Harry Dowding;	WW2;	Sarnia;	7
Lloyd Chadburn;	WW2;	Oshawa;	7

Hugh Godefroy;	WW2;	Toronto;	7
Douglas Hall;	WW2;	Timmins;	7
Harry Mitchell;	WW2;	Port Hope;	7
Tom Patterson;	WW2;	Toronto;	7
Joseph Robillard;	WW2;	Ottawa;	7
Joseph Sabourin;	WW2;	St. Isidore;	7
James Sommerville;	WW2;	Toronto;	7
John Greene;	WW2;	Toronto;	7
Clarence Kirkpatrick;	WW2;	Hamilton;	7
Gord Duncan;	WW1;	Hamilton;	7
Robert Eyre;	WW1;	Toronto;	7
Earl Hand;	WW1;	Sault Ste. Marie;	7
George MacKay;	WW1;	Toronto;	7
Lewis Ray;	WW1;	Toronto;	7
Ernest Joy;	WW1;	Toronto;	7
Ernest Morrow;	WW1;	Toronto;	6
Gerry Bell;	WW1;	Ottawa;	6
Dan Galbraith;	WW1;	Carleton Place;	6
Edward Grange;	WW1;	Toronto;	6
Charlie Green;	WW1;	Oakville;	6
D'Arcy Hilton;	WW1;	St. Catharines;	6
John Page;	WW1;	Brockville;	6
Henry Rath;	WW1;	Tweed;	6
Charles Ridley;	WW1;	Toronto;	6
Tony Spence;	WW1;	Toronto;	6
Ken Watson;	WW1;	Malton;	6
Tom Brannagan;	WW2;	Windsor;	6
Greg Tunnicliffe;	WW2;	Toronto;	6
Walter Conrad;	WW2;	Melrose;	6
Charles Edinger;	WW2;	Barrie;	6
Don Morrison;	WW2;	Toronto;	6
Guy Mott;	WW2;	Oil Springs;	6
Dan Noonan;	WW2;	Kingston;	6
Alfred Ogilvie;	WW2;	Ottawa;	6
George Pepper;	WW2;	Belleville;	6
Don Pieri;	WW2;	Toronto;	6
Fred Johnson;	WW2;	Thunder Bay;	6
Oscar Martin;	WW2;	Ottawa;	6
Alister McLaren;	WW2;	Ottawa;	6
J.G. Boyle;	WW2;	Castleman;	6

Bill Downer;	WW2;	Wybridge;	6
Doug Husban;	WW2;	Toronto;	6
James Kerr;	WW2;	Campbellford;	6
Milt Jowsey;	WW2;	Ottawa;	5
Charlie Magwood;	WW2;	Toronto;	5
Newton May;	WW2;	Guelph;	5
Fred Murray;	WW2;	Windsor;	5
Frank Cochrane;	WW2;	Brantford;	5
Vernon Williams;	WW2;	Hamilton;	5
Russ Bouskill;	WW2;	Trout Creek;	5
Bill Breithaupt;	WW2;	Toronto;	5
Phil Charron;	WW2;	Ottawa;	5
Malcolm Graham;	WW2;	Exeter;	5
Harold Oaks;	WW1;	Preston;	5
H.L. Symons;	WW1;	Toronto;	5
Harold Molyneur;	WW1;	Toronto;	5
E.S. Meek;	WW1;	Sanford;	5
Austin Fleming;	WW1;	Toronto;	5
John McNeaney;	WW1;	Hamilton;	5
A.E. McKay;	WW1;	London;	5
Bill Craig;	WW1;	Smiths Falls;	5
E.B. Booth;	WW1;	Toronto;	5
Bill Duncan;	WW1;	Toronto;	5

Québec Aces

Name;	War;	Home;	Score
George Beurling;	WW2;	Verdun;	32
Wilfred Beaver;	WW1;	Montreal;	17
Carl Falkenberg;	WW1;	Quebec City;	15
Robert Fumerton;	WW2;	Fort Coulonge;	14
Bill Jenkins;	WW1;	Montreal;	13
Peter Huletsky;	WW2;	Montreal;	13
Dave McIntosh;	WW2;	Stanstead;	12
Gerry Birks;	WW1;	Montreal;	12
Stan Stranger;	WW1;	Montreal;	11
Andy MacKenzie;	WW2/Korea;	Montreal;	9
Dave Ness;	WW2;	Westmount;	9
Dick Dawes;	WW1;	Lachine;	8
Jack Rutherford;	WW1;	Montreal;	7

Dave McGoun;	WW1;	Westmount;	6
George Foster;	WW1;	Montreal;	6
Joseph Laricheliere;	WW2;	Montreal;	6
John Christie;	WW2;	Montreal;	6
Omer Levesque;	WW 2/Korea;	Montreal;	5
Phillipe Etieene;	WW2;	St. Lambert;	5
Harlow Bowker;	WW2;	Granby;	5
Peter Leggat;	WW2;	Montreal;	5
Gord McGregor;	WW2;	Montreal;	5

Saskatchewan Aces

Name;	War;	Home;	Score
Mike McEwen;	WW1;	Radisson;	27
Bill Shields;	WW1;	Lipton;	23
Wally McLeod;	WW2;	Regina;	22
Earl Boal;	WW2;	Wayburn;	17
Edward Charles;	WW2;	Lashburn;	16
Edmund Tempest;	WW1;	Perdue;	14
Jim Edwards;	WW2;	Nokomis;	14
Rod Smith;	WW2;	Regina;	14
Les Bing;	WW2;	Regina;	13
John Mitchner;	WW2;	Saskatoon;	11
Wilfred Banks;	WW2;	Hazenmore;	9
Conway Farrell;	WW1;	Regina;	8
Frank Gorringe;	WW1;	Prince Albert;	8
John Malone;	WW1;	Regina;	8
Les Gosling;	WW2;	Battleford;	8
Ian MacLenna;	WW2;	Regina;	7
William Boak;	WW2;	Regina;	7
Charles Vaessen;	WW2;	Leipzig;	6
James Wright;	WW2;	Rosthern;	6
Mike Askey;	WW2;	Saskatoon;	5
Tom Hoare;	WW2;	Lang;	5
John Ritch;	WW2;	Saskatoon;	5
Ernie Davis;	WW1;	Oxbow;	5
Ernest McNab;	WW2;	Regina;	5
Hugh Tamblyn;	WW2;	Watrous;	5

Aircraft Glossary

WORLD WAR 1

ALBATROS D-3 — This was the workhorse of the Germans in WW1. Armed with two guns, it could fly 110 miles per hour. It was a good ship but suffered from an inability to pull out of a dive quickly. This meant that the pilot had to score a kill on his first pass or risk having the enemy get on his tail while he tried to check the momentum of his dive.

ARMSTRONG-WITHWORTH — Alan McLeod won a VC in this big two-seater, which had a forward-firing gun for the pilot and a Lewis weapon for the rear-gunner. It could reach ninety miles per hour but was a slow climber. Nevertheless, it was a good bomber and proved surprisingly capable of defending itself against fighters.

CURTIS H. 12 — The "Large American," as it was called, was the best seaplane of WW1. Leckie used it to great effect against submarines, zeppelins and enemy planes. Equipped with two 275-hp Rolls Royce engines, it could only fly eighty-five miles per hour but it carried a five-man crew and six machine guns. It could stay airborne for up to seven hours, had pontoons to land on water and could sustain a great deal of battle damage without going down.

FOKKER TRIPLANE — This was the most famous German fighter of the war, mainly because it is associated with the Red Baron. Although relatively slow at high altitudes, it made up for its lack of speed with its incredible turning ability. Few pilots could stay on its tail for long because its three wings made it more agile than most fighters.

FOKKER D -7 — The D-7 appeared after the triplane and was, without question, the best German fighter of the war. Like almost all German planes, it had two machine guns, but it was also very easy to fly, could climb to 18,000 feet and reach 120 miles per hour.

NIEUPORT 17 — Built in 1916 by the French, this sleek little single-seater was Billy Bishop's favourite plane. Powered by a 110-hp LeRhone motor, it had a top speed of 107 miles per hour. Although a little slower and less heavily armed than the best German fighters, it was more manoeuvrable than most of the planes if faced. It had a ceiling of 17,400 feet and an endurance of two hours, which was longer than that of most World War One aircraft. With a wing span of just twenty-seven feet and a length of only nineteen, it was a small machine that veterans say was a delight to fly.

SE5A — One of the greatest Allied machines of WWI, it was used by several aces, including Bishop. Although not especially agile, it could climb to 22,000 feet and had a top speed of 125 miles per hour. It also came with two guns. Visibility in the cockpit was good, and Bishop found the plane to be an outstanding gun platform.

SOPWITH CAMEL — Easily the most famous plane of WW1, it had two guns, an uncanny ability to turn to the right and a top speed of 125 miles per hour. With a LeRhone engine it could reach a ceiling of 24,000 feet. Brown, Collishaw and Barker all scored most of their kills in the Camel.

SOPWITH TRIPLANE — Made famous by Ray Collishaw and the Canadians of the "All-Black flight," the triplane was the tightest-turning machine on the front when it appeared in early 1917. It was tiny, even by the standards of the day, with a wing span of twenty-six feet and a body length of eighteen feet, ten inches. Powered by a Clerget engine, it could fly 115 miles per hour and reach a ceiling of 20,000 feet, both good numbers for the period. Its main drawback was the fact that it had only one machine gun compared to the twin guns carried on most German fighters.

SOPWITH SNIPE — The Snipe was the best Allied fighter of the war, but it appeared only during the last weeks of fighting and saw very little action. It is best remembered as the plane Barker used in his classic last stand against fifty enemies. Armed with two guns, its 230-hp Bentley engine gave it a speed of 125 miles per hour and made it an exceptionally fast climber. It was also extremely agile, making it a deadly dogfighter.

WORLD WAR TWO

FOCKE-WULF 190 — This was the top German fighter of WW2, with a speed of 416 miles per hour, four cannons, two machine guns and a radial engine that gave it good diving speed and turning ability.

GLOSTER GLADIATOR — The last of the biplane fighters, this plane was old and slow when war broke out. Nevertheless, with good turning ability and four machine guns, it could be deadly with an ace like Vernon Woodward at the controls. Its top speed was only about 340 miles per hour.

JUNKERS 88 — This twin-engine ship served as a bomber in the first half of the war and as a night-fighter in the last half. A versatile plane, it had a top speed of 280 miles per hour and a ceiling of 32,000 feet. As a bomber, it was defended by five machine guns and carried a load of 4,000 pounds of bombs. As a night-fighter, it had three cannons and three machine guns. Without its bombs, it could fly 311 miles per hour.

MACCHI 202 — A highly manoeuvrable Italian fighter that was capable of taking a lot of punishment, the Macchi had a top speed of 312 miles per hour and a ceiling of 29,000 feet. It was a rugged, agile ship that suffered from a lack of firepower, coming equipped with only two machine guns.

MESSERSCHMITT 109 — The best known German fighter of the war, it could fly 390 miles per hour and had a ceiling of 37,000 feet. However, it had only one cannon and two machine guns. Although a dangerous opponent during the first half of the war, it was out of date by mid-1942.

MOSQUITO — This twin-engine fighter was a deadly opponent in the hands of an ace like Russ Bannock. Made of plywood, it could fly 400 miles per hour with a ceiling of 36,000 feet. When it first appeared, it could outrun any German fighter. And it had an incredible range of 1,700 miles.

SPITFIRE — Flown by Beurling, Levesque, McNair and several other aces, it had a ceiling of 37,000 feet, a speed of 374 miles per hour and a range of 470 miles. Easily the most famous fighter of the war, it was armed with two cannons and four machine guns. Pilots loved it, claiming it was wonderful to fly.

KOREAN WAR

F-86 Sabre — The Sabre had six machine guns, a top speed of 601 miles per hour at 35,000 feet and of 679 miles per hour at sea level. With a ceiling of 48,000 feet, it was a swift climber, capable of reaching 40,000 feet in 10.4 minutes.

MIG-15 — The MIG was better than the Sabre in most respects. Its top speed at 35,000 feet was 625 miles per hour and, at sea level, 668 mph. It also had a higher ceiling — being able to reach 51,500 feet — and could climb faster, achieving 40,000 feet in just 6.4 minutes. Its main drawback was its armament. It had poor gun sights and its cannons were much slower-firing than the Sabre's machine guns.

Endnotes

Introduction

[1] Dodds, Ronald. *The Brave Young Wings*. Stittsville: Canada's Wings Inc., 1980, p. 3.
[2] *Aeroplane Magazine*. London: Vol. 4, 1917.

Chapter One

[1] Roy Brown file, Hitchen's Aviation Collection. University of Western Ontario library.
[2] Carisella, P.J. and Ryan, James. *Who Killed the Red Baron?* New York: Avon Books, 1979, p. 78.
[3] Titler, Dale. *The Day the Red Baron Died*. New York: Ballantine Books, 1970, p. 102.
[4] Richthofen, Manfred von. *The Red Baron*. New York: Ace Books, 1969, p. 112.
[5] Carisella and Ryan. p. 70.
[6] Dodds, Ronald. *The Brave Young Wings*. Stittsville: Canada's Wings Inc., p. 109.
[7] Ibid.
[8] Nowarra, H.J. and Brown, Kimbrough. *Von Richthofen and the Flying Circus*. Los Angeles: Aero Publishers, 1964, p. 114.
[9] Wise, Sydney. *Canadian Airmen and the First World War*. Toronto: University of Toronto Press, 1980, p. 515.
[10] Richthofen. p. 135.

Chapter Two

[1] Collishaw, Ray and Dodds, R.V.. *Air Command*. London: William Kimber and Co. Ltd., 1984, p. 3.
[2] Ibid. p. 26.
[3] Greenhous, Brereton. *A Rattle of Pebbles: The First World War Diaries of Two Canadian Airmen*. Canada: Ministry of Supply and Services, 1987, p. 109.
[4] Nowarra and Brown. p. 66.
[5] Wise. p. 418.
[6] Collishaw and Dodds. p. 209.

Chapter Three

[1] Unidentified newspaper clipping. Hitchen's Aviation Collection. University of Western Ontario Library.

[2] Ibid.

[3] Dodds, Ronald. *The Brave Young Wings.* Stittsville: Canada's Wings Inc., 1980, p. 177.

[4] Whitehouse, Arch. *The Years of the Sky Kings.* Garden City, New York: Doubleday and Co. Inc., 1959, p. 239.

[5] Ibid. p. 240.

[6] Machum, George. *Canada's V.C.'s.* Toronto: McClelland and Stewart Ltd., 1956, p. 98.

Chapter Four

[1] Harris, Norman. *Knights of the Air.* Toronto: The MacMillan Company, 1958, p. 24.

[2] MacMillan, Norman. *Offensive Patrol.* London: Jarrolds Publishers Ltd., 1973, p. 25.

[3] Ibid. p. 108.

[4] Wise. p. 470.

[5] Ibid. p. 568.

[6] Ibid.

[7] Machum, George. *Canada's V.C.'s.* Toronto: McClelland and Stewart Ltd., 1956, p. 137.

[8] Whitehouse, Arch. *The Years of the Sky Kings.* Garden City, New York: Doubleday and Co. Inc., 1959, p. 137.

Chapter Five

[1] Norman, Aaron. *The Great Air War.* New York: The MacMillan Company, 1968, p. 381.

[2] Ibid.

[3] Ibid. p. 382.

[4] Dodds, Ronald. *The Brave Young Wings.* Stittsville: Canada's Wings Inc., 1980, p. 132.

[5] Ibid. p. 127.

[6] Norman, Aaron. *The Great Air War.* New York: The MacMillan Company, 1968, p. 366.

[7] Ibid. p. 407.

[8] Ibid.

Chapter Six

[1] McCaffery, Dan. *Billy Bishop: Canadian Hero*. Toronto: James Lorimer and Company, Publishers, 1988, p. 3.

[2] *Liberty magazine*, Dec., 1939.

[3] Bishop file, Department of National Defence, Ottawa.

[4] McCaffery. p. 15.

[5] Bishop file.

[6] Ibid.

[7] McCaffery. p. 22.

[8] Wise. p. 406.

[9] Bishop file.

[10] Ibid.

[11] Bishop, William. *Winged Warfare*. Toronto: A Totem Book, 1976, p. 158.

[12] Ibid. p. 159.

[13] Schroder, Hans. *A German Airman Remembers*. London: Greenhill Books, 1986, p. 180.

[14] Bishop file.

[15] Ibid.

[16] Ibid.

[17] Bishop, Arthur. *The Courage of the Early Morning*. Toronto: McClelland and Stewart Limited, 1965, p. 198.

Chapter Seven

[1] Beurling, George and Roberts, Leslie. *Malta Spitfire*. Toronto: Oxford University Press, 1943, p. 3.

[2] *MacLean's*, 1943.

[3] Ibid.

[4] Beurling and Roberts. p. 56.

[5] Ibid. p. 102.

[6] Ibid. p. 104.

[7] Lucas, Laddie. *Wings of War*. London: Hutchinson and Company, Ltd., 1983, p. 182.

[8] Ibid.

[9] Beurling and Roberts. p. 139.

[10] Author correspondence.

[11] Ibid.

[12] Lucas. p. 183.

[13] *MacLean's*, 1943.

[14] Lucas. p. 359.

[15] Ibid. p. 357.

[16] Ibid. p. 359.

[17] Nolan, Brian. *Hero: The Buzz Beurling Story*. Toronto: Lester and Orpen Dennys Publishers, 1981,, p. 71.

[18] Beurling and Roberts. p. 215.

[19] Lucas. p. 183.

[20] *MacLean's*, 1948.

[21] Cosgrove, Edmund. *Canada's Fighting Pilots*. Toronto: Clarke Irwin and Company, 1965, p. 162.

[22] Nolan. p. 105.

[23] Ibid. p. 177.

Chapter Eight

[1] Cooksley, Peter. *Flying Bomb*. London: Robert Hale, 1979, p. 61.

[2] Bowyer, Chaz. *Fighter Pilots of the RAF, 1939-45*. London: William Kimber and Co. Ltd., 1984, p. 139.

Chapter Nine

[1] Bowyer, Chaz. *The Men of the Desert Air Force, 1940-43*. London: William Kimber and Co. Ltd., 1984, p. 54.

[2] Halliday, Hugh. *Woody: A Fighter Pilot's Album*. Toronto: Canav Books, 1987, p. 110.

Chapter Ten

[1] Unidentified newspaper clipping. Hitchen's Aviation Collection, University of Western Ontario Library.

[2] Thurston, Arthur. *Bluenose Spitfires*. Hantsport: Lancelot Press, 1979, p. 46.

[3] Ibid. p. 52.

[4] Ibid. p. 55.

[5] Ibid.

Chapter Eleven

[1] Author interview.

[2] Ibid.

[3] Thurston, Arthur, *Bluenose Spitfires*. Hantsport: Lancelot Press, 1979, p. 19.

[4] Ibid. p. 21.

[5] Johnson, J.E. *Wing Leader*. Toronto: Clarke, Irwin, 1956, p. 202.

[6] Ibid. p. 209.

[7] Ibid. p. 215.

[8] Ibid.
[9] Ibid. p. 236.
[10] *Regina Leader Post*, Oct., 1988.
[11] Johnson. p. 205.
[12] Ibid. p. 268.
[13] Ibid. p. 274.

Chapter Twelve

[1] *Air Classics, Sept. 1979.*
[2] Ibid.
[3] Ibid.
[4] Ibid.
[5] Ibid.
[6] Melady, John. *Korea: Canada's Forgotten War*. Toronto: MacMillan of Canada, 1983, p. 119.
[7] LaFrance, Claude. *The Korea Air War*. Canadian Fighter Pilots' Association booklet, Ottawa: 1983, p. 93.

Bibliography

Books

Allward, Maurice. *F-86 Sabre*. New York: Charles Scribner's Sons, 1978.

Beurling, George and Roberts, Leslie. *Malta Spitfire: The Story of a Fighter Pilot*. Toronto: Oxford University Press, 1943.

Bishop, Arthur. *The Courage of the Early Morning*. Toronto: McClelland and Stewart Limited, 1965.

Bishop, William. *Winged Warfare*. Toronto: A Totem Book, 1976.

Bowyer, Chaz. *The Men of the Desert Air Force, 1940-1943*. London: William Kimber and Co. Ltd., 1984.

Bowyer, Chaz. *Fighter Pilots of the RAF, 1939-1945*. London: William Kimber and Co. Ltd. 1984.

Collishaw, Ray and Dodds, R.V. *Air Command*. London: William Kimber and Co. Ltd., 1973.

Cosgrove, Edmund. *Canada's Fighting Pilots*. Toronto: Clarke Irwin and Company, 1965.

Carisella, P.J. and Ryan, James. *Who Killed the Red Baron?* New York: Avon Books, 1979.

Cooksley, Peter. *Flying Bomb*. London: Robert Hale, 1979.

Drew, George. *Canada's Fighting Airmen*. Toronto: The MacLean Publishing Company Ltd., 1931.

Dodds, Ronald. *The Brave Young Wings*. Stittsville: Canada's Wings Inc., 1980.

Forrester, Larry. *Fly For Your Life*. London: Frederick Muller Ltd., 1965.

Fuller, G.A. and Griffin, J.A. and Molson, K.M. *125 Years of Canadian Aeronautics: A Chronology 1840—1965*. Willowdale: The Canadian Aviation Historical Society. 1983.

Greenhous, Brereton. *A Rattle of Pebbles: The First World War Diaries of Two Canadian Airmen*. Canada: Ministry of Supply and Services, 1987.

Halliday, Hugh. *The Tumbling Sky*. Stittsville: Canada's Wings Inc., 1978.

Halliday, Hugh. *Woody: A Fighter Pilot's Album*. Toronto: Canav Books, 1987.

Harris, Norman. *The Knights of the Air*. Toronto: The MacMillan Company, 1958.

Hastings, Max. *The Korean War*. London: Michael Joseph Ltd., 1987.

Melady, John. *Korea: Canada's Forgotten War.* Toronto: MacMillan of Canada, 1983.

Jablonski, Edward. *The Knighted Skies.* New York: G.P. Putnam & Sons, 1964.

Johnson, J.E. *Wing Leader.* Toronto: Clarke, Irwin, 1956.

Lucas, Laddie. *Wings of War.* London: Hutchinson and Company Ltd., 1983.

Machum, George. *Canada's V.C.'s.* Toronto: McClelland and Stewart Ltd., 1956.

MacMillan, Norman. *Offensive Patrol: The Story of the RNAS, RFC and RAF in Italy 1917-18.* London: Jarrolds Publishers Ltd., 1973.

McCaffery, Dan. *Billy Bishop: Canadian Hero.* Toronto: James Lorimer and Company, Publishers, 1988.

Norman, Aaron. *The Great Air War.* New York: The MacMillan Company, 1968.

Nolan, Brian. *Hero: The Buzz Beurling Story.* Toronto: Lester and Orpen Dennys Publishers, 1981.

Nowarra, H.J. and Brown, Kimbrough. *Von Richthofen and the Flying Circus.* Los Angeles: Aero Publishers, 1964.

Schroder, Hans. *A German Airman Remembers.* London: Greenhill Books, 1986.

Richthofen, Manfred von. *The Red Baron.* New York: Ace Books, 1969.

Shores, Christopher. *Duel for the Sky.* Garden City, New York: Doubleday, 1985.

Spick, Mike. *The Ace Factor.* New York: Avon Books, 1989.

Thurston, Arthur. *Bluenose Spitfires.* Hantsport, Nova Scotia: Lancelot Press, 1979.

Titler, Dale. *The Day the Red Baron Died.* New York: Ballantine Books Inc., 1970.

Whitehouse, Arch. *The Years of the Sky Kings.* Garden City, New York: Doubleday and Co. Inc., 1959.

Whitehouse, Arch. *Decisive Air Battles of the First World War.* New York: Duell, Sloan and Pierce, 1963.

Wise, Sydney. *Canadian Airmen and the First World War.* Toronto: University of Toronto Press, 1980.

Journals, Magazines, Newspapers and Booklets

Cross and Cockade Journal (USA) 1960-1973
Cross and Cockade Journal (UK) 1983-1989
Canadian Fighter Pilots Association booklet, 1983
Popular Flying
MacLean's, 1943 and 1948

Air Classics, 1979
Toronto Star
The Globe and Mail
Regina Leader Post
Vancouver Sun
Ottawa Citizen
London Times
Leipzig Neueste Nachrichten (Germany)
The Valetta Times (Malta)